# church
# alive

by William Sanford LaSor

A Division of G/L Publications
Glendale, California, U.S.A.

Published by
Regal Books Division, G/L Publications
Glendale, California 91209, U.S.A.

Library of Congress Catalog Card No. 78-185799
ISBN 0-8307-0145-1

To the Saints of
The First Presbyterian Church
Ocean City, New Jersey
and
The Green Ridge Presbyterian Church
Scranton, Pennsylvania
whose Pastor I was
in the years 1934-38 and 1938-43
respectively
who demonstrated the fruit of the Spirit
— especially patience —
this work is affectionately dedicated

# Contents

Preface

A teaching and discussion guide for use with this book is available from your church supplier.

# Preface

Another book on Acts? Yes—but don't go away, please. Give me just a few minutes to tell you why.

The Church in Acts was closer to God than it has been at any time since then. I don't mean it was perfect. God didn't establish the Church for perfect people. The Church was a fellowship of sinners who were being saved (Acts 2:47).

Perhaps that needs a bit of explaining, for we usually say, "I was saved," or "I am saved." Now, those statements are not incorrect. Let's think of ourselves as passengers. We buy an airline ticket and we are put on the manifest. That makes us a "passenger," and we can walk through the gate marked "Passengers Only." We board the plane and we are passengers. We come in for the landing and we are still passengers, until we finally reach our destination. Being saved is like being a passenger—it goes on until we get where God has promised to take us.

This, after all, is what the Church is all about. The Church isn't heaven. It's just the heavenly vehicle. It is the means used by the Spirit of God to get us from here to there. It isn't perfect. Its members include Peter and John and Ananias and Sapphira and Barnabas and Dorcas and Mark and Timothy and Paul and Apollos and Priscilla and Aquila and Judaizers and Bereans and Simon Magus and the Philippian slave girl, and Luke and Demas, and— well, it's a motley crowd. You name it and we can probably find it in the Early Church. Some of them got off before they reached the end of the line, but most of them stayed.

There are many today who tell us that the Church has failed. Some of them don't really know what the Church is. They think it's that organization that meets in that big—and nearly empty— building on the corner. Some of them have no idea of what the Church is supposed to be doing—so how do they know that it has failed?

Now if the Church is supposed to be a fellowship of sinners, I submit that it hasn't failed at all. It is doing very well, indeed. The sinners in the Church today are just as qualified and capable as were the sinners in the last generation or in the first generation. And if the Church is the fellowship of sinners who are being saved by God's gracious work, then we cannot speak about failure. If we were trying to save ourselves, if we were trying to keep ourselves airborne and moving forward by our own power, then we might speak of failure. But if we are passengers and God's Spirit is responsible for our heavenly journey, then we simply trust God. We relax and leave the flying to Him.

But—and here is the big problem—what if we don't really trust God? What if we don't really know Him? How can we trust someone we don't know?

This is why I have written this book. I would like to help you have that vital, dynamic faith, that confident knowledge of God, that they had in the Early Church.

Other men have written on Acts—a very great number. To not a few of them I am greatly indebted. I haven't the slightest illusion that I shall replace any of them. Campbell Morgan's thorough exposition, Lenski's strongly Lutheran doctrinal exegesis, Bruce's use of classical materials in his exposition of the text, Pierson's devotional study of the Holy Spirit in Acts, the almost exhaustive scholarship of the Lake-Jackson five-volume work—these, and many others that could be named—represent various approaches to the study of Acts. Each work makes significant contributions. I have greatly profited from them all.

It is my conviction that the Church today needs to study anew the Book of Acts. Now this may not strike you as one of the Church's most important tasks. When I first took up the book to lead my people in a series of studies—I think that was in 1935—it was a strange book. Sometimes I found it tedious. Sometimes I found it puzzling. But as I read it and reread it (I think I read it some ten times in a month, each time in a different English translation), I came to appreciate its value. Soon I was enjoying it. The people of my church were enjoying it. We were getting closer to God.

Since then I have taken many groups through Acts: Sunday school classes, church congregations,

Bible-study groups, college- and seminary-level classes, students trying to learn Greek—and each time I have felt that it brought me closer to God.

That's because it is, beyond all other books in the Bible, the book of the Holy Spirit. And God gave us His Spirit to help us get closer to Him. It is by the work of His Spirit that we shall finally become what He intended us to be.

If there are any pastors who have stayed with me this far, let me add one word: Take your people through Acts. Spend weeks, even months, on it. Get them to read Acts over and over. Get them to know the problems of the Church in Acts. Get them to know the people they meet in Acts. Get them to know the Spirit they meet in Acts.

If there are any young people, or people who think and feel young, who feel that the Church today needs something to make it relate to your generation, read Acts. If you think our generation has failed you—and it has—look at the first generation of the Church. What did they have that we don't have? And when you have found the answers to questions like these, be sure you pass on the experience to the next generation. We have failed because we didn't really know God. We had the radio turned up so loud we couldn't hear Him. But we could have known Him. He was here all the time. We just didn't recognize Him. Acts will help you to recognize Him.

In a preface an author is supposed to acknowledge his various debts and express his gratitude. He is supposed to give credit for every borrowed idea while taking the blame for any misrepresentation or misunderstanding. I would gladly do so. But when you have lived and worked with a subject for thirty-five years and more, it is almost impossible to know just where your indebtedness to others leaves off and where your originality begins. So I would like to alter this just slightly.

I would like to express my gratitude to all who have helped me know something of the nature of the Church: parents who brought me up in the Church from my earliest days, Sunday school teachers, pastors, professors, congregations I pastored, fellow Presbyters, authors of many works, colleagues of differing persuasions—the list is almost endless. For as I came to know the Church better, the Book of Acts became richer in its meaning. The Church of our Lord Jesus Christ is very large and very complex. The tendency of most of us is to be rather small and simple. If we have trouble adjusting to the relatively few who are traveling with us, think of the cultural shock we shall experience when we land on that distant shore with multitudes that cannot be numbered, of all nations and races and kinds!

Finally, I would express my thanks to Louise Hoffman, Sharon Srouji, and especially to Janice Tuttle, for typing successive drafts of the manuscript. Paul does not list "typists," but I think the category of "helpers" in 1 Corinthians 12:27-29 is sufficient to justify the conclusion that one of the Spirit's gifts in the Church is a good secretary.

William Sanford LaSor
Altadena, California

# PART I

# How the Church Began

# CHAPTER 1

# The Early Church and Its World

The Book of Acts begins in Jerusalem (1:12) and ends in Rome (28:14). In the intervening chapters, many places are visited: Judea and Samaria, Syria and Cilicia, Asia Minor, Macedonia, Achaia and the islands of the sea lanes. Many persons are mentioned by name, and quite a few are identified by some title or office. From the mass of details we are able, by careful reference to other historical materials, to get a fairly satisfactory picture of the world in which the story of Acts took place.

We call the book "Acts." Actually, we have no idea of the original title, if indeed there was one. The present title was added in the second century.

In the English Bible the title usually occurs as "The Acts" or "The Acts of the Apostles." "The Acts" doesn't tell us much—the acts of what? "The Acts of the Apostles" suggests that the author is trying to record all of the acts of all the apostles—and obviously he isn't. In the Greek New Testament the title is simpler: "Acts of Apostles." In this book the author has recorded some of the acts of some of the apostles. We shall call the book simply "Acts."

The people we meet in the opening chapter of Acts are Jews. Jesus (1:1), who was born of the virgin Mary, was a Jew according to the flesh, and died on the cross under the placard "Jesus of Nazareth, the King of the Jews" (John 19:19). All of the original disciples were Jews. Most of the persons we meet in the first nine chapters of Acts are Jews. But then we notice a gradual shift, and by the end of Acts Paul is saying to Jews at Rome, "Let it be known to you then that this salvation of God has been sent to the Gentiles; they will listen" (28:28—the entire summary statement, 28:25-28, should be read).

The Early Church, as we shall call the church in Acts, began at Jerusalem as a congregation of Jews who believed that Jesus was their Messiah. By the end of Acts, the Early Church was spread across much of the Roman Empire, and while it included a large number of Jews, it was by that time predominantly Gentile.

*The Jewish World.* What do we know about the Jews of the first century A.D.? With the destruction of Jerusalem by the Babylonians (597-586 B.C.) the

4

Jewish Dispersion had begun. Some Jews had already fled to Egypt and set up a colony there. Many Jews were taken to Babylonia as exiles. Cyrus the Great of the Medo-Persian empire had permitted the Jews to return to Jerusalem and rebuild the temple, beginning in 538 B.C., but many had chosen to remain in Babylon. This colony developed into a strong Jewish center that contributed much to the rise of Judaism, notably in the production of the Babylonian Talmud. Likewise the large Jewish colony in Alexandria, Egypt, made a significant contribution to the development of Judaism—but in an entirely different way, for it had produced the Greek version of the Old Testament commonly called the Septuagint. During the intervening centuries Jewish individuals and families had spread throughout the Roman world and the Middle East. This was the "dispersion," or, to use a word taken over from Greek, "the Diaspora."

But the Jews always thought of Jerusalem as their true center. The Temple, destroyed by the Babylonians, had been rebuilt by Zerubbabel and was known as "the Second Temple." Five hundred years later, Herod the Great began a program of completely reconstructing and adorning the Temple, and this rebuilding continued right down to the day it was destroyed by the Romans in A.D. 70—but it was still known as the Second Temple.

After its downfall in 586 B.C., the kingdom had never really been restored. There was a brief period of independence in the days of the Hasmonean kings, or the "Maccabees." Herod the Great, in whose days Jesus was born, was an Idumean (or

Edomite), but he had been given the title "King of the Jews" by the Roman senate, and the Jews, for the most part, accepted him as their king. He reigned from 37 to 4 B.C. After him there were a number of "Herodian kings," of varying authority and extent of reign. We meet some of them briefly in Acts. "Herod" (4:27) was Herod Antipas (4 B.C.–A.D. 39), also called "Herod the Tetrarch" (Luke 3:19), in whose days Jesus was crucified. "Herod the king" (12:1) is known in history as Herod Agrippa I (A.D. 41-44), who was brought up in Rome and had been given his title by the emperor Gaius (Caligula). "Agrippa" (25:13), before whom Paul made his well-known defense, was Herod Agrippa II (A.D. 50–c.93), in whose days the Jewish War and the destruction of Jerusalem occurred.

The Jews of Palestine were divided into a number of sects—the number varies, anywhere from seven to twelve. We have heard of the Pharisees (5:34; 15:5, etc.) and the Sadducees (4:1; 23:6, etc.), and lately, because of the discovery of the Dead Sea Scrolls, we have heard a lot about the Essenes—although they are not mentioned by name in the Bible. We also know by name the Zealots (1:13). It would not be accurate to call the Samaritans (8:9) a sect of the Jews, for even though both groups claimed the same Lord and the same Law of Moses, the reasons for this division were deeper than a simple sectarian schism. The Ebionites, the Dositheans, the Therapeutae, the Sabians, the Sampsaeans and others, however, were sects within Judaism.[1]

The sect that dominated the political life of the

Jewish people was that of the Sadducees. They maintained control of the Sanhedrin or council (22:30ff.), the highest Jewish tribunal, composed of rulers (chief priests), elders and scribes (4:5). However, this control, which had once been exclusive, had gradually weakened, first when Queen Alexandra (76-67 B.C.) had added Pharisees, then when Herod the Great sought to limit the power both of the Sadducees and of the prominent families from whom the high priests were selected. Still, because of the great influence of the high priests— the acting high priest and the former high priests— the Sadducees had powers beyond their numbers. The following description helps us understand some of the situations described in the New Testament: "In manner the Sadducees were rather boorish, being rude to their peers as to aliens, and counting it a virtue to dispute with their teachers. They had no following among the populace, but were restricted to the well-to-do. They were more severe in judgment than other Jews."²

In their religious tenets, the Sadducees accepted only the written word and rejected all oral tradition. Since much of Pharisaism and later Judaism made use of oral tradition, this led to a marked cleavage between the two sects. Specifically, the Sadducees rejected all tradition concerning the continued existence of the soul or the resurrection of the body, an after-life with rewards and punishments, or angelic and demonic beings.

At first the office of high priest (or chief priest, Matt. 26:3, etc.) was hereditary, but since the time of Onias III (174 B.C.) it had become an item of patronage to be conferred by the ruling power. In Acts we find reference to the following chief priests: Annas (A.D. 6-15), Caiaphas (A.D. 18-36), under whom Jesus had been condemned (cf. John 18:13), John and Alexander, of whom we know nothing further (4:6), and Ananias (A.D. 47-48), who presided when Paul was "tried" (23:2).

It should be noted that most of the priests, but not all, were Sadducees, and that there were scribes of the Sadducees as well as scribes of the Pharisees.[3]

The Pharisees were, according to Josephus, the largest of the Jewish sects, numbering about six thousand. However, this was a small minority, since the population of Jerusalem in the first century A.D. was possibly fifty thousand,[4] and Palestine Jewry numbered between five hundred thousand and six hundred thousand. While the Sadducees emphasized the importance of worship in the Temple and the priestly functions, the Pharisees stressed the importance of personal adherence to the Torah (Law —understood as instruction). This was an additional point of tension.

The Sadducees disappeared after the total destruction of Jerusalem in the Second Revolt (A.D. 132-135), but the Pharisees survived and became the architects of later Judaism.

One of the greatest of the Pharisees was Rabban Gamliel, or Gamaliel (5:34), under whom Paul studied to become a rabbi (22:3). Gamaliel was a grandson of the famous Hillel, and the first of a very few rabbis to be called by the highest title "Rabban." According to the Mishnah, "When Rab-

8

ban Gamaliel the Elder died, regard for the Torah ceased, and purity and piety died."[5]

Because of the conflicts between Jesus and the Pharisees recorded in the Gospels, many tend to have an entirely negative attitude toward the Pharisees. It is well to be reminded of the fact stated by F. F. Bruce, "A Pharisee might become a Christian without ceasing to be a Pharisee (cf. 15:5); a Sadducee could not become a Christian and remain a Sadducee."[6]

We come into contact with Diaspora Judaism almost at once in Acts. On the Day of Pentecost (2:1), Jewish pilgrims were present in Jerusalem who had come from the east and the west, from the north and the south (2:9-11). The Day of Pentecost, better known in the Old Testament and among the Jews as the Feast of Weeks, occurred fifty days after Passover (cf. Lev. 23:16). Passover (12:3) was a more important religious occasion, but it usually came late in March or in the first half of April like our Easter, which was too early for safe travel by sea. Accordingly, the Feast of Weeks, which was seven weeks later, therefore late in May or in June, was the occasion when the largest number of Jewish pilgrims returned to Jerusalem. A third holy season was in the fall, including the Day of Atonement, referred to as "the fast" (27:9), and the Feast of Booths (Tabernacles) (Lev. 23:26-36) —but since that came usually in October, the weather was again an adverse factor.

Another reflection of Diaspora Judaism is the use of the term "Hellenists" in contrast to the "Hebrews" (6:1, etc.). The Hellenists were Greek-speaking (that is, non-Hebrew-speaking) Jews; these "Hellenized" Jews lived in the gentile world, or in some cases in Jerusalem as returnees from the Dispersion. The Hellenists who lived in Jerusalem tended to keep to themselves. (Probably the feeling was mutual, for the Hebrews would not want to be "contaminated" by the Hellenists!) They worshiped in synagogues rather than at the Temple.' If it seems anomalous to us that there should have been synagogues in Jerusalem—for the synagogue is often defined as the place of worship for Jews in the Dispersion—we must keep in mind the fact that many Diaspora Jews returned to Jerusalem to live out their days and to be buried in the Valley of Jehoshaphat.

We become most aware of the Dispersion, however, as we trace the outward progress of the gospel, for we find synagogues in almost every city. In the gentile world, synagogues are mentioned at Damascus (9:2), Salamis (13:5), Antioch of Pisidia (13:14), Iconium (14:1), Thessalonica (17:1), Beroea (17:10), Corinth (18:4), and Ephesus (19:8).

The synagogue, which was under the care of the "ruler of the synagogue" (13:15), was a place of worship, of education, and of government of the life of the Jewish community. Worship on the Sabbath consisted of five parts: the Shema or creed (Deut. 6:4-9, to which were added Deut. 11:13-21 and Num. 15:37-41), prayers (such as the Eighteen Benedictions), the reading of an appointed portion of the Torah, the reading of the portion of the Prophets appointed to be read with that selection of the Torah along with exposition and exhortation, and the benediction. Sacrifice, which could only be performed at the Temple in Jerusalem, was replaced by prayer and works of charity ("deeds of righteousness").

Since Hebrew was rapidly becoming an unknown language to Diaspora Judaism, the "interpreter" became an important personage in the synagogue, and "targums" (or Aramaic translations) were common. From the widespread use of the Greek versions of the Old Testament we must assume that Greek translations were used, perhaps even more than Aramaic targums, in the portion of the Dispersion that we meet in Acts.

Mixed marriages, so severely castigated by Ezra (Ezra 10:1ff.), had again become more common, and in addition to the mixed marriage of Aquila and Priscilla, Timothy's parents were a mixed marriage, for his mother was a Jewess whereas his father was a Gentile (16:1). We may be a bit more surprised to learn that Drusilla, the wife of the Roman procurator Felix, was a Jewess (24:24), the younger daughter of Herod Agrippa I and the sister of Bernice the wife of Herod Agrippa II (25:13).

Yet we must not jump to the conclusion that the wall of separation between Jew and Gentile was being removed. Not at all! Much of the problem faced by the Early Church when it began to move out into the gentile world stemmed from this exclusiveness. The Jerusalem church debated the question, "Must a Gentile become a Jew to become a Christian?" (15:1,5). Warnings carved in stone pronounced the death penalty for Gentiles who might invade the sacred Temple area.[8]

11

*The Gentile World.* It is already apparent that the world of the Early Church was the Roman Empire—perhaps at its finest hour. The provincial system had just been completed and a uniform supervisory authority, resulting in *Pax Romana*, extended over the entire Mediterranean area. The excesses and brutality that would characterize many of the later emperors were at this time the exception rather than the rule.

The Roman Empire was ruled by the emperor and the senate. Gaius Julius Caesar Octavianus, grandnephew and adopted son of Julius Caesar, had taken the Caesar family name and was given the title "Augustus" by the Senate in 27 B.C. We know him as Caesar Augustus (27 B.C.–A.D. 14), in whose days Jesus was born (Luke 2:1). His successor was Tiberius Caesar (A.D. 14-37), in whose reign the ministry and crucifixion of Jesus took place (Luke 3:1, etc.). Other Caesars of the period covered by Acts were: Gaius (Caligula), 37-41; Claudius, 41-54 (Acts 11:28; 18:2); and Nero, 54-68 (Acts 25:8).

In 27 B.C., Augustus divided the provinces into "senatorial" and "imperial" provinces. Senatorial provinces did not require the presence of a standing army, and they were governed by former consuls and praetors for a one-year term. The governor was known as "proconsul." Acts mentions Sergius Paullus, proconsul of Cyprus (13:7),* and [L. Junius] Gallio, proconsul of Achaia A.D. 51-52 (18:12).

All provinces added after 23 B.C. were imperial provinces and required military garrisons. They were for the large part governed by "legates" appointed by the emperor, usually for a three-year term. If two legions were garrisoned in the province, the legate was of senatorial rank; if only one legion or none, the legate was of praetorian rank. In a number of special cases, provinces were administered by men of equestrian rank, known as "prefects" until the reign of Claudius, and thereafter as "procurators."[10] In the New Testament, three of these officials are named for Judea: Pontius Pilate, A.D. 26-36 (Matt. 27:2, etc.), Antonius Felix, A.D. 52-59 (Acts 23:24), and Porcius Festus, A.D. 59-62 (24:27). Their official residence was at Caesarea and their authority was limited, being subject to the legate of the province of Syria.

The main responsibilities of government included: (1) military security and public order, (2) revenue, and (3) jurisdiction.[11]

Paul's arrest by the Roman tribune (21:33) illustrates the first responsibility for order, and the census-tax at the time of the birth of Jesus, the second (Luke 2:1). In a different form, the responsibility of revenue is illustrated by the Alexandrian grain fleet (Acts 27:6; 28:11) that supplied Rome with Egyptian cereal. Jurisdiction was left in the hands of local authorities, as the town clerk was careful to point out to the rioting crowd in Ephesus (19:38), but there was always the threat that the imperial power would intervene (19:40). For the Roman citizen, there was of course the right of appeal to Caesar (25:10-11).

The backbone of the Roman military system was the Roman Legion, nominally 6,000 men divided into 10 cohorts and 60 centuries. Augustus reorganized the army of defense into the legions, composed of Roman citizens, and the auxiliaries, consisting of subjects in the provinces. The troops in Palestine were normally auxiliaries, and the term "legion," used with reference to the Roman Army, does not occur in the New Testament. Two cohorts are mentioned by name, the "Italian" (10:1), and the "Augustan" (27:1). The New Testament always refers to Roman centurions in a favorable way. Centurions Cornelius (10:1) and Julius (27:1) are mentioned by name in Acts.

It would not be inaccurate to say that the empire was held together by its network of highways and sea lanes. The highways can be seen even today in some places (e.g., at Philippi and south of Rome), and certainly were traveled by Paul and other Christians of the Early Church. The route from Neapolis to Philippi and Thessalonica (16:11ff.) follows the Egnatian Road which continued on to the Adriatic Sea. Likewise the route from Puteoli to Rome (28:13-14) follows the Appian Way.

Travel by sea was more difficult and hazardous, although the Roman ships had pretty well cleared the Mediterranean of pirates. The sea was closed to navigation from November 11 to March 10, and was dangerous after September 14, as the statement in 27:9 indicates. In addition to his famous voyage to Rome (Acts 27:1–28:13), Paul must have traveled often by sea, for when he wrote 2 Corinthians 11:25 (around A.D. 55), he had already been shipwrecked three times. Luke's knowledge of ships and shipping is so accurate that some think that he may have been at one time a ship's surgeon.

The gentile world was polytheistic in religion—that is, there were many gods and goddesses, although worship might in places be confined to a single deity. Athens was full of statues to many gods (17:16), including one "To an unknown god" (17:23). At Lystra, Barnabas was called "Zeus" and Paul was called "Hermes," because of their works and their message (14:12). The Ephesians worshiped Artemis of Ephesus (the Earth-Mother goddess, to be distinguished from the Greek Artemis) and had built a magnificent temple in her honor (19:27). Paul and Luke sailed from Malta in a ship that had a carved prow of Castor and Pollux (the "Twin Brothers"), astral deities who were looked upon as the ship's patrons.

It was a day of widespread superstition, magical spells, and related ideas. Simon "the Great" practiced magic in Samaria, and sought to buy the power to confer the Holy Spirit (8:9-24). Paul was opposed by Elymas the magician at Paphos (13:8). A slave girl, who had a "spirit of divination," had the evil spirit exorcised by Paul at Philippi (16:16-18). Perhaps the most extreme forms of belief in magical powers were found at Ephesus, and there we find Paul was given the power to perform "extraordinary miracles" (19:11) in order that the power of God might be seen as greater than the satanic powers of evil spirits (cf. 19:11-20).

There was at the same time, a great discontent among the Gentiles, a longing for something better than the old superstitions, and a movement toward the God of the Jews. The loss of faith in the old gods is noted by a number of pagan writers, and with it there was the hope of a "golden" or "glorious" age, when the gods or sons of the gods would come to earth, or when "men coming from Judea" would rule the world."

In the New Testament we find evidence of this movement from paganism in the large numbers of Gentiles that attended the synagogues to hear the gospel. In fact, the great crisis that confronted the church, as described in the fifteenth chapter of Acts, was brought about, as we shall see, by the objections of Jews to the ingress of "uncircumcised" men into the church.

The Jews did not object to the conversion of Gentiles. As a matter of fact, there were provisions for such conversion, and not a few Gentiles had Judaized, accepting the sign and the ritual obligations of the Mosaic convenant. These were known as "proselytes." But a very much larger number of Gentiles were apparently unwilling to take upon themselves the yoke of the Law, and nevertheless wanted to serve the God of the Jews. These are known in Acts as "God-fearers" or "you/those that fear God." The Ethiopian official may have been a proselyte; he certainly was a worshiper of God (8:27-28). Cornelius, on the other hand, was a "God-fearer," an uncircumcised Gentile who worshiped the God of Israel (10:1ff.; 11:3). At Antioch of Pisidia, gentile converts were present in the synagogue when Paul told the good news that in Christ men were freed from the law (13:39,43), and this message so excited the Gentiles that on the following Sabbath a crowd of uncircumcised Gentiles came to the synagogue to hear Paul's message

(13:44). From then on, we find Paul regularly addressing his message to both Jew and Gentile.

*Summation.* Such was the world of the Early Church. It was a day of relative peace and security, of freedom to travel, of many opportunities for the young church to press forward in its evangelistic purpose. It was a day of hopes of a Messiah and longings for a deliverer. It was the God-given moment for launching of the Christian Church. In Acts we see how the Church responded to that opportunity.[13]

## Footnotes

1. For a survey, see W. S. LaSor, *Dead Sea Scrolls* (1962), 200-203.

2. A. Gelston, "Sadducees," *New Bible Dictionary*, p. 1124.

3. The expression "scribes of the Pharisees" seems to imply the existence of "scribes of the Sadducees"; cf. Matt. 2:16; Luke 5:30; Acts 23:9.

4. T. W. Manson, *The Servant Messiah* (1953), p. 11, estimates 30 to 35,000. J. Jeremias, *Jerusalem in the Time of Jesus* (1967), p. 252, estimates 25 to 30,000.

5. *Mishna Sota* 9:15.

6. *New Bible Commentary Revised*, p. 1004.

7. According to one tradition, there were 480 synagogues in Jerusalem when it was destroyed in A.D. 70. *Jerusalem Megillah* 73d.

8. Two of these inscriptions have been found by archeologists.

9. The L. Sergius Paullus, propraetor of Galatia, A.D. 72-74, was probably his son. An inscription has been found at Paphos, dated A.D. 55, with the words "in the time of the proconsul Paulus"—cf. S. L. Caiger, *Archeology and the New Testament* (1939), p. 119.

10. *Encyclopedia Britannica* (70) 18:691-693.

11. Cf. E. A. Judge, "Roman Empire," *New Bible Dictionary*, p. 1100.

12. Cf. Tacitus *History* 5.13, Suetonius *Vespasian* 4, and especially Virgil *Eclogue 4*, 4-54.

13. See also my chapter on "The Fullness of Time" in *Men Who Knew Christ* (1971), pp. 1-14.

17

CHAPTER 2 / (Acts 1:1-5)

# The Author and His Work

"How did Christianity get started?" Perhaps Theophilus asked Luke this question—at any rate Luke seems to be answering it. If we have read the Gospel of Luke, we have already met Theophilus (Luke 1:3), and a comparison of the opening part of Acts (Acts 1:1-5) with the opening of the Third Gospel (Luke 1:1-4) makes it plain that the same man wrote both works for Theophilus.

*The Author.* Who wrote the Gospel of Luke and Acts? According to tradition, it was Luke—but the name Luke does not occur in either book; in fact, it is found only three times in the New Testament. In

Colossians 4:14 Paul speaks of "Luke the beloved physician." In Philemon 24, he refers to Luke as a fellow worker. And in 2 Timothy 4:11 (Paul's last writing, while he was in prison momentarily expecting the death sentence), he writes "Luke alone is with me."

Turn to Colossians 4:10-14 and read it carefully. After naming Aristarchus, Mark and Jesus Justus, Paul adds, "These are the only men of the circumcision among my fellow workers" (4:11). Then he goes on to name Epaphras, "who is one of yourselves" (i.e., a Colossian), and Luke and Demas, who join Paul in sending greetings. The clear meaning of the passage is that the first three were Jewish Christians and the latter three were Gentiles. Luke, then, was a Gentile, and the only Gentile writer, so far as we can determine, in the entire Bible.[1]

Some Bible scholars are convinced that Luke was put to death with Paul. They go on to suggest that Luke planned three works, the Gospel, Acts, and an unwritten volume, since Luke refers to the Gospel as the "first" treatise (Acts 1:1). This would explain why Acts ends without telling us the outcome of Paul's appeal to Caesar. But we cannot press all of this into the use of the word "first," for the Greeks, just as we ourselves, often used "first" when only two are being compared.[2] Moreover, we ask, what would have been the subject of the third volume? In Acts the author gives every indication that his goal was to tell how the gospel got to Rome.[3]

Luke was a companion of Paul during part of Paul's missionary journeys. Three portions of Acts are called "we-sections": 16:10-17; 20:5—21:25; and

19

27:1—28:16. In these three sections, the first person pronouns ("we," "us") are used; all the rest of Acts is written in the third person. The logical inference is that Luke was with Paul during the periods covered by the "we-sections."

In 1882 W. K. Hobart published *The Medical Language of St. Luke,* in which he attempted to prove that some 400 terms in the Gospel and Acts were "medical terms" that only a physician would know. Even the great critical scholar A. von Harnack was impressed with this evidence and wrote a book entitled *Luke the Physician* (1907). Recent scholars have shown that Hobart's claim went far beyond the evidence, and that any well-educated man of the period could have known the words used by Luke.[4] However, it cannot be denied that Luke shows a keen interest in medical matters, and this is in keeping with Paul's reference to him.[5]

The author of Acts gives every evidence of being a careful and artistic writer. His details have been painstakingly checked and rechecked, and scholars have repeatedly classed him among the best historians of his time. His literary ability is abundantly demonstrated by the Gospel and Acts, which are written in the finest Greek in the New Testament. His artistic nature can be seen in his arrangement of material and in the way he develops and presents his theme. His devotion to Jesus Christ is never obscured. In his first treatise to Theophilus, Luke claims that he has "traced the course of all things again accurately" (see Luke 1:3) in order to write his Gospel. There is abundant evidence that he has done no less in writing Acts.[6]

20

*The Addressee.* We know nothing of Theophilus, other than the fact that he is addressed as "most excellent" in Luke 1:3. The suggestion has been made that "Theophilus" (meaning "friend of God," or possibly "beloved of God") was not an individual, but rather Luke's address of any friend of God who happened to read his two-part work. This is unlikely, for in that case the term "most excellent," which is really a term used to address only those of high position (see Acts 23:26; 24:2; 26:25), would be quite inappropriate. On the other hand, it seems obvious that Luke was writing a work for more than a single individual. A further suggestion has been made that, since the epithet "most noble" is used in the Gospel but omitted in Acts, Theophilus had become a Christian between the writing of the former and the latter works. This is possible, but it remains only a conjecture.

Further suggestions, such as the theory that Theophilus was a trial attorney, or someone close to Caesar, or some other person who would be influential in Paul's case before the emperor, are ingenious—but hardly likely. The content of the Gospel would seem to have no particular relevance to the trial, and the content of Acts would go far beyond the arguments of the case. In a word, if Acts was written for such purpose, it is far too subtle to achieve that purpose. The most we can say is that Luke has included a number of semiofficial and official statements (such as Gallio's decision, 18:14-15, and the words of Agrippa and Festus, 26:31-32) that would offset claims that Christianity was an illegal or subversive movement.

*The Date.* Modern scholars incline to date Acts somewhere between A.D. 80 and 90. This is based on theories which require a longer time for the composition of the Gospel than would be allowed by the traditional date of A.D. 63-70. The fact that Luke never refers to Jerusalem in a way to suggest that it no longer stands is a strong argument for a date prior to A.D. 70. This is particularly true when we consider the fact that he ended the "Jerusalem phase" of Acts (1:1–8:3) with violent persecution, and likewise concluded the "Judea-Samaria phase" (8:4–12:25) with violent persecution. Had the destruction of Jerusalem already taken place, he would surely have used that to underscore the thesis that gentile Christianity was here to stay (28:28).[7]

The story in Acts ends two years after Paul's arrival in Rome (28:30), which can be dated c.60. If Luke was put to death when Paul was—and this is only a hypothesis built on the fact that Luke was with Paul when 2 Timothy was written (but he could have been attending him as a slave-physician!)—then Acts must have been written before c.67. We suggest a date between 63 and 67 for Acts.[8]

*The Purpose.* Turn again to the opening words of Acts and compare them with the opening words of the Gospel. The Gospel was written to set forth the "truth" in an "orderly account" (Luke 1:3-4). Or, to use the words of the prologue of Acts, the Gospel "dealt with all that Jesus began to do and teach" up to the day of His ascension (Acts 1:1-2). We might assume, and the contents of Acts would support the assumption, that Acts is intended to deal with all that Jesus *continues* to do after the Ascension. We could paraphrase it, "In this second book, Theophilus, I am dealing with all that Jesus continued to do and teach through His Spirit in the Early Church, from the Ascension until the gospel reached Rome."

If we read the prologue of Acts again, we realize that Luke is putting the emphasis not on Jesus but rather on the Holy Spirit. Jesus gave commandment to the apostles "through the Holy Spirit" (1:2). He charged them not to leave Jerusalem, but to "wait for the promise of the Father" (1:4), and this promise is defined as being "baptized with the Holy Spirit" (1:5).

Of course, this does not deny or in any way minimize the historicity of Jesus Christ. If we compare the end of the Gospel (Luke 24:44-53) with the opening of Acts (1:1-5), we find that it is the same story. The "many proofs" of the Resurrection which Jesus gave through His forty-day post-resurrection appearances (Acts 1:3) are included in representative part in the last chapter of Luke. The Ascension took place at Bethany (Luke 24:50) which is on the Mount called Olivet (Acts 1:12), and the disciples who witnessed the event heard the commission to be "witnesses" (Luke 24:48; Acts 1:8) beginning from Jerusalem (Luke 24:47; Acts 1:8), and then they returned to Jerusalem (Luke 24:52; Acts 1:12). There is no doubt that Luke intends to continue the same story, dealing with the same historical Jesus.

Still, there is a difference. The post-resurrection appearances ended—certainly the Ascension means at least this! Jesus was no longer visibly and bodily present. But He was present in the Spirit. So the era of the Incarnation has been replaced—temporarily (Acts 1:11)—with the era of the Holy Spirit. As we study Acts, we shall be impressed with the number of references to the Holy Spirit. We shall also notice that frequent mention is made of the crucifixion and the resurrection of Jesus. If we mark these items as we meet them, it soon becomes obvious that Luke is telling about the deeds and teaching of the crucified, risen Jesus through the Holy Spirit.

*The Sources.* Where did Luke get his material? It is generally agreed that he had copies of the actual documents referred to in Acts 15:23-29 (the Apostolic Decree) and 23:25-30 (the letter of Claudius Lysias). He probably had some sort of transcript of Stephen's defense (Acts 7:2-53). For the "we-sections," he very likely had a diary in which he recorded events soon after they happened. For Paul's experiences when Luke was not present, Luke could of course get the accounts from Paul, particularly during the two-year imprisonment at Caesarea and during the long voyage to Rome. At Antioch Luke had access to disciples (13:1; 21:16), and at Caesarea he had ample opportunity to consult Philip and his daughters (21:8) and many others. It has been suggested with good reason that Luke wrote his Gospel—at least the first draft of it—during this period at Caesarea. In Jerusalem he would have been able to talk with eyewitnesses of several events (e.g., Acts 21:17). And he certainly had opportunity to talk with Mark (Col. 4:10-14; Philem. 24) and with Silas (Acts 16:10ff.).

There are eighteen speeches in Acts, comprising about twenty per cent of the book.* Scholars have pointed out that these sermons, addresses and other speeches have a ring of authenticity that is little short of amazing. Peter's sermons contain words and ideas found in First Peter and nowhere else in Luke's writings. Stephen's "defense" is full of Aramaisms not generally found in the classical language of Luke. Gamaliel speaks in language typical of the rabbis of the day. There are remarkable parallels between James' summarizing speech in Acts 15 and the Epistle of James. Paul's writings have been compared with his speeches in Acts and many points of similarity have been noted. It is a fair assumption that Luke has gotten the actual speeches from reliable sources.

But are these messages verbatim or merely abstracted? In most cases they appear to be far too short for actual sermons and other speeches. That shorthand records of the speeches could have been made cannot be denied, for shorthand had long been in use and the speeches of Greek and Latin orators were taken down in full in shorthand.[10] But we can hardly claim that a stenographer was present when Peter preached his sermon on the Day of Pentecost, or when Paul preached in the synagogue at Pisidian Antioch. We must rather assume that the messages were abstracted from memory.

Does this violate our doctrine of inspiration? Not at all, for the Spirit who inspired the Scriptures also worked on the memories of those involved in the process of inscripturation (see John 14:26). We need only ask, "What was the Spirit's purpose? Was

25

it to give a full transcript of the message, or to give the substance?" In all cases where the substance was sufficient for the divine purpose, we need ask for no more.

*The Accuracy of Acts.* We have already said enough to indicate that there is a high degree of accuracy in Acts. The great British scholar, Sir William Ramsay, who had been brought up in the school of rationalistic criticism, was at first fully convinced that Acts was a second-century document. As a brilliant young scholar he went to Asia Minor for research in 1881, and in the following 34 years he made extended trips to Asia Minor.[11] He summarizes his complete change of attitude toward the book as follows: "That the Acts contained and described a series of improbable incidents was a view that has not been tenable or possible since 1890 except through total disregard of recent advance in knowledge."

Other scholars have checked other details. The book contains many personal and place names, geographical and cultural notes. It covers a period of about thirty turbulent years, when the political scene shifted often. But Luke never makes a mistake. Rackham says, "Such accuracy would have been almost impossible for a writer compiling the history fifty years later."[12] James Smith made a careful and detailed study of Acts 27-28, and came to the conclusion that it must have been written by one thoroughly familiar with sailing, ship terminology, winds, currents, geographical details of the trip, and other items.[13]

We should not infer inspiration from accuracy,

although the opposite (inspiration cannot lead to inaccuracy) is logically acceptable. The most accurate volume in our day is probably the telephone directory. It has more names, addresses, and numbers (all factual details) and fewer errors than any work I know. But it is not inspired. Acts is both inspired and accurate. Its inspiration is due to the Holy Spirit who moved upon the author so that his work was the word of God. Its accuracy is due to the great care of Luke, who was the kind of man God's Spirit could use for a work requiring such accuracy.

*The Deeper Reason for Acts.* Let's go back to the question, "Why was Acts written?" It was written, we have said, to tell Theophilus the story of Jesus' continuing work and teaching through the Spirit in the Early Church. But is this a sufficient answer? Did Luke have to go into such detail, did he have to produce a work of a high degree of accuracy and beauty of artistic arrangement, just to get his friend, perhaps newly converted, well grounded in the faith? Perhaps. If so, that in itself ought to be a lesson to us. Cheap evangelism is always cheap. We owe our best to the Lord in everything we do.

But there certainly is something more in Luke's purpose. The first generation of Christians (the eyewitnesses) was about to pass away. A change was coming over the empire in its attitude toward Christianity. Formerly, Christianity had been tolerated under Roman law as a sect of Judaism, but in the future Christianity would be looked upon as a new religion and would come under the ban against new religions. Men would be swayed by that fact.

27

And the eyewitnesses would not be present to help set the record straight.

If the gospel was to hold the minds and the lives of men, the full truth must be told: the truth about how it came into the world, how it gradually developed from a Jewish sect to a universal religion, how it shifted its center from Jerusalem to Antioch to Rome, and how it influenced men of all walks of life, rich and poor, nobleman and commoner, educated and simple. This is not mere history; rather it is history with an apologetic, history designed to convince men of the truth.

Theophilus was the representative of the Western mind. Luke was out to convince him and all others like him, that the good news of Jesus Christ was for them—for us. Charges being brought against the Christian religion were not new; they had been raised from the beginning, and they had been answered. Luke presents the charges in detail, and records the replies to the charges. The officials had been unable to convict the apostles of any crime. Moreover, under persecution the Christians had always remained loyal to their Saviour. The cumulative impact of these facts is astounding!

*Summation.* In an "educated age," when men take pride in cultural attainments and scientific accuracy, when all sorts of accusations are leveled against the gospel of Jesus Christ, the Book of Acts deserves careful study and wide publication. Master it, to satisfy your own mind! Master it, so you can present it to any Theophilus you know who wants to be convinced! Master it, so you can answer the critics of Christianity!

# Footnotes

1. Rom. 3:2 refers to the Old Testament Scriptures, for at that time the New Testament was in process of being written. Hence this passage must not be used to press the argument that all of the Bible was written by Jews.

2. "First" is, strictly speaking, a superlative, implying at least three. The more correct word would have been "former."

3. Note Acts 19:21; 22:26f.; 23:11; 25:11f.; 26:32; 27:24; 28:14,30-31.

4. H. J. Cadbury rejects the theory entirely in *The Book of Acts in History* (1955), p. 36.

5. Cf. C. S. C. Williams, *A Commentary on the Acts of the Apostles* (1957), p. 4.

6. For a fuller account of Luke, see my *Men Who Knew Christ* (1971), pp. 119-126.

7. This is not the place to enter into a discussion of theories of the date of the Third Gospel. However, lest I be charged with ignoring a strong argument, I must mention that some theory of a "proto-Luke," (a first edition prior to A.D. 70) or some theory making significant room for catechetical (oral) tradition, can be made consonant with a pre-70 date for the Gospel and Acts.

8. F. F. Bruce, *Commentary on the Book of Acts* (1954), finds the period 64-70 best suited to the apologetic nature of Luke's writings (pp. 22-23). C. S. Dessain, in *Catholic Commentary on the Holy Scriptures* §156, suggests that the great fire of July A.D. 64, which unloosed the Neronian persecution, may have been the cause of the hurried ending of Acts.

9. *Catholic Commentary on the Holy Scriptures* §816b.

10. Shorthand was in use by 63 B.C. and was used to record speeches of Cicero and Seneca. A system of "speed writing" was used in Greece in the fourth century B.C. *Encyclopedia Britannica* (1952) 20:576.

11. This is told at length in W. M. Ramsay, *The Bearing of Recent Discovery on the Trustworthiness of the New Testament*, pp. 35-52. The book was originally published c. 1913, reprinted in 1953.

12. R. B. Rackham, *The Acts of the Apostles* (13th ed., 1947), p. xlv.

13. J. Smith, *The Voyage and Shipwreck of S. Paul* (4th ed., 1880), p. xlvi.

# The First Fellowship

Luke did his writing approximately thirty-five years after the church was founded.[1] The generation that lived through the events he describes was passing away. Younger Christians wanted to know such things as: "What did you do when Jesus left you?" "How did the first church come into being?" "Who preached the first sermon?" "How rapidly did the young church grow?" "Was there opposition to it in those days?"—and many, many other things.

The first seven chapters of Acts might be headed "How the Church Got Started."[2] This topic can be subdivided into seven "firsts" of the Early Church:

Note the artistic way Luke has developed his story. With the *first fellowship*, there is at once a division of the world into two groups: those within the fellowship, and those outside. The *first preaching* is the effort of the First Church to reach those outside the fellowship. The *first opposition* is the reaction of those outside against this preaching. With the first preaching comes growth, and with growth come the *first problems* of the church. Also with growth comes a more determined opposition amounting to the *first persecution*. At the same time, as the first fellowship reacts to the first problems it develops its *first organization*. Finally, as the opposition increases in strength, and as the organization provides time and manpower for more preaching, the crisis is reached with the *first martyr*.

*The First Church.* This is the First Church—not the First Presbyterian Church nor the First Baptist Church, not the First Church of Jerusalem nor the First Church of Ocean City; it is the very First Church. There is a church in Rome (St. John Lateran) which is called "the mother of all churches in Rome and in the world." But that is a mistake, for all churches in the world are daughters of the

First Church described in the first chapter of Acts. What was it like?

Well, it was like all churches in some ways. It had its times of blessing, and its times of difficulty. It had its believers, and it had its doubters. We shall see these things as we pursue our study in Acts. But for the moment let us concentrate on the concept of "fellowship."

Strangely enough, the word occurs only once in Acts (2:42), although it is the dominant theme of the entire book. The Greek word is *koinōnía* and may be translated "fellowship, communion, communication, distribution," and in several other ways. The noun form occurs nineteen times in the New Testament.[3] It is used with reference to the Communion or Lord's Supper (1 Cor. 10:16), to the generous sharing of goods (2 Cor. 9:13), and to fellowship with the Father (1 John 1:3), with the Son (1 Cor. 1:9), with the Spirit (2 Cor. 13:14), and with one another (1 John 1:7). It is used of fellowship in the gospel (Phil. 1:5) and fellowship in Christ's sufferings (Phil. 3:10).

The root meaning of the word is the idea of "oneness." It can refer to oneness of persons, oneness of experience, oneness of goods, or oneness of purpose. Our word "common" conveys the idea, especially in the expression "in common." Certainly the basic element of the First Church was oneness. We shall see the Church in its oneness with its Lord and in its oneness of membership. We shall see a oneness of purpose, and for a while at least a oneness of material goods. We shall see what happens when that oneness is broken. We shall see oneness in the "communion of saints," from the Communion Table to common every-day life.

*Fellowship with the Risen Lord.* The First Church began with fellowship with the risen Lord. After the Crucifixion, His disciples (except John and Peter) were scattered. When the first reports of the Resurrection came to their ears, they were frightened. But gradually, as Jesus appeared and re-appeared to them, they came to realize that what He had predicted had in fact happened.

For an all-too-brief period—a mere forty days— they experienced this fellowship with the risen Jesus. But this was enough to overcome their fears and give them the boldness—built on "many proofs" (Acts 1:3)—that would characterize the preaching of the Early Church. During this period, Jesus also taught them about the Kingdom of God. He "charged them not to depart from Jerusalem, but to wait for the promise of the Father," the baptism with the Holy Spirit (1:4).

Then came the day when the fellowship ended. No, it really did not end—but they still had to learn that lesson. Jesus led them as far as Bethany (Luke 24:50), and gave His farewell message. Then, "as they were looking on, he was lifted up, and a cloud took him out of their sight" (Acts 1:9). We call this the "Ascension."

During the forty days after the Resurrection, while His disciples were talking about Him, Jesus would suddenly appear (cf. Luke 24:36). Or while they were talking with Him, He would vanish (cf. Luke 24:31). Yet, if they had any questions about His identity, He clearly showed them that He was the same Lord (cf. Luke 24:38-39). What was He trying to teach them?

Jesus was teaching them—as we shall see in the account of the Early Chuch—that fellowship with Him in this new age was to be the same, and yet different. It was to be fellowship with the same Lord, but in a spiritual, nonmaterial form. They were to learn by these experiences that He was always present, even though unseen.

Do we all recognize the divine wisdom behind this truth? If Jesus had continued to be visually present on this earth, He would also have been geographically localized. Where would He be today? In Jerusalem? Then He would not be in Los Angeles! Would He be in the Episcopal Church? Then He would not be in the Methodist Church! Or, rather, let us say that if men *saw* Him in one place they would not *believe* that He was in another place at the same time. He wanted His Church to know that He is *with* us, wherever we are. So the *visible* presence must be replaced by the *spiritual* presence—which is no less real!

During the forty days, Jesus spoke of the Kingdom of God (1:3). This was a favorite subject during Jesus' earthly ministry. What more was there to say about the Kingdom in this post-Resurrection ministry?

We can be sure that He did *not* teach them when it would appear. And when on that last day they asked Him, "Will you at this time restore the kingdom to Israel?" He said bluntly, "It is not for you to know times or seasons which the Father has fixed by his own authority" (1:7), and He went on to say,

"But you shall receive power . . . and you shall be my witnesses . . ." (1:8).

"Not to know . . . but to get . . . and to be." There are many things that God wants us to know, but the time of the Second Coming of Christ is not one of them. During the present age it is our responsibility to take what He gives (power of the Holy Spirit), and to be what He wants us to be (His witnesses).

What did Jesus teach them about the kingdom? It is in their preaching, in Acts and in the Epistles of the New Testament. Yet, strange as it may seem, the term "Kingdom of God" rarely occurs in Acts.⁴ It was the substance of apostolic preaching, for Philip "preached good news about the kingdom of God" (Acts 8:12), and Paul went about "preaching the kingdom of God" (20:25, cf. 28:31). Jesus gave His disciples no esoteric teaching about the Kingdom. What He taught them, they have given us in the Scriptures. We look for no "hidden books"—we need only study the writings of His inspired apostles.

Speakers often refer to "the Great Commission," usually meaning Matthew 28:19-20 or the parallel in Mark 16:15 (*KJV*). If the words, "Go ye into all the world . . ." are the Great Commission, the words of Acts 1:4 are the Greater Commission: "Don't go until you have received the power of the Holy Spirit!" And the Greatest Commission is found in Acts 1:8: "You shall receive power [of] the Holy Spirit . . . and you shall be my witnesses."

Men and women have no business preaching the gospel to anybody until they themselves have received the power of the Holy Spirit. After that, they

35

have no business keeping silent. Paul said it for all of us, "Woe to me if I do not preach the gospel!" (1 Cor. 9:16).

We notice three things in the Greatest Commission. First, the *power* comes from God's Holy Spirit. In the next several studies, we shall see the Holy Spirit at work in the members of the Early Church, and we shall be able to study this power.

Second, we are to be *witnesses*. This term will be used a number of times in Acts,[5] and we shall have lots of opportunities to see what His witnesses are and say. Witness is of two kinds: *evidence* and *testimony*. In a trial, the evidence is often more important than the testimony, for what the witnesses say may be distorted or falsified. As the Lord's witnesses we must remember that the evidence we present in our lives is often of far greater significance than the testimony we present by our words. We are witnesses even when we are silent—and sometimes what we are contradicts what we say. In Acts we shall see the evidence of the witnesses and we shall hear their words.

Third, this witness is *to begin where we are* when the Spirit comes upon us, and then *to extend to the end of the earth*. It is a common mistake of new converts to think that they must right away rush to Africa or India or China to carry out the Great Commission. The disciples in the First Church started right there in Jerusalem. It is also a common mistake of older Christians to believe that the gospel need not be taken beyond their own circle of friends. "We have so much to be done here at home, why send missionaries to other countries?" is the common objection to any plea for missions. Now the First Church almost got into that rut. In fact, God had to stir up a persecution against the church, to get them out of Jerusalem (Acts 8:1). But we can thank God most sincerely that the Early Church set its sights on the uttermost part of the earth—for otherwise we would still be lost souls ignorant of God's salvation.

*Fellowship with Each Other.* After Jesus was taken up to Heaven, the apostles returned to Jerusalem. The words of the two heavenly messengers were still sounding in their ears: "This same Jesus, who was taken up from you into heaven, will come in the same way as you saw him go into heaven" (1:11). They never forgot this promise. It became the blessed hope, the purifying hope, of the Early Church. But there was something to be done other than to stand there waiting.

The apostles were all there—all, that is, except Judas. They are named in 1:13. Mary the mother of Jesus was there, and His brothers, and "the women," certainly including the women who were at the cross and who went to the tomb early on the first day. Luke tells us that there were "in all about a hundred and twenty" (1:15) in the "upper room" (1:13). Someone has suggested that there probably was no home in Jerusalem with an upper room able to accommodate 120 persons, and that the First Church probably met in an area of the Temple precincts. This is entirely likely, for later we find them at the Temple.

They were in "one accord" and in "prayer." These two elements are essential to true Christian fellowship. It was at that time that Peter proposed the selection of a successor to Judas. Some question Peter's wisdom in this suggestion. G. Campbell Morgan,[6] for example, is quite convinced that Peter acted without divine guidance, and that Paul should have been the twelfth apostle. Morgan particularly objects to the method used, namely, casting lots. But let us study the text carefully before coming to any conclusion.

What was the apostolate? We find the lines laid down in Mark 3:9-14. Jesus called to Him from among His disciples (3:9), "those whom he desired" (3:13) and appointed twelve of them to be apostles.[7] The apostle was first a disciple. Not all disciples became apostles. The *disciple* is one under discipline, one being taught. The *apostle* is one who has been sent. No one is sent without first being taught. Not all who are taught are sent. Now let's read Mark 3:14 again, and note two qualifications: "to be with him," and "to be sent out to preach." These are the basic qualifications for the apostolate. Now look at Acts 1:21, and notice Peter's statement of the qualifications: "one of the men who have accompanied us during all the time that the Lord Jesus went in and out among us," and 1:22, "one of these men must become with us a witness to his resurrection."

Are these not the same qualifications? Jesus established two requirements for the apostle, (1) personal, firsthand experience of Himself, and (2) mission. Peter said two things were necessary for the successor of Judas: (1) personal experience of Jesus, and (2) witness.

38

Peter carefully defines the time of this firsthand experience: from the baptism of Jesus by John to the Ascension (Acts 1:22). Paul could not qualify as one of the Twelve under these terms. He could witness to the risen Christ, for he had seen Him. But Paul could not witness to the life and ministry of the Lord Jesus in the days of His flesh.

Some have raised the question, Why was not James (the brother of Jesus) appointed to succeed James the apostle after the latter had been killed by Herod? (In fact, some think that he was so appointed, even though the Scripture is silent on the matter.) The answer is obvious, in my opinion: James the brother of Jesus, an unbeliever before Calvary, had not been with Jesus, and could not qualify.

Others could be "apostles" in a broader sense, in that the Lord had sent them, through the Spirit, to do an apostolic work. Barnabas, Saul, and others are so called in the Bible. But none of them could (or did) qualify under the terms laid down by Jesus and reiterated by Peter.

Why were only Joseph Barsabbas and Matthias put forth for the selection (1:23)? Was this a mistake on the part of Peter and the First Church? I do not so understand the record. Rather, it seems to me that these were the only two men to qualify. How many would there have been who could claim that they were followers of Jesus from the very beginning, from the baptism of John? Certainly not many! Jesus had few followers during the first year of His ministry. The Gospel record indicates that His rise in popularity did not come until about the middle of His ministry (around the time of the miraculous feeding of the five thousand). If there had been three or thirty who could have qualified, and only two were put forward by the fellowship, then I might be inclined to agree with Campbell Morgan that the method was open to question. On the other hand, if only two could qualify, then there is no objection.

What about the choice by lot? Well, note the steps. First, the men were selected because they could fill the qualifications laid down by Jesus and restated by Peter. Then, the fellowship prayed that God would make His will known in the choice. And then the lots were cast. Actually, no matter how the lot fell, the man so chosen would be qualified for the office, for only qualified men were put up! Personally, I am not ready to reject the selection of Matthias as the successor to Judas.

One thing we must admit: the First Church was of one accord, and it was in prayer. Under those conditions, I am much more confident that it acted in the will of the Lord than I would be of some of the elections in modern-day churches!

Well, we can almost hear Luke saying, this is how the First Church started. Some might object to using the word "Church" at this point. According to some teachers, *The* Church was born at Pentecost. That is a matter of the use of terms. However, there is no discontinuity. The fellowship that was with Jesus in the days of His flesh, that was with Him after His death and resurrection during the forty days, and upon whom the Spirit fell at Pentecost— it is the same fellowship. There is no break in the line. No new group was formed on the day of Pentecost. Only a new power was given: the power for the work for which they had been chosen.

*Summation.* Since that first fellowship, the Church has passed through many generations and undergone many changes. There have been changes in ritual, changes in language, changes in forms of government, and in many other elements. But it is still the same fellowship with the Lord Jesus Christ and with all who are His. If not—then it is no true church! There was no new church formed when it split into its Eastern and Western branches, nor when the Protestant Reformation took place. It is impossible to form a new church. There is only one Church of the Lord Jesus Christ: the one that maintains fellowship with Him and with His.

We belong to that Church as we meet that qualification.

GOLDEN HILLS
COMMUNITY CHURCH

## Footnotes

1. This assumes a date of 63-67 for the writing of Acts.

2. C. R. Erdman, *The Acts* (1930), p. 15, refers to it as "the Founding of the Church." I have taken a number of his terms to describe the "firsts" of the Church.

3. Acts 2:42; Rom. 15:26; 1 Cor. 1:9; 10:16; (2x); 2 Cor. 6:14; 8-4; 9:13; 13:13; Gal. 2:9; Phil. 1:5; 2:1; 2:10; Philem. 6; Heb. 13:16; 1 John 1:3 (2x),6,7.

4. After 1:6 the expression is found only at 8:12; 14:22; 19:8; 20:25; 28:23,31.

5. The word occurs 13 times in Acts, 9 times in the first 10 chapters. My word counts are generally taken from R. Morgenthaler, *Statistik des neutestamentlichen Wortschatzes* (1958).

6. *The Acts of the Apostles,* (1924) p. 21.

7. The words, "whom also he named apostles" are not well supported in the Greek of Mark 3:14, but Matt 10:1 uses the word "apostle" in Matthew's account of the same event.

41

# The First Preaching

Luke puts stress on the events connected with the first preaching of the First Church. He ended his Gospel with the commission to preach (Luke 24:47), and the stern charge to "stay in the city, until you are clothed with power from on high" (24:48). He opens Acts with reference to this same promise of the Spirit and the same charge "not to depart from Jerusalem, but to wait for the promise of the Father" (Acts 1:4). Then—lest we forget, it would seem—he is careful to report the words of Peter towards the end of the first sermon, "and having received from the Father the promise of the Holy Spirit, he [Jesus] has poured out this which you see and hear" (2:33).

So we might summarize the events: they waited, the promise was fulfilled, and then they began preaching.

*The Day of Pentecost.* It was Pentecost (2:1), the fiftieth day after Passover (the word Pentecost comes from the Greek word for "fifty"). Since the Ascension took place forty days after the Resurrection (1:3), we can assume that this was about ten days after the Ascension. According to the Sadducees, Pentecost was reckoned from the first Sunday after Passover ("the morrow after the Sabbath," Lev. 23:11), and therefore occurred on Sunday. This seems to lie behind the Christian tradition of Whitsunday. On the other hand, the Pharisees reckoned Pentecost from the day of Unleavened Bread, which varied according to the day of the New Moon and therefore could occur on any day of the week. Modern Judaism follows the Pharisee tradition.

Pentecost is called the "Feast of Weeks" (Exod. 34:22; Deut. 16:10). It is also called the "Feast of the Harvest" (Exod. 23:16) and the "Day of the First Fruits" (Num. 28:26). The appropriateness of these latter two names to the occasion of the first preaching of the gospel by the First Church is obvious.

According to Jeremiah (31:31-34), the law on tablets of stone was to be replaced by the law on the fleshly tablets of the heart. We may therefore look upon Pentecost as the time of the initial fulfillment of this promise, and the New Testament counterpart of the giving of the Law at Sinai. The New Testament counterpart of the Passover, we might add, is the death and resurrection of Christ, for He is "our passover" (1 Cor. 5:7, *KJV*).

Pentecost was one of the important festivals of the Jewish year, and originally required the attendance at the sanctuary of every male Israelite (Lev. 23:21). With the Dispersion, this requirement, of course, was possible only for those making a pilgrimage to Jerusalem. There were two other annual holy days that had the same requirement (Exod. 34:23), Passover, in early spring, and the Feast of Ingathering or Feast of Booths (Tabernacles) in the fall. Because of the danger of sailing in bad weather, as we have seen, the Mediterranean was closed to shipping, making travel by sea impossible for Passover and Tabernacles. Pentecost, therefore, came to be the occasion when the greatest number of pilgrims would be present in Jerusalem, as Luke indicates (Acts 2:9-11).

*The Gift of the Holy Spirit.* The believers "were all together in one place" (2:1). There is no indication that they had had any advance notice that the event was to take place on this particular day; they had simply been told to wait for the promise. We may therefore assume that they had remained constantly in fellowship, waiting for the promise. Then, suddenly, it happened!

First, there was a roaring sound that filled the house, and apparently also the entire city (2:2,6). Then, almost simultaneously, "tongues as of fire" appeared on each of them (2:3). In other words, both audible and visible signs were given to show that the promise had been fulfilled. The third sign, however, was far more important: they were filled

44

with the Holy Spirit (2:4). How did they know this? "They . . . began to speak in other tongues, as the Spirit gave them utterance" (2:4).

It is important that we understand exactly what happened. The visible and audible signs were "objective"—i.e., they could be tested with the senses of others, and did not depend upon the person undergoing the experience. The crowds heard the sound. The disciples could see the tongues of flame on each other's head. But what was the objective sign of the filling of the Spirit? On the Day of Pentecost it was the phenomenon of speaking with tongues, technically known as "glossolalia."[1]

The crowd heard the Spirit-filled believers speaking (2:7), each in his own language (2:8), in the tongues (languages) of the hearers (2:11), telling the mighty works of God. Glossolalia was repeated in the case of Cornelius at Caesarea (10:45), and in the case of the disciples of John at Ephesus when they were baptized in the name of the Lord Jesus and the Holy Spirit came upon them (19:6).

Did the Spirit-filled disciples speak their own language, with the miracle occurring in each hearer so that he heard the message in his own language (2:7-8,11)? Or did they speak in the languages of the hearers, the miracle occurring in the speakers? Or did they speak in some unknown tongue ("other tongues," 2:4), which each hearer heard as his own language, the miracle occurring both in the speakers and in the hearers? We cannot say dogmatically, and perhaps we should not attempt to answer the question. In the case of Cornelius and in the case of the disciples at Ephesus, there was no reason to

45

speak in foreign tongues, for no foreigners were present. Yet Peter describes the phenomenon at Caesarea as the same as that which occurred on the Day of Pentecost (10:47).[2]

Did this phenomenon occur whenever the Spirit came upon new converts? There is no evidence in Acts or elsewhere in the New Testament to lead to this conclusion. Peter's experience with Cornelius was not described as similar to occurrences with Jewish converts, but "just as on us at the beginning" (11:15). Paul did not defend his gentile ministry before the Jerusalem council by appealing to the evidence of tongues. We should be slow to set up any "rule" that would require speaking in tongues as evidence of baptism with the Spirit.

Is this the same phenomenon as the "speaking with tongues" that Paul discusses in First Corinthians? A careful study of the lengthy passage (1 Cor. 12:11—14:40) will show that there was no communication to foreign-speaking persons. Moreover, the tongues were unintelligible without the "gift of interpretation" (1 Cor. 12:10; 14:6-19; 14:27-28). We should hesitate to equate the phenomenon at Corinth[3] with that which occurred at Jerusalem on the Day of Pentecost.

Is the modern phenomenon of "speaking in tongues" to be compared with the event on the Day of Pentecost? On this point there are severely different opinions, and a high degree of emotionalism generally gets into any discussion of the point. Personally, I am unwilling to lay down any principle that would seem to limit the power of the Holy Spirit. Sincere believers testify that they speak in tongues by the power of the Spirit. I accept their word. On the other hand, can we call this phenomenon by the name "pentecostal?" Does it fit the descriptive characteristics or serve the same purpose as the pentecostal miracle?

Speaking with tongues in Acts seems to have occurred only on special occasions. The first occasion was on the day when the Spirit was poured out and the first preaching of the Gospel occurred. The second occasion was when the first Gentiles were brought into the young church. And the remaining occasion was when there was a difficult problem arising out of a misunderstanding of the nature of Christian baptism.

*Peter's Sermon.* The pentecostal miracle produced three results. Some of the crowd reacted in amazement, and truly wanted to know what this was all about (2:12). Others openly ridiculed the event (2:13). Peter looked upon it as the sign that the promise of the Father had been conferred and therefore that it was time to begin the preaching of the gospel.

Peter's sermon can be divided into three parts.' First, he explained what happened (2:14-21). Then, he explained why it happened (2:22-28). Finally, he gave the proof from Scripture of all this (2:29-36). We might summarize it in a sentence: The signs came from the Holy Spirit; the Holy Spirit came through Jesus; Jesus could confer the Holy Spirit because He is Lord and Christ.

Peter used the approach, "Begin where your hearers are." He took up the statement of the mockers, and reduced it to nonsense (2:15). Then, he

47

went on (for it is not enough merely to ridicule your opponents), and explained the event by turning to the Scriptures. Specifically, he quoted Joel (Acts 2:17-21=Joel 2:28-32).

Wasn't there any Holy Spirit before Pentecost? Of course there was! The Old Testament frequently mentions the Spirit of the Lord. The Lord Jesus breathed the Spirit on the apostles after the Resurrection (John 20:22). What, then, was the difference in the pentecostal experience? There are two differences, which can really be looked on as one: the Holy Spirit henceforth is to be poured out on all flesh, and whoever calls on the name of the Lord shall be saved.

Before Pentecost, the Spirit was a special possession for a special purpose. The Spirit came upon men to enable them to construct the Tabernacle, to compound incense for the holy service, to prophesy, etc. From Pentecost on, the Spirit was to be the common possession of the Lord's people. Sons and daughters, even male and female slaves, would perform the office formerly limited to the prophets (2:17,18)! Before Pentecost the Holy Spirit was not looked upon as belonging to all Israelites (otherwise Joel's prophecy would be pointless). After Pentecost, the gift of the Spirit belonged to all believers.

Here, as so often in the Bible, the word "all" must be studied carefully in its context. Quite often it does not mean *all!* "All flesh" (Acts 2:17; Joel 2:28) certainly does not mean all living things; it does not even mean all human beings in the world. But does it mean all believers? From a careful reading of

Acts 2:17-18, I cannot see how this can mean less than all who are in the covenant of faith. Does Scripture make a distinction between believers with the Spirit and believers without the Spirit? Is there such a thing as "receiving the Holy Spirit after" you have believed? Or does the Holy Spirit belong to all believers? We must keep our mind and our eyes open as we continue our study in Acts.

What about the second statement, that "whoever calls on the name of the Lord shall be saved"? Is this new? The new thing since Pentecost, I believe, is the opportunity it affords. With the outpouring of the Spirit on all flesh, and with the once-for-all sacrifice of Christ and the coming of the hour when men no longer need to go to Jerusalem to worship, the good news of God's salvation can quickly be spread to men of all nations everywhere. In fact, we might almost say that, before Pentecost, if God wanted a Gentile brought into the Kingdom, He had to do it in some special way. Since Pentecost, the responsibility has been placed on all of us.

How can this be? This is one of the results of the Incarnation. When the Son of God took upon Himself human form, He entered into the human race. When He sent forth the Spirit, after the Incarnation, He sent the Spirit into the redeemed human race. The Church of Christ here on earth is, in a sense, an extension of the Incarnation. We are the body of Christ. Just as the Spirit of the Holy God could dwell in the blessed Son of God, so He can dwell in all who by virtue of the Son's redeeming work are sons of God. We have become the temple of the Holy Spirit.

The second point in Peter's sermon is rooted in history. This is also true of Paul's preaching, and we should pay careful attention to what the apostles did. Apostolic preaching is rooted in the history of God's dealings with Israel, and particularly in the culmination of His work in Jesus Christ. But the apostles do not merely cite events of history; they indicate the witnesses to those events. This is especially true with reference to the death and resurrection of Jesus. Peter calls his hearers witnesses of the mighty works of Jesus (Acts 2:22), and he sets forth the apostolic company as witnesses of the Resurrection (2:32).

It is important to note the ultimate reason for the death of Christ. Well has it been said: "We are not saved by the murder of a Man. We are saved by the death of the One Who was delivered up by the determinate counsel and foreknowledge of God."[5] The mere fact that Jesus died would save no one. It is the fact that He died according to the Scriptures (1 Cor. 15:3), that is, according to the will of God. This was God's appointed way of saving the world. Christ's blood was shed for our sins, not just because it was His blood, but because this was the Father's will (Matt. 26:36-46). There was no other way. And to prove that this was so, God raised Him from the dead. Thus Paul can say that His resurrection was "for our justification" (Rom. 4:25).

But if this was the Father's will, then it must have been revealed in the Law and the Prophets. The final test of truth is always this: Does it agree with what is revealed in the Word of God? So Peter quotes from Psalm 16:8-11, and points out that

David could not possibly have been saying those things about himself. He was speaking of the resurrection of the Davidic Messiah.[6] Quoting also from Psalm 110:1, Peter makes it clear that David foretold the Ascension and heavenly enthronement of Christ (Acts 2:34-35). And the proof that Jesus has ascended into heaven is found in the fact that He poured out the Spirit which He had promised—"which you see and hear" (2:33).

If, then, Jesus occupies the scriptural place of the Messiah and if Jesus has entered into Heaven with the very power of the Lord, then God has indeed "made him both Lord and Christ" (2:36)—even though this is the one they had crucified!

Notice how Peter has put this message together. He has supported his claims by the Old Testament Scriptures. He adds to this the apostolic witness to the Resurrection. And to both of these points he adds the knowledge of those whom he is addressing. This is indeed a strong presentation!

*The Effect of the First Preaching.* What was the result of this strong message?

First, there was the conviction of helplessness and need. "What shall we do?" (2:37). Preaching should appeal to the head and to the heart. But unless it also appeals to the will, it falls short of its purpose. It is not enough to sway the hearer's emotions or to satisfy his intellectual curiosity. That man must be led to want to do something. Otherwise, it is only entertainment.

Peter was ready with the answer. "Repent . . . be baptized" (2:38).

The first step toward salvation is repentance, and

without true repentance, faith is valueless. But what is repentance? The Greek word means basically "to change your mind or purpose." Often it means to turn away from the former way to a new way. The Hebrew word used as its equivalent in the Old Testament means "to turn"—"return." We do not distort the word if we say that the person who has not repented is going away from God, is acting contrary to God's will. On the other hand, the person who repents changes his mind, his attitude, his direction, and returns to God. When the prodigal son made the decision to go back to his father (Luke 15:18), he was truly "repenting." So it is clear that repenting is more than feeling sorry for yourself; it is even more than feeling sorry for your sins. It is making a definite commitment of the will to turn back to God.

Peter's hearers were struck with the force of what they had done. Seven weeks earlier they had consented to the crucifixion of Jesus, because they thought He was an impostor and a blasphemer. But in the light of the evidence now presented, they recognized that He was the Son of God. Therefore they had to change their attitude toward Him.

But far more basic was the matter of sin. If it had been God's will to accomplish redemption in this way, and if this will had been revealed beforetime in the Scriptures, then they were sinners against the revealed will of God. Therefore they must repent.

But repentance is not enough. They must also express their faith in the Lord Jesus—and this was to be done by public baptism in His name (2:38). This has been the rule of the Church ever since, and it is based not on the words of Peter, but on the words of Jesus (Matt. 28:19). This is not to say that baptism is necessary for salvation. It is necessary as the prescribed means of expressing faith in Christ.

If there is sincere repentance, understood in the biblical sense of the term, and if there is confession of faith in Jesus, then there is forgiveness of sins, and the gift of the Holy Spirit will be conferred on the believer (Act 2:38).

God's seal of approval was placed on Peter's sermon by the Holy Spirit. Hearts were turned to the Lord, and "about three thousand souls" were added to the First Church that day (2:41). And the Church had only been preaching the gospel for one day!

Is it enough just "to repent and be baptized"? Yes—and no. It is enough to receive God's pardon. But the New Testament makes clear the fact that there should be growth in the Christian life. This is underscored right at the outset (2:42), for those who were baptized devoted themselves to the things that produce Christian growth: apostolic doctrine, fellowship with other Christians, the Communion, and prayer (2:42).

With such results from the very first, "fear came upon every soul; and many wonders and signs were done through the apostles" (2:43). The believers were filled with fear. The apostles were filled with power. Their sense of fellowship—of oneness—developed, so that they counted even their material possessions as common property (2:44-45), and their life was both a constant expression of praise to God, and a good witness to those outside the fellowship (2:47). Is it hard to believe that the Lord gave steady increase to such a church?

*Summation.* The story of the First Preaching serves not only to satisfy curiosity. It is itself a witness to every Christian fellowship, whether it is a church or a small group of individuals. It serves as a model for all preaching. True proclamation of the gospel puts the death and resurrection of Jesus Christ at its center. It draws its authority from the Scriptures and from the apostolic witness. Perhaps if the Church had limited itself to this apostolic kind of preaching, the word "preach" would not have fallen into such disrepute. Apostolic preaching is positive, telling of the length to which God was willing to go in order to bring us to Him.

But this is not only a witness concerning the nature of preaching. It is also a witness concerning the nature of the fellowship that is to do the preaching. This fellowship is united with the Lord who made its existence possible, and it is united in its very being by the Holy Spirit of power. Can we for a moment believe that this is the same Peter who, on the night of Jesus' trial, cursed and denied that he ever knew Jesus? What changed Peter? The power of the Holy Spirit and the knowledge of the Resurrection. But obviously, Jesus knew that the knowledge of the Resurrection by itself would not be enough for He told His disciples to wait for the power.

Finally, note that the outward expressions of fellowship (2:43-47) are the results, not the initial steps. Too many churches today seek to impose the results without having first of all proclaimed the gospel and received the Spirit. These results are what Paul calls "fruit of the Spirit"—and you can't get fruit without first planting and cultivating. The seed is the Word of God, and the development of that planting is the work of God's Spirit.

## Footnotes

1. It might be worth noting that when the Holy Spirit came upon Jesus at the Baptism, there was a visible sign (the dove descending upon Him) and an audible sign (the voice from Heaven).

2. We might note that in 10:46 "they heard them speaking in tongues and extolling God," and in 19:6 "they spoke with tongues and prophesied."

3. While there is no mention of speaking in tongues anywhere else in Paul's letters—nor anywhere else in the New Testament, from Paul's personal testimony we may assume that he often spoke "in tongues" (1 Cor. 14:18).

4. A very fine treatment of Peter's sermon will be found in J. B. Phillips' expanded version in his *Young Church in Action*, pp. 82-86.

5. G. C. Morgan, *Acts of the Apostles*, p. 64.

6. The Greek word *christós* is the exact equivalent of the Hebrew word *māsîᵃh* (Messiah). Both words mean "anointed, the anointed one."

# The First Opposition

After the story of the Day of Pentecost, with the powerful preaching of Peter and the tremendous growth of the First Church, we might assume that nothing will be able to stop this church. And if we add to the events of that day the splendid fellowship of First Church members, their deep devotion to God and their loving unselfishness with each other, this conclusion is doubly underscored.

But life is not so simple. The law of "action and reaction" applies not only in physics but also in human relationships. "If they persecuted me, they will persecute you," Jesus told His disciples on His last night before the Crucifixion (John 15:20). The rulers who had condemned Jesus to death now had to act again to stamp out this new "heresy," or they would have a worse situation than when Jesus was teaching. At that time, they really had to do only with the "Master," for His followers were not upsetting the world. But now they had suddenly become like Him. A reaction is inevitable. The only question is, when and how will it occur? Luke is careful to give us a very full account.

The story is divided into four clearly marked parts: (1) the miracle (3:1-10); (2) the explanation, or Peter's second sermon (3:11-26); (3) the arrest and trial of the apostles (4:1-22); and (4) the effect upon the First Church (4:23-31).

Luke prepares for the story by writing a transitional paragraph (2:43-47), which summarizes the previous portion and prepares for the next step in the development of Luke's record. Such transitional paragraphs are one of the characteristics of Luke's excellent literary method. In this summary we see the *koinōnia* in the oneness of persons (2:44,45). In the story that follows, we shall learn something about oneness in suffering (Phil. 3:10; cf. 1 Cor. 12:26). It is impossible to be a member of the Body of Christ and not experience the sufferings of that Body!

*The Miracle.* The story opens simply. Peter and John were going to the Temple to pray. Two things impress us. On the one hand, there is the continuity with the old. The First Church did not break off from Judaism but was faithful in carrying on the old forms of worship—at least until God caused the Temple to be destroyed. On the other hand, there is the appearance of the new. In the Gospels it was never "Peter and John"—never, that is, until the Resurrection. It was "Peter and Andrew, James and John." Peter and John, as many Bible students have pointed out, were possibly of different ages, very likely of different social backgrounds, and certainly of different temperaments. But in the experience of the risen Christ they have found a new oneness. Christ is indeed the great Equalizer!

At the "Beautiful Gate" of the Temple sat a lame beggar asking alms of all who passed by. The beggar was over forty (4:22), and probably for years he had been brought daily to the Temple to beg. He was known to the people and was quickly recognized (3:10). Only a few months before Jesus had passed by that gate. He must have seen the beggar many times; it is quite likely that the beggar had asked Him for alms. Why had Jesus not healed him? For one reason, Jesus did not come in His First Advent to heal all diseases. But in this case, there was a second reason: Jesus had reserved this man's cure for the time when He would be working not in the flesh but in the Spirit through His apostles.

The man was lame from birth (3:2). Therefore this was not one of those "miracles" where a person with an imaginary ailment is "cured." Moreover, we may conclude that the man had so despaired of health that he did not even ask to be cured. He asked for alms—which is another way of saying that he was merely asking to be supported in the condition in which he was.

It is important to note this fact in the light of

Peter's answer (3:6). If the statement about selling their goods and sharing the proceeds (2:45) is to be taken at its face value, then Peter's statement about not having silver or gold was not exactly true. He may not have had any money with him, but if he had been so led, he certainly could have gotten the money from the Fellowship. Therefore we must join the first part of his reply to the second. What he is saying, it seems to me, is this: "We do not have money to keep you in your present condition but we do have something to get you out of this condition."

This is a very important point! It is not the Church's business in this world simply to make the present condition more bearable; the task of the Church is to release here on earth the redemptive work of God in Christ.

Now Luke gives the details of the miracle. Peter took the man's hand and lifted him to his feet (3:7). The man's feet and ankles were immediately healed (Dr. Luke's medical interest seems to be apparent) (3:7). He could walk at once (3:8). After even a few months in bed a man must learn again to walk— and this man had never walked before! He went to the Temple to praise God, all the while leaping and walking around and around (3:8). The people saw him, recognized him, and were filled with amazement (3:9-10).

*Peter Preaches Again.* The gathering crowd in Solomon's portico (3:11) set the stage for Peter's second sermon. Just as there had been other miracles (2:43) which Luke omitted in order to get to the most significant one, so there must have been other sermons. It is impossible to believe that the Spirit-filled apostles had been silent! But it was this particular proclamation of the gospel which brought on the opposition, so Luke gives the details.

Peter's sermon has two parts:

I. This miracle was done by the power of Jesus (3:11-16).

II. You acted in ignorance and now have the opportunity to repent (3:17-26).

Those who believe that all good sermons have three parts suggest that Peter was arrested before he got to the third point. But what would the third point have been? Peter said all that was necessary.

First, Peter disclaimed any personal credit for the miracle (3:12). It was not the apostle's power or piety that had worked the cure; it was Jesus (3:16) who had been glorified by God (3:13) who was able to do this. Once again, we note that historical details are the basis for the deeper faith: Jesus—you delivered up and denied—Pilate had decided to release him—you asked for a murderer (Barabbas)—you killed the Author of life—God raised Him from the dead—we are witnesses (3:13-14). These are all facts! The people were confronted not with theories or theologies but with facts. From my experience as a chaplain and then as a college professor I know something of the problems and doubts of young men, and I am convinced that their doubts arise largely because they have never faced the evidence. We spend entirely too much time talking about the theories of our faith, and not enough time talking about the factual foundations. Let us remember this: the apostles did not believe in the Resurrection because it was an article of faith; it became an article of faith because they had seen the risen Lord!

Peter's second point was the personal application: You and your rulers acted in ignorance. The Law made provision for sins of ignorance, but deliberate sins, sins of the "high hand," were not covered by the sacrificial system.[1] The Law provided for sins done in ignorance[2]—but those deeds were still sin, and therefore needed to be forgiven. These men had acted ignorantly, hence they had the opportunity to repent and turn again (the two words mean almost exactly the same thing) and receive forgiveness (3:19).

Some may conclude that Peter, by his careful presentation of the Old Testament witness, is trying to prove that these people had no reason for ignorance. But the truth in the Old Testament is sufficiently obscure that the fuller revelation of Christ and the apostles is necessary in order to understand it. These verses are rather an attempt on the part of Peter to remove obstacles that might be in the way of faith. The people had stumbled over the facts of Jesus' life, particularly over His ignominious death, because these facts did not seem to be in accord with what was taught in Scripture. Peter is attempting to show them that Scripture foretold the coming of the Messiah, even in the details that seemed to be stumbling blocks. The problem lay in confusing the glories of the Second Advent (3:20) with the humiliation of the First Advent (3:18).

Moses had foretold the coming of the greater prophet (3:22; Deut. 18:15-16), and had warned the Israelites against refusing to hear him (Deut. 18:19; Lev. 23:29). All the prophets had foretold the days that had come to Israel. God's servant (using a term familiar to them in Isaiah 42—53) was the seed of Abraham through whom all the families of the earth were to be blessed (Gen. 22:18; cf. Gen. 12:3). This Servant had been sent first to these very people whom Peter was addressing (Acts 3:26).

If the officials had not intervened at that point, the people would have been smitten in conscience. They would have asked, "What shall we do?" Peter's answer could only have been what it was in 2:38. There is no other gospel. There is no other salvation. The presentation varies with the audience and the occasion. The witness will depend upon the experience of the one witnessing. But once the presentation has been made, once the will has been moved, then the message is the same: repent, believe, make public profession of your faith in Christ by being baptized in His name.

Why do we need to know this? Isn't it the responsibility of the minister? No; it is the responsibility of the witness, and according to the word of Christ, we are all witnesses. Once we have given our witness, we need to know how to lead the inquirer to Christ. We will learn this by watching the witnesses in Acts.

*The Arrest.* Peter never got to say these things, for the officials arrested him and John (4:1-3). The apostles had gone to the Temple at the ninth hour, or 3 p.m. (3:1). The miracle, the gathering of the crowd, and the apostolic preaching had taken some time. Sunset would be perhaps at 6:30 at this time of the year (it was probably June or July), and it was against their law to hold a trial after sunset.

Notice the reason for the arrest: the rulers were annoyed because the apostles were teaching the people and proclaiming in Jesus the resurrection of the dead (4:2). F. F. Bruce points out:

> It is particularly striking that neither on this nor on any subsequent occasion (so far as our information goes) did the Sanhedrin take any serious action to disprove the apostles' central affirmation—the resurrection of Jesus. Had it seemed possible to refute them on this point, how readily would the Sanhedrin have seized the opportunity! Had they succeeded, how quickly and completely the new movement would have collapsed![3]

The force of this argument is frequently over-looked.

Arresting the apostles, however, did not halt the reaction of the people. Many believed, and the number of men in the First Church came to about five thousand (4:4).

It is important to note the details of the hearing. There was no charge presented against the apostles (what charge would have been made?); they were simply asked how they did the miracle. This was a leading question, designed to get them into a trap so that a charge could be made. Peter avoided the trap, because he was filled with the Holy Spirit. He first parried the question, in a way reminiscent of his Master (John 10:32). Then he proceeded to give his witness that it was in the name of Jesus Christ of Nazareth, whom they had crucified and whom God had raised, that the lame man was healed. Note the blunt statement of historical facts! Because of Jesus Christ of Nazareth—whom you crucified and God raised (who else could?)—this man is standing before you well. It is impossible to argue against facts! Peter went on to declare that Jesus was the only source of salvation (4:12).

It was probably not more than three months before this that Jesus had stood in this very room before these very officials, and Peter in the courtyard outside had blasphemed and cursed and said, "I never knew Him!" Look at Peter now! Do we need further proof of the resurrection of Jesus? Even the officials were impressed with the boldness of Peter and John (4:13).

The officials were also impressed by the fact that these men, who had had no formal education (doubtless meaning no rabbinic training) were skillfully handling the Scriptures. They also recognized that the apostles had been with Jesus. So they put the apostles outside while they deliberated. And their statements are worth careful observation.

The Council admitted that the miracle had been performed and had been witnessed by many. Moreover, the beggar was well enough known that the entire city would quickly have the story. It would be folly to attempt to deny the fact (4:16). The Council therefore decided that the best action would be to apply pressure on the apostles. This they did (4:18).

But Peter was a witness, and a witness is under oath to tell "the truth, the whole truth, and nothing but the truth." So he replied, "We cannot [do anything else than] speak of what we have seen and heard" (4:20).

There was no way to punish them, so the Sanhedrin threatened them further and let them go (4:21).

*The Effect.* What was the effect upon the First Church? Peter and John, of course, gave a full account of what had taken place (4:23), and the Church immediately went into a time of prayer.

First of all, they recognized the sovereign will of God (4:24-26). From time to time we meet Christians who seem to think that God is responsible only for the good things that happen. It is exceedingly important for us to recognize that God is completely in control in this universe; nothing happens apart from His permission. During the present age, for reasons known to Himself, He allows His rain to fall on both the just and the unjust. He allows the wicked to prosper and the righteous to suffer. Do we resent that teaching? Then we must read carefully: It was by His determinate counsel and foreknowledge that the Righteous One was delivered up (2:23). If God allowed His own Son to suffer unjustly, can we deny that God allows even the most righteous ones of us to suffer? God permitted the unholy alliance of Herod, Pilate, the Gentiles, and the unbelieving Jews to gather against Jesus, "to do whatever thy hand and thy plan had predestined to take place" (4:28-29). We who believe God's Word must first of all recognize the sovereignty of God.

At the same time, the Church recognized the threats of the enemies. There was a grim reality in what had happened. Jesus had forewarned His apostles (John 16:32-33). If the Master was not beyond the brute force of scoffers and unbelievers, neither were His disciples. If the Sanhedrin—the chief priests, rulers, and scribes of Israel—could condemn the innocent Son of God to death, that same Sanhedrin was not powerless before two of the apostles. The present situation was only a foreshadowing of things to come. The First Church was now alerted to that grim reality, and girded itself spiritually for the attack.

What would we have prayed for under the circumstances? Would we have asked what the fellowship prayed for: "Grant to thy servants to speak thy word with all boldness" (4:29)?

How did God answer their prayer? The place was shaken with an earthquake, they were all filled with the Holy Spirit, and they spoke the word of God with boldness (4:31). They had asked for boldness; they were granted boldness.

*Summation.* We who live in the twentieth century seem to think that the age of martyrs is over. But it will never be over until the Lord Jesus comes again. Moreover, toward the end of this age, an outburst of satanic opposition against Christ and His Church will make martyrs as common as they were in the bloodiest days of the Roman tyrants! But what about us in the present day?

It costs even us something to be faithful to the Lord Jesus Christ! Oppositions may be more civilized and persecutions more subtle, but they are present. What is our reply? Do we soft-pedal our witness? Or do we ask for boldness?

But we had better not ask the Lord for boldness unless we are willing to be bold—for He may answer our prayers the way He answered the prayers of the First Church!

## Footnotes

1. Num. 15:27-29,30-31.
2. Cf. Lev. 4:2,27; 5:18; 22:14; Heb. 9:7 and 10:26; Luke 23:34; 1 Cor. 2:8; 1 Peter 1:14.
3. *Commentary on Acts*, (1954), p. 103.

# The First Problem

Luke has been telling us something about the fellowship *(koinōnía)* of the First Church, and we are learning that it is an ever-growing concept. Just about the time we think we have grasped the idea, we find that it is still larger. In fact, there are areas of life in which we have not entered into fellowship at all.

There is oneness in faith. We think we have this—provided, of course, that we limit ourselves to the essentials of the faith. We still have not learned enough of the truth revealed in Christ to have perfect oneness in all points.

We believe we have oneness with Christ. But there are still manifestations of the sinful nature in most of us, and these result in thoughts and deeds which, we know, will not enjoy the blessing of fellowship of Christ.

Oneness with other believers? Well, that is a more difficult point. If we limit ourselves to believers of our own nationality, our own race, our own denomination, our own general interests, etc., we can speak of fellowship. But we must admit in candor that there are lots of believers with whom we could find it difficult to have true fellowship.

Fellowship in the sufferings of Christ? Most of us would definitely prefer not to have too much of this kind of fellowship. We like all men to speak well of us. We are not really anxious to enter into the fellowship of Christ that would result in men reviling us, spitting upon us and cursing us, ridiculing us, or just ignoring us. Oh, we occasionally sing about this kind of valiant courage in our hymns. But don't take our hymns too seriously! They are poetry, you know.

Fellowship of goods? Do you mean Communism? Now, wait a minute! . . . But before we get into an argument over this point, let's study the passage in Acts.

*The koinōnia of Goods.* The First Church grew suddenly—from 120 to 3,000 on Pentecost, and not long after that to 5,000 men (Acts 4:4). The fellowship of this large group is described in striking words: They "were of one heart and soul." The rest of that statement introduces an element that has led to great confusion and misunderstanding: "No one said that any of the things which he possessed was his own, but they had everything in common" (4:32).

Some writers have called this practice of the Early Church "communism," and the statement can be found in not a few books that the Early Church attempted to practice communism and failed. Other scholars have suggested that the Church should today practice some form of communism as the only Christian ideal. Obviously the same passage of Scripture cannot teach contradicting ideas, so a careful study is called for.

All students of the Old Testament will admit that it stresses voluntary offerings rather than compulsory giving. Likewise, Jesus encouraged voluntary giving. In fact, enforced giving would have been the opposite of the principles of religion which He taught, for He opposed any kind of legalism.

If, therefore, the First Church had decided to institute compulsory community of property, it certainly would have had to make that fact clear—for such an innovation would need defining and defending. The early chapters of Acts would be the place to look for such teachings.

But the expression of the principle is made in such a way that personal volition is underscored: "No one said that any of the things which he possessed was his own . . ." (4:32); "as many as were possessors . . . sold . . . and brought the proceeds . . . and laid them at the apostles' feet" (4:34). Peter certainly recognized the right of private property when he said to Ananias: "While it remained unsold, did it not remain your own? And after it was sold, was it not at your disposal?" (5:4). Only by

70

the most distorted interpretation can this passage be made to prove that Ananias was punished because he had refused to comply with a church rule enforcing common property!

Communism and *koinōnía* have a root idea in common—but after that they go in opposite directions. Communism says, "What is yours is mine; I'll take it." *Koinōnía* says, "What is mine is yours; I'll share it." The one forcibly invades the right of private property; the other voluntarily relinquishes the right of private property. The one is enforced by law; the other is enforced only by love.

We are not attempting here to say that communism (as a political system) is anti-Christian, or that a Christian cannot live in a Communist society. We are simply trying to disprove the notion that only communism is Christian. The Christian church would cease to be acting in the Spirit of Christ if it attempted to coerce anyone into unwilling contribution. Freedom is an essential part of the gospel, and love is the whole law of Christ.

The historian Kent says, "The absence of any trace of communism in the later history of Palestinian Christianity or elsewhere in the early Christian church, until the alien tendencies toward asceticism and monasticism gained a foothold within it, substantiates the testimony of Acts."[1]

How did the practice of selling property and donating the proceeds come about? It has been suggested that as the First Church grew it found itself composed of an increasing number of poor. Perhaps many of them were Jews of the Diaspora who had come to Jerusalem for some religious occasion, heard the gospel, were converted, and settled there. Others were of the lower economic strata of the land, for whom Jesus showed special concern (as, indeed, does the entire Bible). It is quite possible that some were beginning to feel the persecution by unbelieving Jews that later became widespread against those who had accepted Jesus as Messiah. And sometimes it has been suggested that the Early Church was so sure that the return of Christ was imminent, that its members got rid of their possessions and "waited" for His coming.

There are probably elements of truth in all of these explanations. Later, the poverty of the Jerusalem Church became so great that offerings taken in other parts of the world were sent to Jerusalem. But it would be a mistake to conclude, on the basis of Acts 4:34, that the First Church stripped itself of all property and so became destitute. Luke makes it clear that Barnabas (4:37) and Ananias (5:1) sold only part of their holdings.

*One Who Gave of His Possessions.* Luke takes this occasion to introduce us to Barnabas. Since he will become a key figure later, we would do well to get acquainted with him. We might also take this opportunity to note that Luke tends to introduce important persons in advance, so that when they step into the spotlight we have already met them.[2]

His name was Joseph, but the apostles called him "Barnabas." Just what this word represents in their language (Aramaic), we are not sure, but Luke translates it for us as "Son of *paraklesis*." The difficulty is that this Greek word cannot be easily translated into English. Sometimes it means exhortation,

72

and sometimes encouragement, consolation. In John 14:16, the Holy Spirit is called the "Paraclete"[3] which is translated "Comforter." The word could also be translated "Advocate" (one called to the side of another).

At any rate, we have a general idea of what it meant: Barnabas was good at exhorting, encouraging, comforting. He must have been a wonderful man to have been given such a wonderful name!

Barnabas was a Levite, and a Cypriot[4] (native of the island of Cyprus). According to the Law, a Levite was not supposed to own property—but that law had not been strictly observed for several generations, perhaps even longer. Barnabas had lived in Jerusalem for an undisclosed period of time, owned property there, and even had relatives there (see Acts 12:12; Col. 4:10). It is possible that he lived with his aunt Mary and her son John Mark. When the need of his fellow believers became apparent, he sold his property, and brought the money to the apostles.

*Two Who Got Out of Fellowship.* In our printed Bibles, chapter 5 begins with the word "but." Now, this word cannot stand alone; it must refer to something before it. As a matter of fact, there should be no chapter division here.[5] The chapter should begin either at 4:32 or at 5:12. If we start at 4:32, and read it as a connected story, the outline is like this: "Now the company of those who believed were of one heart and soul. . . . Thus Joseph . . . sold a field . . . and brought the money. . . . But a man named Ananias . . . sold a piece of property, and . . . kept back some of the proceeds." It holds together, doesn't it? All of them were of one heart and soul—but Ananias and Sapphira.

Somewhere, somehow, this man and wife had gotten out of true *koinōnía*, the oneness of the First Church. Instead of thinking about the fellowship and their relationship to it, they began to think more about themselves, and the benefits they could get from the fellowship. If we read the story carefully, we will notice that the deed was done in full knowledge of both man and wife (5:2), that it was a deliberate attempt to deceive (5:3), and that it was the representation (or misrepresentation) of part as all (5:3). Moreover, it was not done to avoid giving part of the proceeds of the sale, for Peter clearly stated that the property was theirs to do with as they wished: to sell or not to sell, to give part of the proceeds or to give all (5:4). Therefore, there is only one possible explanation: This man and woman wanted to get credit for being more generous than they really were.

We can almost reconstruct their plot. Everyone was talking about the generous act of Barnabas. Sapphira said to Ananias (or the reverse; it makes no difference): "That was nice, what Barnabas did, wasn't it? Didn't the church make a fuss over him? Why don't we do something like that?" Ananias replied: "We can't afford it; not if we are going to enlarge the living room." Sapphira said, "But couldn't we sell a field, and keep some of the money to enlarge the house?" Ananias answered, "Yes; but the church would think we were selfish, keeping some of the money when so many poor people don't have enough to eat." And Sapphira said, "But who would

74

know how much we got for the field?" So they worked out their satanic plan (5:3), in order that no one would ever know. But some One did know.

Perhaps we can even go a bit further in reconstructing the story. That three-hour interval between the entrance of Ananias and Sapphira (5:7)—had it been pre-arranged? The fact that Sapphira had not heard what had happened—does that suggest that she was staying out of sight until time for her dramatic entry? That Peter had no mercy on her—does that suggest that she was the one who concocted the whole thing? We do not know, and perhaps we should not speculate.

We do know that the sin was hypocrisy—pretending that they were something they were not. In the Greek theater the actor wore a mask; what he was under the mask was something entirely different from what he was to the audience. The word "hypocrisy" comes from the Greek word for play-acting, and suggests that the hypocrite is only playing a part.

The sin of Ananias and Sapphira was like the sin of Achan in the book of Joshua. In fact, Luke may have been thinking of this parallel, for the word he used, translated "kept back" (Acts 5:2), is the same as the word used in the Greek version of Joshua 7:1. Bruce suggests that "The story of Ananias is to the book of Acts what the story of Achan is to the book of Joshua. In both narratives an act of deceit interrupts the victorious progress of the people of God."[6]

The sin was premeditated. Sapphira's answer to Peter's question (5:8) could only indicate that Ananias and Sapphira had agreed together in advance to represent the specified sum (not mentioned by Luke) as the total amount received for the field.

Premeditated deceit, hypocrisy—what is the penalty? In the case of Ananias and Sapphira it was sudden death.

Why was the penalty on Ananias and Sapphira so severe? They were the first (but not the last) hypocrites in the Church, and God intended it to serve as a warning for coming generations. Often in Scripture the first event or the first person in a new situation assumes a representative character. To the person who has no certain conviction of Divine Providence, this is often dismissed as some kind of typological fantasy. But some of us believe we see God's purpose: "These things happened to them as a warning, but they were written down for our instruction" (1 Cor. 10:11).

*Summation.* Fellowship is a sacred reality, not to be taken lightly. If we really believe in the oneness of the body of Christ, then we must live and think according to that belief. And as we explore the fullness of meaning of oneness, we shall discover that there are no limits. Oneness cannot be divided at any point, or it ceases to be oneness. The ideal is found in the words of our Lord's fervent prayer: "That they may be one even as we are one, I in them and thou in me, that they may become perfectly one, so that the world may know that thou hast sent me and hast loved them even as thou hast loved me" (John 17:22-23).

# Footnotes

1. C. F. Kent, *The Work and Teachings of the Apostles*, (1916), p. 43.

2. See the chapter on Barnabas and Mark in my book *Men Who Knew Christ* (1971), pp. 109-116.

3. *paráklētos* used of Christ (1 John 2:1) and of the Spirit (John 14:16,26; 16:7).

4. The monastery of Hagios Varnavas (St. Barnabas) near the ruins of Salamis, Cyprus, marks the traditional place of his burial.

5. Chapter divisions are not found in the manuscripts. They were added in the Middle Ages, and are in no way to be considered as inspired.

6. F. F. Bruce, *Commentary on Acts*, p. 110. For a discussion of the complex ethical problem in the story of Ananias and Sapphira, particularly as it involves Peter, read Bruce's comments, pp. 110-112. It is well to read the story of Achan also (Josh. 7:1-26).

CHAPTER 7 / (Acts 5:12-42)

# The First Persecution

There is some similarity between the story in this part of Acts and that told in Acts 3:1–4:31. This has led some critical scholars to speak of "parallel sources," and to conclude that only one such incident could have happened. But such criticism is naïve on two counts. First, it fails to realize that the experiences of the Early Church were rich and varied. A series of similar events can be found in historical developments of the present day or any day. But even more, this criticism fails to take into consideration the great artistic ability of Luke. By his arrangement of material, he manages to convey a great deal more without using more space. It is not necessary to present an exhaustive account of all that happened to the First Church; there was a noticeable pattern that made representative selection sufficient. At the same time, there is progress in the sequence. The outcome of the trial in chapter 4 was a warning; the outcome in chapter 5 is punishment. Repetition is one of the basic laws of composition. Perhaps critics fail to recognize this because they are critics and not artists!

*Miracles in the First Church.* In another transition paragraph, Luke summarizes the events in First Church before proceeding to discuss at length one climactic event. From the summary we get the impression of great power in the young church (5:12,15-16), of great respect for the church by those outside (5:13), and of phenomenal growth (5:14).

What do we mean by "phenomenal growth"? Well, 3,000 were added on the Day of Pentecost (2:41); more were added daily after that (2:47), until the number came to about 5,000 (4:4); now Luke (and probably the First Church) gave up trying to keep count, and says simply, "more than ever believers were added to the Lord, multitudes both of men and women" (5:14). Does that mean 10,000? We should not even try to guess. At last it will be "a great multitude which no man could number, from every nation, from all tribes and peoples and tongues" (Rev. 7:9).

What does the statement mean, "the people held them in high honor"? (5:13). Luke doesn't elaborate on it, but there must have been some feeling that almost approached awe of the divine, for "none of the rest dared join them" (5:13). In the dark

79

days of the Roman Empire, those who despised Christianity were forced to admit, "Behold, how these Christians love one another!" If it is by our love that all men shall know that we are the Lord's disciples (see John 13:35), then we may conclude that it was the love which they had for one another that marked the First Church.

What about the statement, "Many signs and wonders were done among the people by the hands of the apostles"? (Acts 5:12). Where Luke says "signs and wonders," we would probably use the word "miracles." Luke leaves little doubt about the widespread extent of the apostles' healing ministry, for he records that sick were brought to Jerusalem from outlying towns, "and they were all healed" (5:16).

We live in a "scientific" age, when men do not believe in miracles. But let us not forget that Luke was a physician. From what we know of physicians, even in those days,[1] we cannot assume that Luke would gullibly accept stories of "miraculous healing" without investigating them.

Did the Early Church continuously perform miracles? We should repeatedly ask this question as we study the record in Acts and the Epistles. From Paul's statement in First Corinthians (12:9), we must assume that only certain persons were given this spiritual power. In our present study, Luke seems to limit the power of healing to the apostles, with special emphasis on Peter.

Does the church today have the power to work such miracles? There are some who believe that miracles, tongues, prophecy, and other *charismata* (spiritual gifts) were limited to the apostolic age, and when the last apostle died, these powers ended. Others believe that these spiritual gifts can be found whenever and wherever there is particular emphasis upon the works of the Spirit. Some miracles in modern times seem to be well authenticated.[2]

Personally, I believe that the Holy Spirit is able to confer special *charismata* on men in any age. If the church today shows less signs of power than it did in apostolic times, can it be because we have less faith in the Spirit's power than they had? I further believe that these gifts of the Spirit given as He wills, are not particularly to be sought, nor to be given a higher rating than other gifts of the Spirit, especially the gift of love (see 1 Cor. 12:31 and 13:1).

Luke calls these miracles "signs and wonders." In the New Testament, there are three words used for such unusual (or superhuman, or supernatural) deeds. One word, always in the plural, conveys the idea of "wonders." It may properly be translated miracles, since wonder is the meaning behind our word miracle. The second word, usually in the plural, may be translated "power(s), mighty work(s)." The third word means simply "sign(s)." It is significant that the word "wonders, miracles" is never used by itself, but always with the word "signs," and twice in the expression "mighty works and wonders and signs" (Acts 2:22; 2 Cor. 12:12). We may therefore conclude that the New Testament never is concerned with miracles except as they are "signs" of something more than the mighty work that has been done.[3]

Neither Jesus nor the apostles ever performed a miracle for the miracle's sake. A miracle was always a sign. We would do well to remember this lesson.

*Official Opposition.* As the report spread, crowds came to Jerusalem, including sick and demon-possessed who were brought by their loved ones seeking healing. This news, of course, reached the official ruling body, the Sanhedrin[4] and they were impelled to act. After all, they were not only responsible for the religious government of Judaism, but they also had limited civil and legal responsibility. The majority of the Sanhedrin were Sadducees, who may have had mixed motives for their action, partly due to jealousy for their position, and partly due to their rejection of almost everything "supernatural."

Accordingly, the apostles were arrested and thrown into prison, to be brought to trial the next day. But during the night "an angel of the Lord" let them out of prison (5:19). Just what is meant by "an angel of the Lord" cannot positively be stated. It implies divine intervention, but, as Rackham points out, "it may have been connivance on the part of an officer, or the help of a friend."[5] In a later incident we shall see that a superhuman being is involved, but in the present account this is not necessarily the case.

When the Sanhedrin sent to have the prisoners brought in, they received the report, "We found the prison securely locked and the sentries standing at the doors, but when we opened it we found no one inside" (5:23). The reaction of the Council, understandably, was perplexity.

Almost at once they received a second report: "The men whom you put in prison are standing in the temple and teaching the people" (5:25). This was too much! But, fearful of the people—for the Sadducees were not the popular party, and the young church had gained a measure of success—they used no violence to get the apostles before them. Bruce points out that the apostles apparently made no resistance, on their part, hence, "thanks to the apostles' restraint, there was no breach of the peace."⁶ Those who react violently "against the establishment," while claiming the name of Christ, might do well to follow the apostolic example!

The trial was much the same as before. The Council referred to the previous trial and charge (5:28). The apostles stood on their previous argument: they must obey God, and gave their witness (5:29-32). And the Council burst into a rage, "and wanted to kill them."

This is a time-tested method of silencing noncomformists, and has been used more than once in the church. First, when there is no basis for a charge of insurrection, you order the person or persons to stop what they are doing. When they refuse, you charge them with disobedience. If they can be forced into some kind of action against the first order, you have an additional charge of insurrection to level against them. Thus tyranny develops. We might add that the opposite tactics also work: Do something relatively harmless and force official action. When your resistance reaches the point of subversion or revolution, declare that your "rights of free speech" have been violated!

*Gamaliel's Advice.* One of the Pharisees on the Sanhedrin was the great Rabban Gamaliel.[7] Ordering the apostles to be put out (in other words, going into "executive session"), he urged caution. First he cited other men who had been agitators: Theudas and Judas the Galilean.[8] Their efforts had come to nought, although the Zealot party was a result of the revolt led by Judas. Gamaliel's summary was in keeping with the spirit of his grandfather Hillel and with the Pharisaic party in general: "Let them alone; for if this plan or this undertaking is of men, it will fail; but if it is of God, you will not be able to overthrow them. You might even be found opposing God!" (5:38-39).

*The Disposition of the Case.* The Sanhedrin took Gamaliel's advice—almost. They decided not to try to stop the Christian movement directly. But they did beat the apostles—meaning, probably, that they gave them the customary thirty-nine lashes (Deut. 25:3) which Paul also received on more than one occasion (2 Cor. 11:24). And they ordered the apostles "not to speak in the name of Jesus," and then let them go (Acts 5:40).

Why the officials thought this disposition of the case would be any more effective than the previous one (Acts 4:18-21), is not clear. Perhaps they assumed that the physical torture of the beating—which certainly was administered with exceptional vigor, and usually left the person who received the lashes bleeding and torn—would serve to remind the apostles for many days of the order to be silent.

But the officials did not reckon the power which the apostles had received from God. Luke reports simply, "They left the presence of the council, rejoicing that they were counted worthy to suffer dishonor for the name" (5:41).

If threats won't stop them, and if beatings won't do it, what will? Only one thing is left to try: death. When Luke returns to the story of mounting opposition, he will tell us how successful—or unsuccessful—was the inflicting of the death penalty.

*Summation.* When the Council first ordered the apostles to stop speaking and teaching in the name of Jesus, the apostles said that they simply could not refuse to speak of what they had seen and heard (4:20). When the Council beat them, and charged them not to speak in the name of Jesus, they rejoiced that they were worthy of the beating, and "every day in the temple and at home they did not cease teaching and preaching Jesus as the Christ" (5:42).

Sometimes we ask: Why was the First Church so powerful; why did it grow so rapidly? And implied or stated is the other question: Why is the church today so powerless; why is it growing so slowly? The answer should be evident. In the First Church, when the going began to get rough they prayed and kept on preaching. Today, when the going gets rough we declare a moratorium on preaching; we assume that preaching no longer works and turn to other means of "reaching" the world.

God has ordained that by the foolishness of preaching He is going to save the world. The apostles believed Him and kept on preaching. Do we believe Him?

# Footnotes

1. Hippocrates, the "father of medicine," lived c. 430-c.360 B.C. and Galen, whose medical writings are well-known, lived A.D. c.130-c.200. Luke, therefore, lived at a time when medical science was in one of its great ages.

2. The great surgeon, biologist, and Nobel prize winner, Dr. Alexis Carrell, for example, was convinced that authentic miracles had occurred at Lourdes. Cf. *Man the Unknown* (1935), pp. 148-149.

3. It is interesting that John, in reporting Jesus' miracles, never uses the word "miracles," but always "signs." The expression "signs and miracles" occurs once in John, significantly when Jesus says to the nobleman, "Unless you see signs and miracles you will not believe" (John 4:48).

4. Older dictionaries authorize san-hēd'rin, but recent dictionaries correctly put the accent on the second syllable, san-hē'drin or san-hed 'rin.

5. R B. Rackham, *The Acts of the Apostles*, p. 72. He has an excellent discussion of the problem, pp. 71-72.

6. F. F. Bruce, *Commentary on Acts*, p. 121.

7. See definition of "Rabban" in chapter 1.

8. For more details on these men, see Bruce, *Commentary on Acts*, pp. 124-125.

# The First Organization

Where did church officers come from? Did the
First Church have bishops and archbishops, priests
and deacons, elders and trustees, and all the other
kinds of officials that we have today? Luke does not
treat these questions as we have asked them. Rather, as he swings from the interior life of the First
Church to the exterior reactions and back to the interior life, he reaches the point where the unusual
growth leads to problems. At this point, he describes the first division of duties, or the beginning
of organization as a solution to these problems
(Acts 6:1).

*"Hebrews" and "Hellenists."* First, we must try to understand some of the technical terms that Luke employs.

Since the time of the Babylonian exile, the correct term for the people called "Israelites" or "Hebrews" is "Jews" (2:5). That term is derived from the word "Judean," the people of Judea or Judah. The term "Israel," which was used both for the entire nation (the "twelve tribes") as well as for the northern kingdom (Israel, as contrasted with Judah), was still in use. Peter could therefore address them as "men of Israel" (2:22); and Paul could write, "not all who are descended from Israel [=Jacob] belong to Israel" (Rom. 9:6), thus making a still different use of the word. But the truly definitive word was "Jew."

The Jews were divided into two groups: those who maintained the almost exclusive separation from the gentile world that characterized many of the Jews of Palestine; and those who because of the Dispersion had become integrated into the gentile world, to a greater or lesser degree. Luke calls the first group "Hebrews," and the second group "Hellenists."

This description is perhaps an oversimplification. The Hebrews are often described as "Hebrew-speaking Jews,'" and the Hellenists as "Greek-speaking Jews." This is even more of an oversimplification. But it may serve to help us understand the feeling that was present, not only in Palestine but even throughout the Dispersion.

The process of Hellenization had resulted to a large extent from the ideals which Alexander the

Great had carried with him as he conquered the world. Hellenization had even penetrated the exclusive world of the Jews. Thus we read in the First Book of the Maccabees:

At that time there appeared in Israel a group of renegade Jews, who incited the people, 'Let us enter into a covenant with the Gentiles round about,' they said. . . . The people thought this was a good argument, and some of them went to the king and received authority to introduce non-Jewish laws and customs. They built a sports-stadium in the gentile style in Jerusalem. They removed their marks of circumcision and repudiated the holy covenant. They intermarried with Gentiles, and abandoned themselves to evil ways (1 Mac. 1:11-15 *NEB*).

Of course not all Hellenist Jews went to such extremes. But they were still considered somewhat less than "holy" by the Hebrews. It is interesting that the apostle Paul, even though he was born in Tarsus among the Dispersion, refers to himself as "a Hebrew born of Hebrews" (Phil. 3:5).

There is a third term, which Luke has not yet introduced, but which we should place beside these two, namely "Greeks" (or Hellenes). This term simply means "Gentiles." The "Hellenists" were Jews—at least, so the term is exclusively used in the New Testament.[2]

*The Threat to the koinōnía.* The First Church had some sort of "daily distribution"—perhaps something like a soup kitchen or a bread line, or perhaps a dole. In whatever way it functioned, we can surely assume that this was the distribution of the community of goods which was described in 4:32-37.

But, as so often happens, those who received from the generosity of others began to complain. The Hellenists were murmuring against the Hebrews "because their widows were neglected" (6:1).

This may have been an unfounded complaint. Or, it may have been a just grievance. If the Hebrews were handling the distribution, they may, with the best intentions, have been oversolicitous about their own needy. But this is no time to choose sides. The oneness of the First Church is at stake! Friendships have often been strained to the breaking-point by unintentional oversights. So the apostles acted promptly.

*The Office of the Twelve.* The apostles (the "Twelve") summoned the body of the disciples[3] and defined the division of labor. "It is not right that we should give up preaching the word of God to serve tables" (6:2).

The word translated "tables" needs a bit of elucidation. From the English "to serve tables," we may get the idea that the apostles had actually been waiting on those who came to receive prepared food. As a matter of fact, the Greek word for "bank" *(trápeza)* is derived from the word for "table." In the parable of the pounds, the master says to the wicked servant, "Why then did you not put my money into the bank . . . ?" (Luke 19:23), using the same word here as in Acts.[4] Perhaps we should understand the statement in Acts 6:2 to mean "to conduct the financial affairs."

Let's be sure we understand what the apostles are saying. They are not saying that they are "too good to do menial service." Nor are they making a clear distinction between "clergy" and "laity." I am not certain that they were even concerned about full-time preaching as over against part-time witnessing. We shall soon read about the preaching of Stephen and then of Philip—and they were members of the group that was set up here in order that the Twelve might not be cumbered by the work of caring for the needy. These other distinctions will become significant at a later time. For the present, the main issue is the apostolic witness to the work of Jesus Christ. These twelve were chosen to be with Jesus and to proclaim what they had heard and seen. For such testimony there are no substitutes. Therefore nothing must hinder their work. Before their earthly service is over, they must spread the good news far and wide, first by spoken word and personal life, then by putting the gospel in permanent form for future generations. It is the eyewitness testimony of those who were with Jesus that must become the basis for the faith of the Church.

*The Selection of the Seven.* The apostles suggested the action to be taken and stated the qualifications; the body of disciples (the First Church) selected the men; the apostles prayed and laid their hands upon them. It is important that we note each of these facts, for they help us define further the kind of authority that existed in the First Church. The apostles suggested the course of action; the disciples did the choosing, and then the apostles confirmed the choice and actually appointed the men to office.

In other words, while there was a democratic principle at work, according to which all of the members had a voice in choosing the Seven, there was also a hierarchical principle (using the word in its best sense), according to which there were levels of authority. We often speak of "democracy" as if it were the highest ideal. Actually, in its pure form (all actions taken by the decision of all the people) democracy is not at all ideal. Not all of the people are qualified to handle all of the problems that must be met! The "republic," with representative government elected by the people, is closer to the scriptural system.

We should note the qualifications suggested by the apostles for this office. First, the men were to be "from among you" (6:3), in other words, members of the Fellowship. They were to be "of good repute" (6:3), that is, having a good reputation, well spoken of. Then, they were to be "full of the Spirit" (6:3), meaning, of course, God's Holy Spirit. They were also to be full "of wisdom" (6:3), which may be defined as good, common sense. These should be minimum qualifications for any church officer.

These seven about to be elected are generally called "deacons." But the word "deacon"[5] does not occur in this passage. On the other hand, a cognate word meaning "ministry, service"[6] does occur, both of the daily "ministration" (6:1, *KJV*) and of the "ministry of the word" (6:4). Likewise, the cognate verb "to minister, to serve" occurs in the expression "to serve tables" (6:2). Later, the word "deacon" will be used of church officers (Phil. 1:1; 1 Tim. 3:8,12), but we should be careful not to limit the meaning too severely, for it is also used in the general sense of "helper" (cf. Rom. 15:8; Eph. 6:21; Col. 4:7). Likewise, we should remember that there is no indication anywhere that the "deacons" were released from spiritual service such as preaching the word.[7] There are varieties of ministries (1 Cor. 12:5). The Holy Spirit appoints "helpers" and "administrators" in the Church and it is He who gives a variety of gifts so that they qualify for their appointed offices (1 Cor. 12:4).

The suggestion pleased the "multitude" (another word, it would seem, for the First Church) and they chose the following men: Stephen, Philip, Prochorus, Nicanor, Timon, Parmenas, and Nicolaus (Acts 6:5).

All of these men have Greek names. That may suggest that they were all Hellenists. On the other hand, we must remember that "Peter" is a Greek name, being the translation of the Aramaic name "Cephas" which was conferred upon him by Jesus. Grecized names may have been used of the Seven because Luke is getting ready to introduce the next problem, namely the inclusion of gentile proselytes into the Church.

Nicolaus was not even a Jew—he was a "proselyte" (6:5). We shall learn more about proselytes later; for the present, let's be content to say that a proselyte was a Gentile who converted to Judaism. However—and this is an important point for our study of Acts—a proselyte was no longer considered a Gentile; he had taken on himself the sign

93

and the obligations of the Law of Moses and was henceforth considered a Jew.

*Luke's Summarizing Statements.* At this point Luke inserts a summary statement: "The word of God increased; and the number of the disciples multiplied greatly in Jerusalem, and a great many of the priests were obedient to the faith" (6:7).

That a large number of priests—who were for the greater part Sadducees—would accept Jesus as their Messiah is a startling fact. It testifies to the power of the gospel. At the same time, it helps prepare us for the break between the Church and unbelieving Judaism. We may assume that those who had been "more moderate" in their attitude toward the First Church were largely included in the converts, leaving behind those who were "more extreme." The moderating influence was now largely removed, and the open persecution of the First Church would shortly follow.

*Summation.* The First Church is the body of Christ in its infancy. Nevertheless, it is a body composed of many parts. If one part is in need, other parts are called upon to supply that need. If one part is neglected, the other parts must care for the neglected part before a more serious disease results. Only as each part of the body fulfills its purpose is the body healthy.

How well do we meet the qualifications as members of the body of Christ?

# Footnotes

1. Or "Aramaic-speaking Jews."

2. See H. J. Cadbury, "The Hellenists," *Beginnings of Christianity* (1933), 5:59-74 *Theological Dictionary of the New Testament,* 2:504-516. Cadbury holds that "Hebrews" in Acts 6:1="Jews," and "Hellenists"="Gentiles." I do not find his arguments convincing.

3. It is good to remind ourselves of the distinction between the "apostles" and the "disciples"—cf. the latter part of chapter 3.

4. W. F. Arndt and F. W. Gingrich, *A Greek-English Lexicon of the New Testament* (1956), p. 832. This work will hereafter be referred to simply as "Arndt & Gingrich."

5. diákonos, used in a secular sense (John 2:5,9) and a sacred sense (Col. 1:23). The word "deacon" comes from this Greek word.

6. diakōnía, from which we get "diaconate."

7. Bruce, *Commentary on the Book of Acts,* p. 130, suggests that we should use the term "minister" when it is contrasted with "bishop," and "elder." With reference to the Seven he prefers the term "almoners."

CHAPTER 9 / (Acts 6:8—8:1)

# The First Martyr

I imagine I can hear someone asking Luke, "How did the First Church get out of Jerusalem?" Jesus had told them that they were to be His witnesses not only in Jerusalem, but also in Judea and Samaria, and even beyond that (Acts 1:8). So far, the witness had been confined to Jerusalem. Moreover, there was not the slightest indication that the leaders of the First Church had any intention of moving beyond Jerusalem. Just how did they happen to change their minds?

God has mysterious ways of accomplishing His purpose. Often He achieves great progress by what might seem to be defeat. He turns failure into success. He turns sorrow into joy. It is never easy to pass through the experiences of these mysterious ways—but it is always wonderful to look back over them and to see how God has done His work.

If we had been in Jerusalem just after the death of Stephen, I am sure we would have heard remarks such as: "This is certainly a great tragedy!" or, "This will set the Church back for years; it may halt the work entirely." Others were no doubt saying, "Stephen was such a good man; I can't understand how the Lord could have let that happen!" or, "Wasn't that a terrible waste of life, for one so young and capable to die so soon after he had been ordained!"

Yet, from our vantage point, as we look back over the events, we say: "If Stephen had not prayed, Paul would not have preached" and "If Stephen had not been stoned and the Church had not been scattered, Christianity would never have gotten beyond Jerusalem." How foolish for us to rebel at God's plan, when we know so little, and God knows the end from the beginning!

*Stephen and His Preaching.* Stephen, we have learned, was one of the Seven appointed to "serve tables" (6:2,5).[1] But the first thing Luke records about him is that he "did great wonders and signs among the people" (6:8). How long he served tables, we are not told. At the time he was chosen, he was already known for his faith and fullness of the Spirit (6:5), so there is no reason to insist on a period of spiritual growth. We have already learned that the Seven had Greek names, and were quite possibly Hellenists—i.e., Jews of the Diaspora. This

97

prepares us for the fact that the dispute that had arisen over Stephen's preaching was among the members of the Hellenistic synagogue of the Freedmen (6:9).[2]

The Freedmen were Jews who had been taken captive to Rome by Pompey and afterward released. Those who had returned to Jerusalem had established a synagogue, henceforth called the synagogue of the Freedmen.[3] It is unnecessary to suppose that all who attended the synagogue were Freedmen—but they all were of the Hellenistic spirit and felt ill at ease in the Temple.

Some have suggested that Saul of Tarsus may himself have worshiped in this synagogue during his stay in Jerusalem, and that he may even have listened to Stephen's preaching and entered into the disputes with him. If so, Paul is strangely silent about the fact.

What Stephen was preaching we are not told. Whatever it was, it brought forth dispute. This in itself was a new methodology that would be used quite extensively by the Christians, especially by Paul—to dispute in the synagogues. The disputes would arise, I believe, because of an effort to reinterpret the Old Testament in the light of the Christian gospel. It was not a question of what the Old Testament said, but of what men understood by it: if Jesus was indeed all He claimed to be, then men's interpretations of the Old Testament must be revised, in some cases scrapped entirely. This is not easy. It will cause lengthy disputes, and sometimes hot tempers, and stone-throwing, and perhaps worse.

There were two factors in the Hellenist synagogues that should be noted—though they may seem at first glance to be contradictory.

Jews of the Diaspora learned to appreciate what it meant to be deprived of some of the privileges of their religion. Hence, when they returned to Jerusalem they were often more zealous for their faith than were the "Hebrews" of the homeland. This will explain at least in part why the hostile opposition to the preaching of the gospel reached fanatical proportions in the synagogue before it did in the Temple.

At the same time, and contrastingly, Jews of the Dispersion also learned how unnecessary the Temple and the sacrificial system were to the basic religious concepts of Judaism. This will explain why it was among the Hellenist Jews that the doctrines of Stephen, and later of the converted Saul of Tarsus, could develop. We shall see more of this matter as we study the present passage.

*The Charges.* Two charges were leveled against Stephen: he had uttered blasphemous words against Moses and God, and he had spoken seditious words against the Temple and the Law. We shall be impressed by similarities between the trial of Jesus and the trial of Stephen at several points.' Verses 11 and 13 are probably the initial and final forms of the same charges, for we can equate "Moses" with "Law," and we can equate "God" with "this holy place." In the common speech of a slightly later period, the Jews, in order to avoid any form of the divine name often referred to God as *hammāqôm,* (the Place), or *hashēm* (the Name).

In the charges we can see the truth beyond the half-truth that was used to try Stephen. He was probably preaching a message that contrasted the temporary nature of the Law and the Temple with the permanence of the reality in Christ. This is sound Christian doctrine, and is remarkably similar to the Epistle to the Hebrews.[5] But where did Stephen get such ideas? If we search the teachings of Jesus carefully, we shall find the seeds of all of the ideas that later developed into the doctrines taught by the Spirit-inspired apostles and preachers.

Jesus had denied the validity of blood-relationship to Abraham as a basis of religion (John 8:31-47). This means that those not of the blood-line of Abraham can be his spiritual seed. The contrast, then, must be, not between the physical descendants (Jews) and others (Gentiles), but between those who had the faith of Abraham (believers) and those who had not (unbelievers) (Rom. 4). This truth will become the climax of Stephen's sermon.

Jesus had suggested that true worship of the Father was a matter of the heart, and not a matter of geography. It was to be "neither on this mountain [Gerizim] nor in Jerusalem" (John 4:21). If so, then the permanent validity of Jerusalem as the holy city, and particularly of the Temple as the holy place in Jerusalem, is seriously challenged. If men did not have to go to Jerusalem to worship, but could worship in truth wherever they were, the Temple was indeed doomed! I do not suppose that Stephen said exactly that, but he was moving in that direction. It is quite reasonable to say that Stephen went further along these lines than anyone in the Church up to that time. Saul of Tarsus, of course, went further than Stephen. Stephen stands at the halfway mark between Peter and Paul in the expansion of Christian truth.

Jesus once said that it was impossible to take new wine and put it in old wineskins, for it would burst the skins (Matt. 9:17). What was happening with Stephen and would soon happen with the early Church is simply that the old wineskins of Judaism were bursting.

*Stephen's Defense.* Stephen's speech is the longest in the book of Acts; Rackham points out that it is as long as the three sermons of Paul put together. Actually, it is not a defense of himself at all, but a defense of the gospel he preached. More correctly, it is an "apology"—but the word apology today has come to have a quite different meaning. Originally, an apology was a statement proving that you are right; today it is an admission that you are wrong. Stephen was the first of the long list of Christian Apologists, stalwart champions of the Faith who defended it against all attacks in the early centuries of our era!

At first reading we may be inclined to agree with those who think the speech is long-winded and not at all to the point. However, as we analyze it in detail, we see that Stephen is answering the charges by setting forth the truth of his position, or rather, Jesus' position. In a word, Stephen's argument is based on the progressive nature of God's revelation.

The idea of "progressive revelation" is abhorrent to some Christians. Although it is clearly taught in

Hebrews 1:1, many reject it, insisting that to believe in progressive revelation is to believe that the Bible (or God) is self-contradictory. Nothing could be further from the truth! Those who object are in fact taking the line of Stephen's opponents. Progressive revelation, simply defined, is the proposition that God did not reveal *all* of the truth at once, but has been unfolding it down through the ages.

Stephen points out that God did not give the final form of revelation to Abraham, but simply gave him the promise (Acts 7:5). The promise, even in its initial form, could not be fulfilled for four hundred years—but nevertheless Abraham believed God. Joseph was the man who, in the providence of God, kept alive the hope of that promise by preserving the lives of the sons of Jacob. But his brothers, the physical descendants of Abraham, rejected him (7:9-16). Did Stephen have Jesus in mind? I believe he did.

When the time came for the fulfillment of the initial phase of the promise to Abraham, Moses was the one God chose (7:20). He presented himself to his brothers as the deliverer, but they rejected him too (7:35). Again, it was the one who was rejected who was God's servant.

Moreover, Moses himself had spoken of One to come: "God will raise up for you a prophet from your brethren as he raised me up" (7:37; cf. Deut. 18:15,18). But instead of looking for that coming Prophet, the fathers turned to idols. So for nearly a thousand years of its history Israel was enslaved to idolatry (Acts 7:42).

Up to this point, Stephen has been answering the

charge that he spoke blasphemous words against Moses. He has said, in effect: (1) Moses was but a step in the fulfillment of God's promise, as indeed Abraham had been; (2) your fathers rejected Moses when he came; (3) Moses foretold the coming of a greater Prophet. The implication seems to be: If Moses has been replaced (I would rather say "fulfilled") by Jesus, this is only what Moses himself had foretold. Moses was not the end of God's redemptive revelation.

Now, Stephen turns to the charge concerning the Temple. But he begins with the Tabernacle, which, as we know, was the forerunner of the Temple. The Tabernacle was made in accordance with the instructions given to Moses on the mount (7:44; Exod. 25:9,40). It was therefore God's own plan. If they insisted upon stopping with Moses, they should logically stop with the Tabernacle; for God had not given the Temple plans to Moses!

When the fathers came into the land of Canaan, it was under the leadership of one named Joshua. I wonder if Stephen enjoyed making that point! The names *Jesus* and *Joshua* are actually identical: *Jesus* is only the Greek form of *Joshua*. When Stephen was speaking Greek to the Hellenists, he had to say "Jesus" whenever he referred to Joshua; when he was speaking Hebrew to the Sanhedrin, he had to say "Joshua" when he was referring to Jesus. The two names are really one and the same. The immediate successor to Moses, who led the people into the fulfillment of the promise made to Abraham, was named *Jesus/Joshua*.[e] Stephen seems to be saying that the greater Successor to Moses, who would

103

lead the people into the greater fulfillment of the promise, was Jesus.

When David conceived the idea of building a house to the Lord, the Lord told him that he (David) should not build it, but his son would build it. We cannot help but ask the question at this point: Did God mean that David's son Solomon was to build the house (the Temple), or did God mean that David's greater Son Jesus was to build the house (the Church)? The Temple of Solomon was not the complete fulfillment of the promise—at most, it was a type and foreshadowing of the spiritual Temple. Stephen then quoted from Isaiah 66:1-2 (Acts 7:49-50): the Most High does not dwell in houses!

At this point Stephen turned directly on his hearers. This was no longer a "defense"—it was an offense, and in their minds probably as offensive as it could be. Yet the basis of the words was historical, and Scripture could have been quoted to support the charge—passages such as Exod. 33:3ff; Num. 27:14; Isa. 63:10; Jer. 6:10; 9:26. The people had repeatedly rejected the Prophets who had foretold the coming One. At last they had killed the One Himself (Acts 7:51-53).

*The Stoning of Stephen.* The crowd was filled with rage, blind rage, it would seem (7:54,57), and what began as an orderly trial seems to have become mob action.[7] Stephen, filled with the Spirit, gazing into Heaven, said, "I see . . . the Son of man standing at the right hand of God" (7:56). This was too much! They stopped their ears (the sign that blasphemy was being uttered), rushed on Stephen, cast him out of the city, and stoned him to death. As he was dying under the barrage of stones, they heard him say, "Lord Jesus, receive my spirit" (7:59), and then, in a loud voice, "Lord, do not hold this sin against them" and he fell asleep. The parallels with the words of Jesus on the cross are obvious.

A young man named Saul was present that day, and they laid their garments—or perhaps it should read "his" garments, i.e., the clothes they had stripped from Stephen prior to stoning him—at Saul's feet. Saul never forgot that day or that scene. He referred to it years later (22:20). At the moment, however, his conscience was not touched—except, of course, by the feeling that blasphemy had been uttered.

*The Immediate Results.* Just before the Ascension Jesus had said, "You shall be my witnesses in Jerusalem and in all Judea and Samaria and to the end of the earth" (1:8).

The word translated "witness" has given us our word "martyr." The reason is simple: so many of the early Christian witnesses became martyrs. Stephen was the first martyr of the Church.

That day "a great persecution rose against the church in Jerusalem," and as a result, the believers, with the exception of the apostles, "were all scattered throughout the region of Judea and Samaria" (8:1).

So the period of the First Church comes to an end. No longer will it be a compact fellowship meeting in Solomon's Portico. It is now scattered throughout the southern part of Palestine. If there had been any rose-colored optimism about quickly winning the Jewish people to their Messiah, that was gone. The Church could not expect triumph without a bloody battle. "A servant is not greater than his master. If they have persecuted me, they will persecute you," said Jesus (John 15:20). Devout men buried Stephen, but Saul laid waste the church, dragging men and women from their homes and throwing them into prison (Acts 8:2-3).

We still find men and women who think that the Christian message can be proclaimed in this world without opposition. They attempt to make the program of evangelization easy by removing the distinctives of the message. They attempt to conform to the world, to cooperate with all non-Christian groups and philosophies. But this is not Christianity! It has nothing in common with the gospel of Christ or the Early Church. "The Son of God goes forth to war! . . . Who follows in His train?"

Stephen was the first to follow. "Stephen" in Greek means "crown." To those who follow in the Master's train shall be given a crown of life (Rev. 2:10). According to the book of Revelation, blessings beyond imagination are reserved for the martyrs.

*Summation.* Faithful witness to the Lord Jesus Christ can only be given by those who are willing to be martyrs. Deep-rooted conviction, rather than false bravado, produces heroes. If we have that kind of faith in the Lord Jesus Christ, we need never fear what we will do in the time of stress. A faithful witness will make a faithful martyr! (Rev. 2:13).

God's will is done, even though it may come about through opposition and persecution. The witnesses were driven out of Jerusalem, and I suppose Saul and the members of the Sanhedrin thought that they were at last in control of the situation. But men do not control the Spirit of God! Driving out the witnesses was like scattering flames. These witnesses were men filled with the Holy Spirit. They took that Spirit with them, and soon He would be let loose on all of Judea and Samaria! With the shedding of his blood, Stephen's earthly life came to an end. But, as Saint Jerome wrote, "The blood of the martyrs is the seed of the Church."

## Footnotes

1. See discussion of this expression, under "The Office of the Twelve" in chapter 8.

2. Scholars find from one to five synagogues in 6:9. For a careful discussion, cf. F. F. Bruce, *The Acts of the Apostles* (2d ed., 1952), p. 156. Please note that this book is to be distinguished from Bruce's *Commentary on the Book of Acts*. We shall refer to the latter as *Commentary on Acts*.

3. The older translation "synagogue of the Libertines" is to be rejected, for the word "libertine" today has a connotation of immorality.

4. Read in this connection Mark 14:58 and Matt. 26:61. Bruce reminds us that Caiaphas, who was high priest until A.D. 36, was probably the high priest at both trials. (*Commentary on Acts*, p. 144).

5. Cf. W. Manson, *The Epistle to the Hebrews*, (1951), pp. 25-46.

6. This is obvious in *KJV*, where the Greek form of the name Joshua is translated "Jesus"—see Acts, 7:45, *KJV*.

7. There were "witnesses," indicating it was a trial. Perhaps there was also an official "verdict"—but this has to be inferred from 8:1, "Saul was consenting to his death." This last statement, however, may only mean that Saul agreed inwardly with the action of the mob.

# PART II

# The Period of Transition

# CHAPTER 10

# The Church in Preparation
# for Its World Mission

For seven chapters, Acts has recorded the story of the First Church, the church in Jerusalem. Beginning with chapter 13, the story of the spread of the gospel "to the uttermost part of the earth" will be unfolded. The portion between, Acts 8:1–12:25, is in the nature of a transition.

Transition is a necessary part of growth or development. It is the "adolescent" period of the individual or of the church. An individual Christian usually begins with a faith that is pretty much turned inward. He thinks of his own "salvation." Then he comes to think of those who are close to him. Usually it takes an educational process, through speakers, Bible study, reading, and other experiences, to give him a "world-view" of the gospel. Many Christians never come fully to this stage.

What is true of individuals is also true of churches. Attempts to force maturity can be tragic. Our Lord expressed a true principle: "First the blade, then the ear, then the full grain in the ear" (Mark 4:28). I would suggest that if the Early Church in its first few years had been faced with the problem which resulted from Paul's first missionary journey,[1] a revolution could have resulted that might have destroyed the Church. It simply was not yet prepared to face that problem. What do I mean? Well, let's see. A survey of this transitional period will help us.

*The Steps in the Transition.* Luke has again demonstrated a historian's wisdom and art in tracing for us the principal steps in the transition. He has selected five significant events:

The Expansion into Samaria and Judea (8:1-40)
The Conversion of Saul (9:1-30)
The Conversion of Cornelius (10:1—11:18)
The Church in Antioch (11:19-30)
The Herodian Persecution of the Church (12:1-25)

We cannot date all of these exactly. The last, however, can be dated at A.D. 44,[2] and the first can be dated somewhere between A.D. 32 and 35, probably the earlier date. We can therefore say that this transitional period took about ten or twelve years. Merely listing these does not necessarily show the stages in the transition, so let's look at them again, trying to discover the significance of each event.

We have already seen that for the Jew the world was divided into two categories: Jew and non-Jew (or Gentile). But this is an oversimplification. There were Jews who were born Jews, and there were others who had converted to Judaism (called "Proselytes"). Another subculture traced their ancestry to the Patriarchs, kept the Law of Moses, but, because of historical events in the past, were not "Jews" (Judeans), but rather were "Samaritans." Moreover, there were people who "feared God." That is, they worshiped the God of the Jews, read the Scriptures of the Jews, and, it would seem, even got as close to the Temple or the synagogue as was possible.[3] But they were not Proselytes. Finally, there were non-Jews, or Gentiles, who were completely pagan, with no knowledge of God or the Scriptures.

A second factor to be considered is the background and attitude of the evangelists. For work among Jews, a Jewish Christian is the logical choice; for work among the Samaritans, a Samaritan would have been ideal. For work among Gentiles—whether Proselytes, God-fearers, or pagans—a Hellenist was almost a "must." In time, gentile Christians were ready to undertake the task of evangelizing the pagans.

In Acts we notice that a Hellenist is used to reach the Samaritans, although two of the apostles enter the task and perform commendably. Whether the Ethiopian was a Proselyte or a God-fearer is not clear. In either event, it was a Hellenist who reached him with the gospel. Peter, it is true, was the agent used to reach the God-fearer Cornelius—but it was not without protests from Peter. When we study the account of the conversion of Cornelius we shall see why it had to be one of the Twelve—in fact, the leader of the Twelve—that made this first great leap in the evangelization of the Gentiles.

But when we come to the actual campaigns into the gentile world, we find God raising up a Jew from outside Jerusalem, in fact, outside Palestine— a Jew who was able to move freely among Gentiles, who was able to defend his course of action before the apostles, and who was able to collaborate with gentile Christians in the work of the gospel.

A third factor was the center from which the Early Church would conduct its evangelistic program. Jerusalem was too obviously tied in with Judaism. This would, of course, change with the destruction of Jerusalem and the Second Temple, but for the immediate future, a new center was needed. Where should it be?

The three first cities of the Roman Empire were in order of their importance Rome, Alexandria, and Antioch-on-the-Orontes. Ultimately, Rome would be the center for evangelization of the West—but for the present, the jump was simply too great. Alexandria would be less than ideal for two reasons. First, Alexandrian Judaism had developed philosophically, and Christianity emanating from that place would become highly speculative. The age for speculative Christianity would come later, but at this early stage the gospel must be presented in its historical nature. Christian theology must arise out of the events of God's redemptive work, and not out of the speculations of men.

A second disadvantage of Alexandria as a new center was geographical: it was off the main line. It is true that a strong church developed in North Africa in the first centuries of our era. But where did it go from there? By sea (during the few months the sea lanes were open), it had access to Rome. But otherwise, it was badly limited. Antioch-on-the-Orontes, on the other hand, was on main routes, by land and by sea, and these routes fanned out in all directions. Eastern Christianity as well as Western Christianity developed from the church in Antioch.

But how could a new era in the Early Church, under new leadership and with a new location, come into prominence? There could have been, of course, a major schism—a split. But that would have destroyed the very thing that God was attempting to create in Christ: a unity, a oneness in Christ. Historically, the transition was made gradually. Jerusalem remained the center, but because of persecutions the Hellenist Christians were driven out; finally none of the apostles, it would seem, remained in Jerusalem. The church in Jerusalem became a relatively weak Jewish church under the leadership of James the Lord's brother. At last he was martyred and with the Roman siege, the Jerusalem church was scattered.

*The Planning of the Transition.* Now I do not suggest for a moment that the apostles, or any other person or group of persons in the First Church sat down and planned this strategy. When we study the work of Paul, we shall see several signs of a planned strategy. The apostles were convinced that the Spirit was leading them, blocking the road in some directions, opening great doors of opportunity in other places, and gradually unfolding the plan of God.

Left to their own devices, the apostles might never have gotten out of Jerusalem, and probably would never have attempted evangelization of the Gentiles. But they were not left to their own devices. God was devising a strategy for them. Just as the death of Jesus by the hands of cruel men was in reality the outworking of God's counsel and foreknowledge (2:23), so the development of the body of Christ (the Church) was according to God's plan, even including the persecutions, the martyrdoms, and all the other events recorded and unrecorded.

*Summation.* Obviously, the outward progress of the gospel can be achieved more readily if we seek to evangelize first those who stand closest to our own position rather than attempting to jump at once to the most difficult objective. In the Early Church, the progress will be: first the Jews, then the Samaritans, and after that, the gentile Proselytes, then the "God-fearers" or the Gentiles who worship the God of the Jews without converting to Judaism, and finally, the pagans.

In this transitional period, we can see, if we look for it, the unfolding of God's plan for the Early Church.

## Footnotes

1. It is possible that Luke intended the "First Missionary Journey" to be considered also as part of the transition, thus putting the Jerusalem Conference (chap. 15) at the middle of his outline, and "Evangelization of the Gentiles" would be the second half of Acts, 15:36—28:31.

2. The date of the death of Herod Agrippa I has been determined thanks to the account in Josephus, *Antiquities* 19.8.2, §§ 350-351.

3. At one period, the term "proselyte of the gate" seems to have been used of them. It suggests a "half-converted" state, which Judaism never recognized.

# The Expansion into Judea and Samaria

On the day when Stephen was stoned, "a great persecution arose against the church in Jerusalem; and they were all scattered throughout the region of Judea and Samaria, except the apostles" (Acts 8:1b). This statement forms a watershed in the story. Luke will return to it in several ways (cf. 8:4; 9:1; 9:31; 11:19). It is clear that Luke regarded the persecution and the scattering as an essential part of the history of the Early Church.

What does Luke mean by the words, "they were *all* scattered"? We shall hear further of the church in Jerusalem (8:3, 12:1,5), the disciples in Jerusa-

117

lem (9:26), the circumcision party (11:2), and other indications that the church was not entirely driven from Jerusalem. Most probably Luke means that the Hellenists of the First Church were driven out; the Hebrews remained.[1]

The apostles were not driven out—probably because they, along with the Hebrews, were careful to observe the Law of Moses. But we shall soon notice that they are no longer connected exclusively with the church in Jerusalem. They seem to be establishing churches in Judea.

*The Preaching of Philip.* "Those who were scattered went about preaching the word," says Luke (8:4). The word he uses for "scattered" comes from the same root as the word for Dispersion or Diaspora. But there is a difference: the Diaspora of the Jews had not resulted in evangelization; the Diaspora of the Church did result in evangelization or the proclaiming of the good news.[2]

One of those who had been scattered was Philip —but was it Philip the apostle or Philip, one of the seven new church officers? If the apostles remained in Jerusalem, and this Philip was one of those who had been scattered, he must have been one of the Seven, later called "Philip the evangelist" (21:8). Certainly, Luke's precision of language requires this interpretation! It follows, then, that the appointment to "serve tables" did not exempt the Seven from preaching the Word. Moreover, since both Stephen (6:8) and Philip (8:6) had the power to work miracles, we must conclude that this power was not limited to the Twelve.

Philip went first to Samaria. His preaching and

his "signs" or miracles drew multitudes, and "there was much joy in that city" (8:8).

Among those who were attracted was a man named Simon, a magician who had previously amazed the Samaritan people. Since he had said he "was somebody great" (8:9), he is usually referred to as Simon Magus (or Simon the Great). For "a long time" he had enjoyed great popularity in Samaria. But when Philip came along, many were baptized, and Simon no longer held the center of the stage (8:12). Luke records that "Simon himself believed, and after being baptized he continued with Philip" (8:13).

In the light of what is about to happen, we might well pause here to comment on the fallacy of putting too much stress on baptism, particularly that which is referred to as "believer baptism." Please understand that I am not trying to set forth any particular view. I have my own convictions, but this is not the place to defend them. I am simply trying to understand the Word of God. Some sincere Christians believe in "infant baptism," or the baptizing of infant children of believers. Some who are equally sincere believe that only those who are able to make a meaningful profession of their own faith should be baptized. This latter view is often referred to as "believer baptism," suggesting that those who are so baptized are believers. Well, Simon Magus was baptized with "believer baptism" (8:13). Let's beware of putting stress on anything other than sincere faith in the Lord Jesus Christ and complete dedication to His teachings!

Samaria was a "half-breed" area. When the Assyrians had overrun the land in the sixth century B.C., they deported the most productive Jews, but left the poor and the weak. They moved pagan peoples into the area, following the Assyrian custom of displacing peoples to prevent insurrection. The Samaritans, in general, had resulted from the intermarriage of the poor Israelites with the relocated Gentiles. They had held on to the Scriptures, which at that time consisted only of the books of Moses (the Prophets were only then proclaiming their messages), and they worshiped according to the rites described in the Law. But they had located their temple on Mount Gerizim, some miles south of the city of Samaria.

In a sense, then, the Samaritans were closer to the Jews in their religious beliefs than any other people. It was logical that the first step in the outward progress of the gospel should be to the Samaritans. Still, there was deep-seated prejudice, amounting almost to hatred, standing between the Jews and the Samaritans (John 4:9).

It is true that Jesus had made a Samaritan the hero in one of His parables (Luke 10:29-37). And He had not only talked with the woman at the well in Samaria, but He had even spent two days in her village (John 4:40). Furthermore, He had sent some of His disciples into a village of the Samaritans that He planned to visit—but the feeling of hostility was so ingrained, that when the people of the city would not receive Him, James and John (of all people!) suggested, "Do you want us to bid fire come down from heaven and consume them?" (Luke 9:51-55).

We can therefore believe that it was not easy for the Jewish Christians to evangelize Samaria. Perhaps that is why God used a Hellenist for the task.

*Apostolic Confirmation.* "When the apostles at Jerusalem heard that Samaria had received the Word of God, they sent to them Peter and John" (Acts 8:14). It was still one Church, and the report of conversions in Samaria was the signal for some kind of action by the apostles. Peter and John went to Samaria,* prayed for those who had been baptized, laid their hands on them, and the Samaritan Christians received the Holy Spirit (8:14-16).

This is probably the beginning of the church rite of "confirmation." But was it intended to be set up as a rite? Are we to conclude that the Holy Spirit can only be conferred by the "laying on of hands" by the apostles? Before we become fixed in any conclusions, let's read on in the book of Acts. If the laying on of hands preceded the gift of the Spirit in Samaria, certainly this was not the case in Caesarea! Someone has suggested that the only rule we can establish from Acts is that God does not obey our rules. Still, I would not suggest that He is opposed to order, for He commends order in the Church. (See 1 Cor. 14:40).

There was some kind of supervision by the "mother church" over her offspring, and this supervision of new churches continues in the work of the apostle Paul. We can assume that it should be present whenever new churches come into being.

*Simony.* Simon Magus noticed that "the Spirit was given through the laying on of the apostles' hands" (8:18), and he tried to buy this power. He gave the world a new word, "simony," which is the buying and selling of ecclesiastical offices. But more important, he gave us a lesson that further extends our understanding of the meaning of "fellowship."

What Simon was asking for was the power to confer the Holy Spirit on persons of his own choice. "Give me also this power, that any one on whom I lay my hands may receive the Holy Spirit" (8:19). No man should have such power! No man should have power to determine who should be admitted to the Kingdom of Heaven (which is what birth of the Spirit means, cf. John 3:5) and who should be excluded.

But perhaps Simon was not thinking of his sought-for power in this way. Probably not—but even if we take his words with minimum value, he was still asking to have the power to confer the Spirit's power. And no man can be entrusted with power under such conditions! To give a man untold power, when his will is not thoroughly committed to the will of God, is unthinkable! Simon did not ask for power "that any one who believes" but "that any one on whom I lay my hands" might receive the Spirit. The result of such power would be to fill the world with power-filled unbelievers!

Peter struck at the suggestion with immediate and sharp language. "To perdition with you and your money!' . . . Your heart is not right before God. . . . Repent therefore of this wickedness of yours, and pray to the Lord that, if possible, the intent of your heart may be forgiven you . . ." (8:20-23).

Did Simon repent? He shows early signs of repentance (8:24), but beyond that Luke does not go. In the literature of Early Christianity, Simon Magus assumes almost gigantic proportions, but these traditions have no scriptural basis beyond what we read here.[5]

*The Ethiopian Official.* Philip was led to go to the southern part of the country (Judea), on the road from Jerusalem to Gaza. It is impossible to locate the route precisely, therefore the traditional sites that are shown to the tourist have no validity.

An Ethiopian official (something like the chancellor of the exchequer) had been to Jerusalem to worship, and was returning home. Seated in his chariot, he was reading what appears to have been a Greek manuscript of Isaiah. Philip was led by the Spirit to join him (8:26-29).

Ethiopia in the first century A.D. was located in the Nile Valley, between the First Cataract (modern Aswan) and the confluence of the White Nile with the Blue Nile (modern Khartoum), including parts of present-day Egypt and Sudan. The modern nation of Ethiopia (Abyssinia) is located further east. A popular notion that the church there traces its origin to the Ethiopian eunuch has no foundation in fact.

Just what was the Ethiopian eunuch's religious status? Was he a Proselyte (convert to Judaism), or a God-fearer? Luke does not make it clear. Some scholars say that he could not have been a Proselyte since he was a eunuch.[6] But two objections may be raised to this conclusion. The term "eunuch" was often used to denote an office and did not necessarily signify "castrate." Moreover, the strict regulation concerning the admission of eunuchs to the Congregation of Israel may have been somewhat modified, in the light of Isaiah 56:3-5.

In view of the fact that Luke clearly makes Cornelius the *cause célèbre* of the admission of God-fearers to the Church, it seems unlikely that the Ethiopian was anything less than a Proselyte. Whenever Luke has included the story of a conversion which is significant, it is to highlight a new situation. This is true of the inclusion of Samaritans (8:14), of the inclusion of the God-fearers of the household of Cornelius (11:1), of the evangelization of Gentiles at Antioch (11:22), and, above all, of the widespread gentile evangelization by Paul (15:1-2). It seems to me that the absence of any such inquiry here means that Luke is treating this story as part of the geographical expansion of the Church.[7]

The Ethiopian was reading aloud from Isaiah 53.[8] He had reached the words, "As a sheep led to the slaughter or a lamb before its shearers is dumb, so he opens not his mouth" (8:32), when Philip joined him.

We would do well to notice the varied approaches that are presented in Acts. In just about every situation the evangelizer begins where the hearer is. The question, "Are you saved?" is not used once.

Philip asked him, "Do you understand what you are reading?" The Ethiopian replied with a question (8:31), and followed it with another question, "About whom, pray, does the prophet say this, about himself or about someone else?" (8:34). It was a good question, and scholars have debated the same point for over two thousand years. Philip might have gotten lost in a discussion of the options. Instead, he went immediately to the application of the prophecy to Jesus.

The prophet is not talking about himself as the Saviour. He is talking about someone else, someone who acts savingly or redemptively for the prophet and those included in his words. That other One was "stricken for the transgression of my people" (Isa. 53:8). He was made the "offering for sin" (v.10).

The Servant of the Lord in Isaiah 42–53 can be likened to a triangle or pyramid. The base represents the nation Israel. As the figure narrows down, it refers to the prophet and the righteous remnant. But at last, at the apex, it refers to a single individual.⁹

Philip began there, and proclaimed the gospel of Jesus. How much he told the Ethiopian Luke does not tell us, but we certainly can make a reasonably close guess. Starting with the "sheep led to the slaughter," Philip must have proclaimed the death of Jesus. He surely did not stop with the death, but must have gone on to the Resurrection. He must have mentioned baptism, since the Ethiopian speaks of it in 8:37. But since the message in Acts is always "repent and be baptized," Philip must certainly have preached repentance. This is the same message that the apostles have always proclaimed. Luke does not spell it out because there is really no need to do so.

So Philip baptized the eunuch. What happened next to the Ethiopian we are not told. As for Philip, he was found at Azotus (it would seem by a miraculous event, 8:39), and then he continued preaching until he reached Caesarea. At this point, Luke turns to another part of his story.

*Summation.* What have we learned from this story? Above all, we have learned that the growth of the Church, the spread of the gospel, is by orderly progress. Sudden leaps, instead of gradual transitions, are not the natural thing—and God is the God of the natural far more often than He is of the supernatural. God expects us to do our work in an ever-increasingly outward progress; but He does not expect us to leap over the gulfs that divide cultures and personalities.

It is a fallacy, I believe, and one that has seriously hurt the missionary program of the Church, that men and women should think that they can take the gospel to Africa, or China, or India when they have not yet learned to evangelize men of their own cultural and social and racial kind. By what right do I assume that I will be a success with the Hottentots if I have been a failure with the young people of my own church or school or club? Would I expect to clear the bar at six feet if I have never yet been able to get above four-feet-one? Such a question sounds silly. It is no less silly to think that we can ignore the transitions in Christian witness.

This, however, does not allow us to be content with our present sphere of witness. We have not obeyed the command of the Lord Jesus until our circle of witness is as large as the circle of His will.

# Footnotes

1. For the distinction between these terms see the beginning of chapter 8.

2. The verb translated "preaching" in 8:4 is *evangelizomai* from which we get "evangelize."

3. The expression "came down" is used because one always "went up" to Jerusalem and "came down" from it.

4. J. B. Phillips' translation ("to hell with you and your money") is offensive to many, but it is quite an accurate translation.

5. There is a brief discussion of Simon Magus in Bruce, *Commentary on Acts*, pp. 178-179, with references. For a fuller discussion, cf. R. P. Casey in *Beginnings of Christianity*, 5:151ff., and articles in larger Bible dictionaries.

6. Cf. Deut. 23:1, but see also Isa. 56:3-5.

7. If, on the other hand, Luke's repeated use of the word "eunuch" is significant here, then he may be stressing the relevance of the words of Isa. 56:3-5 to the Messianic Age. In other words, we would be saying, "A eunuch may not be acceptable to Judaism, but he is welcome in the Kingdom of God." But in that case, we would have expected Luke to have included some reference to the passage in Isaiah.

8. Scholars working in the Hebrew and Greek texts of Isaiah 53 recognize at once that the passage in Acts 8:32-33 follows the LXX and not the Masoretic (Hebrew) text.

9. The pyramid-figure of interpretation is discussed more fully in my article, "Interpretation of Prophecy," in *Baker's Dictionary of Practical Theology* (1967), pp. 128-135.

CHAPTER 12 / (Acts 9:1-30)

# The Man for the Gentile Mission

Next to the resurrection of Jesus Christ, it is possible that the second most important event in the history of the world was the conversion of Saul of Tarsus, better known as the apostle Paul.

This sounds like an extreme statement. But think about it. Humanly speaking, Paul had more to do with the establishment of the Christian Church in the Western World than any other individual. He personally carried the gospel into Asia Minor, Greece, and Rome, establishing churches that became ecclesiastical centers of primary significance in the early centuries of our era. He personally (and practically alone) fought against the forces that would have split the Early Church. He wrote almost twenty-five percent of the New Testament.[1]

His letters, particularly those to the Romans and the Galatians, have had profound effect on the thinking and behavior of the world. If you challenge this statement, just check the Library of Congress catalog and see how many books have been written about Paul and his epistles.

Luke would certainly agree that Paul is of very unusual importance, for he devoted about eight percent of Acts to the story of Paul's conversion, including three separate accounts of the event (Acts 9:1-30; 22:3-29; 26:2-31), and two-thirds of Acts is used to tell about Paul's part in the story of the Early Church.

Luke is not merely concerned with telling the story of Paul, for that is contrary to the purpose implicit in his prologue (Acts 1:1-5). Primarily he is concerned with telling the story of the risen Lord. But Paul is one of the great historical evidences of the Resurrection—for it was the appearance of the risen Jesus that brought about Saul's conversion.

That story is our present study.

*Events Leading up to the Conversion.* The story begins with a murderous mission. With the single statement, "still breathing threats and murder against the disciples of the Lord" (9:1), Luke carries us back to the stoning of Stephen (8:1-3). Saul had succeeded in doing great harm to the church in Jerusalem. Now he is seeking to extend this persecution to the refugees in Damascus (9:2).

We must seek to understand Saul, or else we shall never understand Paul. That is probably why, when Paul tells the story of his conversion, he includes a reference to his youth (22:3; 26:4-5).

129

He was a Jew of the Diaspora, born in Tarsus in the Roman province of Cilicia (22:3). Tarsus was an important city, the location of one of the three universities of that day. However, Saul was probably not greatly influenced by Tarsus—not at that time, anyway—for he tells us he was brought up in Jerusalem (22:3; 26:4). His father and mother are never named. They may have died when he was very young, or they may have rejected him when he became a Christian. Saul had a sister living in Jerusalem, and at least one nephew (23:16). He may have lived with them, but this does not seem likely.

His parents were both Jews, and his father at least was of the tribe of Benjamin (Phil. 3:5). Doubtless Saul was named for the Benjamite king Saul, the first king of Israel. His father was a strict Pharisee, and he brought up his son in that tradition (Phil. 3:5; Acts 26:5). Hoping to train him for the rabbinate, the father took or sent Saul to Jerusalem to study under the great Rabban Gamaliel, who also was a Pharisee. We have met Gamaliel, just briefly, in connection with the first persecution of the First Church (Acts 5:34-39). The Rabban was a man of moderation; his disciple Saul was a man of unholy zeal (Phil. 3:6; Acts 26:9-11).

We get additional light on Saul from statements which he wrote in his letter to the Romans. Being exceedingly zealous to keep the Law, he was finding no satisfaction in the Law. It is possible that Romans 7:9-11 tells his preconversion experience, and 7:13-25 his feelings after his conversion. In any event, we see the terrible struggle that was taking place in his soul, as he was driven by the demands

of the Law. "The very commandment which promised life," he wrote, "proved to be death to me"
(Rom. 7:10).

Whether Saul stayed on in Jerusalem when his
training was finished, or went back to Tarsus, we do
not know. Whether he ever saw or heard Jesus, we
do not know—although some would interpret 2 Corinthians 5:16 to mean that Saul had known Jesus in
the flesh. Was Saul a member of the Sanhedrin? His
words, "I cast my vote against them" (Acts 26:10),
are taken by some to mean that he was one of the
Council. The statement does not necessarily require
this interpretation. Was Saul married? At one time,
members of the Sanhedrin were required to be married men. We do not know if that requirement was
yet in effect in Saul's time—and, of course, we do
not know if he was actually a member of the Sanhedrin. When he wrote 1 Corinthians 7:8, he was not
married. If he had been previously married, what
happened to his wife? Did he have any children?
We do not know. His wife and child might have
died in one of the epidemics common to Tarsus. His
wife might have renounced him when he became a
Christian. But of course, we haven't any evidence
that he was married.²

Since we cannot fill in all of the details of the
period preceding the stoning of Stephen, we cannot explain precisely what triggered Saul's reaction.
Perhaps he had been in one of the synagogues of
the Hellenists and had heard Stephen disputing
with them—he might even have participated in the
dispute (Acts 6:9). Or, perhaps he had just come to
Jerusalem for one of the holy days, and "happened"

on the event. We know he was present when they stoned Stephen (7:58). And we know that Saul entered immediately into his diabolical effort to exterminate the members of the First Church (8:3). He once described his violent action against the church in the following way:

I myself was convinced that I ought to do many things in opposing the name of Jesus of Nazareth. And I did so in Jerusalem; I not only shut up many of the saints in prison, by authority from the chief priests, but when they were put to death I cast my vote against them. And I punished them often in all the synagogues and tried to make them blaspheme; and in raging fury against them, I persecuted them even to foreign cities (Acts 26:9-11).

How could a religious Jew, devoutly striving to keep the Law, act like this? Simply stated, he was defending God's name. Blasphemy was the greatest sin. It was worthy of death. Jesus, in Saul's eyes, was a blasphemer. No man could make the claims that Jesus was reported to have made, without blaspheming. We must understand this!

Modern writer-critics try to tell us that the picture of Jesus was gradually built up by the Early Church. "It was the Church that made the Galilean Jesus into a God," they tell us. But this is clearly contradicted by the unanimous testimony of the New Testament record. Jesus was put to death because the claims He made were equivalent to making Himself God. Once, when they tried to kill Jesus by stoning Him, He asked them, "For which of these [good works] do you stone me?" They replied, "We stone you for no good work but for blasphemy; because you, being a man, make yourself God" (John 10:33).

Moreover, His followers were blasphemers. They not only accepted His claims, but they even worshiped Him as the Son of God. Stephen indeed claimed to have seen Jesus standing at the right hand of God!

From his own point of view Saul was right. If Jesus said such things, and was only a man, then, according to the Law of Moses, He deserved to die. And if His disciples accepted His claims and worshiped Him, they deserved to die according to that same Law. Therefore Saul persecuted the Church with fury.

*The Event on the Road to Damascus.* Saul had done his work in Jerusalem (and also in nearby towns, it would seem from Acts 26:11). Now he was on his way to Damascus with authority to carry out the same task (9:2).

A light from Heaven that was brighter than the noon-day sun (26:13) blinded him as he was approaching the city (9:3; 22:6). He fell to the ground and heard a voice saying, "Saul, Saul, why do you persecute me?" (9:4; 22:7; 26:14).

Saul was persecuting the church. Now the identity of Jesus and His Church is firmly established in the New Testament. This is part of the meaning of *koinōnía.* Therefore Saul must realize that by persecuting Christians he is persecuting Jesus. Yet Saul did not know who was speaking. His words, "Who are you, sir?" tell us that.[3] So Jesus declares, "I am Jesus, whom you are persecuting" (9:5).

133

According to Luke's account, the men traveling with Saul heard the voice (9:7). But later Paul said they did not hear the voice (22:9). Is this a contradiction? Well, Luke wrote both statements, even if one was in Paul's words—therefore we rule out the idea that Luke recorded a flat contradiction of his own words. It is equally ridiculous to suppose that Luke recorded contradictory accounts of whether the companions stood (9:7) or fell to the ground (26:14). Probably all of them fell to the ground, but while the others could rise, Saul, who was blinded, could not. As for the voice, Bruce suggests that Luke meant that the companions heard Saul's voice, but could not see who it was he was talking with.'

Saul was instructed to go into Damascus, where he would receive further directions, and he was led blind to the city (9:8-9; 22:10-11).

According to the account given to Festus and Agrippa, the voice from heaven also said, "It hurts you to kick against the goads" (26:14). What did that mean? Some feel that Saul was slowly backing into Christianity—but there is no indication of this in any of the various statements in the New Testament. Others feel that God was gradually preparing Saul for this moment. There had been the training under the gentle Gamaliel, with his advice of caution. Gamaliel was a Pharisee, but he had a remarkable desire to test new ideas. He was a liberalizing spirit, in the best sense. Saul, his disciple, would put into practice this attitude at a later date, but for the present he was resisting it. Then there had been the testimony of Stephen. Later Saul would not only accept many of the principles enunciated by Stephen, but he would even carry them through to their logical conclusion. But at this time, he was "kicking against the goads." There had also been Saul's own conflict with the demands of the Law, which should have driven him to seek for grace. Later, he would recognize that salvation comes by the grace of God and not by human works. But up to now he was resisting.

According to the account which Paul gave in the presence of Festus and Agrippa, God revealed to him at that time what the nature of his ministry to the Gentiles was to be (26:16-18). It seems unlikely that this revelation would have been meaningful to Saul at that time, therefore some scholars feel that Paul telescoped a number of revelations into this one account. On the other hand, the gentile ministry of the apostle was revealed to Ananias in Damascus (9:15-16), hence it is not incredible that God may have revealed His purpose to Saul also at that time.

*Ananias of Damascus.* Saul was only "half-converted" on the road to Damascus. He had to be baptized and receive the Spirit—and these things were reserved by God until Saul was in fellowship with other believers. Certainly God could have bestowed the Spirit at once on Saul, as He poured out the Spirit on the Day of Pentecost. But after Pentecost, it seems to be the scriptural rule that the Spirit is given only when another Spirit-filled believer is present.

Why did Saul remain sightless for three days? I am sure that God had a reason. One of the important lessons that we need to learn is to await God's time and God's way.

There was a disciple at Damascus named Ananias. We know nothing about him other than that he was a "disciple" (i.e., a Christian, 9:10) and "a devout man according to the law, well spoken of by all the Jews who lived there" (22:12).

The Lord told Ananias to go to the house of Judas on Straight Street, and ask for Saul (9:10-12). Ananias had already heard about Saul, about his satanic work in Jerusalem, and about his present mission to Damascus, and Ananias didn't want anything to do with him (9:13-14). (Thus I interpret the word "but" in his reply.)

Nevertheless the Lord said, "Go," and revealed to Ananias some of His plan for Saul (9:15-16). So Ananias went (9:17). Paul doesn't include these details in his accounts (cf. 22:12-13; 26:19-20)—perhaps he did not know them; more likely he did not consider them necessary to his defense.

Ananias greeted Saul at once as "Brother"—fellow Christian—telling him that "the Lord Jesus who appeared to you on the road . . . has sent me that you may regain your sight and be filled with the Holy Spirit" (9:17). The simplicity of faith, in going to the man who had come to destroy the church in Damascus and calling him "Brother" (because he believed that God had spoken to him) marks Ananias indeed as an unusual man.

God had also prepared Saul for this visit. Luke reports it as part of God's message to Ananias: ". . . inquire in the house of Judas for a man of Tarsus named Saul; for behold, he is praying, and he has seen a man named Ananias come in and lay his hands on him so that he might regain his sight" (9:11-12). Was Saul praying during the three days he was without sight? Had he already repented of his former way? We are not told. According to one of Paul's accounts, after Ananias had explained to him the meaning of what had happened on the Damascus road, he added, "And now why do you wait? Rise and be baptized, and wash away your sins, calling on his name" (22:16).

We usually race through the story of Saul's conversion: he had the vision, Ananias came, Saul was baptized, and that's over! Did it take God a day or two to convince Ananias that he should go? Did God have to wait for Saul, while he sat in darkness, praying to a God he hadn't really known, trying to understand what had really happened? Did Saul find it hard to believe, almost impossible to believe, that the crucified Jesus whom he had marked as a blasphemer had actually appeared to him on the road? We don't know. But we do know that the events of those days are deeply etched on Paul's memory. He could never forget that in persecuting the Church he was the chief of sinners, and that to him, who was less than the least of all saints, Jesus had appeared! We can never understand the conversion of Saul, unless we understand all that the word conversion implies.

Did Saul repent? We are not told in so many words. But if "repent" means to turn around, to reverse your mental attitude, then certainly Saul repented. Three days earlier he was breathing out murderous threats against the Church because of its blasphemy in declaring that Jesus was the Son of God. Now, Saul is joining that very Church and immediately proclaiming that Jesus is the Son of God (9:20)! This is repentance.

So Ananias laid his hands on Saul, and Doctor Luke reports, "something like scales fell from his eyes and he regained his sight" (9:18). Saul was baptized and broke his fast by eating some food (9:19). One of the greatest miracles of all time had just occurred. Saul was born anew!

*Saul's Work in Damascus.* The order of events immediately following Saul's conversion is not entirely clear. "For several days he was with the disciples at Damascus" (9:19b). Luke reports that he began at once to preach that Jesus is the Son of God, amazing all who heard him (9:20-21). He increased in strength, confounding the unconverted Jews of Damascus "by proving that Jesus was the Christ" (9:22). And then, "when many days had passed" (9:23), there was a plot against his life, and Saul was forced to escape by night (9:23-25), and he went to Jerusalem.

In his letter to the Galatians, Paul writes, concerning his conversion and the subsequent events, as follows:

"But when he who had set me apart before I was born, and had called me through his grace, was pleased to reveal his Son to me, in order that I might preach him among the Gentiles, I did not confer with flesh and blood, nor did I go up to Jerusalem to those who were apostles before me, but I went away into Arabia; and again I returned to Damascus. Then after three years I went up to Jerusalem . . ." (Gal. 1:15-18).

It is impossible to speak with certainty, but I am inclined to put the visit to Arabia after the "several days" of Acts 9:19, and before the "many days" of 9:23.

What is meant by "Arabia"? The Nabatean kingdom of Aretas IV almost certainly is meant, for Paul mentions Aretas (2 Cor. 11:32) in connection with his escape from Damascus "in a basket through a window in the wall."[5] Therefore, Saul may have merely gone a few miles from Damascus into the kingdom of Arabia. Or he may have gone to the Nabatean capital at Petra.[6] A number of writers have suggested that Saul went to Mount Sinai.

How long was Saul in Arabia? It was three years after his conversion that he went to Jerusalem (Gal. 1:18). The record seems to imply that he spent most of this period in Damascus, hence we may assume that Saul spent only a few weeks or months in Arabia.

What was he doing in Arabia? Well, if I had held the theology that Pharisees held, and if I had held the view of Jesus and the Church that Saul had held, and then I had been confronted with the living Jesus, I am sure that I would need some time to rethink my previous theological convictions. He had seen Jesus alive in the glorious effulgence of the Godhead—how then could Jesus be a blasphemer? God would certainly never exalt a blasphemer to Heaven. Then what Jesus claimed for Himself must be true. If salvation could be reduced to repenting and believing in Jesus Christ, then what was the Law of Moses for? What was the

Temple for? Now, I have no idea what Saul did in Arabia. But I am certain that he was reworking his understanding of the Old Testament. For when he returned to Damascus, he "confounded the Jews . . . by proving that Jesus was the [Messiah]" (9:22).'

After his return to Damascus, Saul engaged actively in preaching and disputing in the synagogues. This continued for "many days" (9:23), until serious opposition developed, and "the Jews plotted to kill him" (9:23). The hunter has now become the hunted! It would seem that even the civil government was involved in the plot (2 Cor. 11:32-33). But Saul's disciples helped him escape through a window in a house built on top of the city wall (9:24-25), and he went to Jerusalem.

*Saul's Visit to Jerusalem.* First, Saul "attempted to join the disciples," but that failed, for "they were all afraid of him" (9:26). Word of his conversion does not seem to have spread to Jerusalem as rapidly as word of his persecuting the Church had spread to Damascus.

Barnabas, however, had faith in Saul, and he "brought him to the apostles" and told them the story of Saul's conversion (9:27). Once again, we have difficulty piecing together the events as they are related in Acts and as Paul tells them in Galatians. Paul says: "Then after three years I went up to Jerusalem to visit Cephas [Peter], and remained with him fifteen days. But I saw none of the other apostles except James the Lord's brother" (Gal. 1:18-19). Luke, however, suggests that more than two weeks were involved. Saul "went in and out among them at Jerusalem, preaching boldly in the

140

name of the Lord" (Acts 9:28-29a). Taking up where Stephen had been stopped, Saul even went and "disputed against the Hellenists" (9:29b), until they wanted to kill him also.

In his speech before the people, on his final visit to Jerusalem, Paul refers to a trance he had in the Temple, in which he was warned to get out of Jerusalem (22:17-21). Whether this occurred at this time, or during the "famine visit" (11:30), we cannot say for sure; some scholars are of the opinion that it fits better on the later occasion.

In his defense before Agrippa, Paul says he "declared first to those at Damascus, then at Jerusalem and throughout all the country of Judea, and also to the Gentiles" the message of repentance (26:20). But this seems to telescope the events of years, hence we need not suppose that it contradicts Galatians 1:22.

We must admit that the precise details and schedule of this visit to Jerusalem are beyond our ability to reconstruct. It would seem that Saul's work in Jerusalem on this occasion was principally with the unconverted Hellenists, and that the decision to kill him came from that group (9:29). The work of Stephen and his fate certainly were on Saul's mind (22:20)!

When the determination to kill Saul came to the attention of the Jerusalem church, they took him to Caesarea, and sent him on to Tarsus (9:30).

*Summation.* In this day of pragmatic concern, someone asks, "What is the practical lesson in this story?" Well, what can we learn of Washington at Valley Forge? Is not the fact itself, with its significance for all subsequent history, practical? The fact

141

that you and I are Christian, that our Western civilization has countless benefits that have directly come to us from the Christianizing of the West—are these not a practical result of the conversion of Saul? How many languages have been reduced to writing, how many alphabets have been modified or adapted to write these languages, by Christian missionaries emulating the apostle Paul? Is this a "practical" result of his conversion? A historian who attempts to trace all of the results of Saul's conversion would probably be branded as fanatical —but a historian who attempts to deny them is certainly perverse!

Why was Saul's conversion experience so unusual? Well, Saul was an unusually strong-willed man. And when God goes out to get a strong-willed man, He has to use unusual methods.

## Footnotes

1. On the basis of the number of words in the NT, Paul wrote 23.5 percent.

2. A number of novels about Paul have appeared. Various suggestions have been made in them, similar to those I have included. Since many people assume that everything in a "historical novel" is true, I have dealt briefly with some of the questions they raise.

3. The word *kyrie* in Greek, like the word "lord" in English, can be used both of a man ("my lord") and of Deity ("my Lord"). I see no reason to capitalize the word in Saul's first use of it; he did not yet know who was speaking to him.

4. *Commentary on Acts*, p. 197. Another explanation is that the companions heard the sound of the voice, but did not hear the words (cf. John 12:29).

5. Aretas IV reigned c. 9 B.C.–A.D. 40. The view that requires a date after A.D. 37 for Paul's escape from Damascus can no longer be held. See *New Bible Dictionary*, pp. 80-81.

6. See *New Bible Dictionary*, p. 55; but I see no reason for this conjecture.

7. Bruce (*Commentary on Acts*, p. 204), following K. Lake (*The Earlier Epistles of St. Paul*, pp. 320ff.), suggests that Paul may have engaged in some form of Christian witness in Nabatean Arabia. But there are times when it is more important to "Be still and know that I am God" than it is to speak. I feel that this was one such time.

142

# Peter's Ministry
# at Lydda and Joppa

Well, Saul of Tarsus, the great persecutor of the Church, has gotten converted, and has now gone back to Tarsus. How did that affect the fortunes of the Early Church? Luke gives us a "summarizing statement" (9:31), to tell us in brief the immediate effects of Saul's conversion. Meanwhile the work of the apostles continues, and Luke returns to report several important events. Then, when God's plan has been worked out, he will resume the story of Saul.

*The Church and the Churches.* Luke refers to "the church throughout all Judea and Galilee and Samaria" (9:31). The word "church" suggests that it was all one church, even though it was spread over much of Palestine. Luke might have said "the churches"—that would have been just as accurate, and just as scriptual. (cf. Rev. 1:20 with 2:1-3:22.)

There is an individuality about each local congregation that meets in the name of Christ. Each group of believers has the right to call itself a "church."[1] The Lord knows the strength and weakness of each church, just as He knew the strength and weakness of each of the seven churches in Asia (cf. Rev. 2:2-4).

At the same time, there is a corporate nature of the Church of Christ that makes it impossible for one local group to say to another, "We are the church; you are not." If the local church is truly part of the Body of Christ, then it is part of the Church universal. What is true of the individual members of the Body of Christ, as set forth in 1 Corinthians 12:12-26, can in effect be said of the individual churches of the Body of Christ. Some present-day denominations stress the idea of the local church; others stress the corporate nature. If only we could get a clear understanding of both usages of the word, how much better it would be for the Church and the churches!

Luke reports that the Church "had peace and was built up." The word "built up" literally referred to the erection of a building. Then it came to be used figuratively, something like our word "edify." Here Luke means the Church "was strengthened, firmly established." That he is not merely talking about size is clear, for he adds the words, "and walking in the fear of the Lord and in the comfort of the Holy Spirit it was multiplied" (9:31).

Two things are evidence of healthy life in the Church: growth in size and organizational maturity.

144

Some will dispute each of these points. "We should not be concerned with increase in numbers," we are told. If your child does not grow, you worry and finally you take him to the physician. A healthy child should grow. So should a healthy young church.

"Organization is not necessary in the church; we are led by the Spirit," another person will tell us. Well, go study your New Testament. God requires of each church that "all things should be done decently and in order" (1 Cor. 14:40). At a certain point the human body ceases to grow in size, but if it is healthy, it continues to mature in a well-coordinated manner. It is well "organized." Let the man who argues against Spirit-led organization in the church bring forth his scriptural evidence for that view! Of course, there are churches that are top-heavy with organization and have no knowledge of the Spirit—but I am not speaking of that kind of organization!

Rackham makes the following observation: "To walk in the way the Christian needs two helps: *the fear of the Lord* drives him to keep the commandments, and *the help (paraclesis) of the Holy Ghost* enables him to do so."[2]

*Peter at Lydda.* The apostles had not been driven out of Jerusalem by the persecution that had followed upon the martyrdom of Stephen (Acts 8:1), but they went out of Jerusalem nonetheless. Perhaps they were exercising some kind of supervision over new churches. Certainly they were preaching the gospel. At any rate, Luke tells us specifically that Peter's visit to Lydda was incidental to the fact that he "went here and there among them all" (9:32).

Lydda was a town not far from the sea on the Plain of Sharon—today it is known as Lod, where the principal airport for the State of Israel is located.

Luke calls the members of the believing community "saints" (9:32). His first use of this term with reference to Christians was in the mouth of Ananias of Damascus, and referred to the believers at Jerusalem (9:13). The term will be found often in Paul's writings. For some strange reason the word "saint" has come to mean someone who is very holy and very dead. A church "canonizes" its saints only after a long period of time has elapsed, possibly hundreds of years, and then only after a thorough investigation of the life and works of the ones to be canonized. But in the New Testament, saints are not always very holy and they are very much alive, Paul even refers to the sinners at Corinth as "saints" (1 Cor. 1:2)!

Among the saints at Lydda was a man named Aeneas, who had been a paralytic for eight years. In fact, he could not get out of bed (Acts 9:33). Peter said, "Aeneas, Jesus Christ heals you; rise and make your bed" (9:34).[3] Aeneas got up at once.

*The Raising of Dorcas.* About eleven miles from Lydda, on the sea, was the village of Joppa. One of the real, live saints in the church at Joppa was a woman named Tabitha—which means "Dorcas" in Greek (9:36) or "Gazelle" in English. This blessed woman "was full of good works and acts of charity which she did" (9:36).[4] Some of these deeds of righteousness were sewing and distributing coats and garments, which her fellow-saints at Joppa were wearing. The words "showing coats and garments" would appear to mean "wearing" (or show-

146

ing by wearing) these items of clothing.

Dorcas fell sick and died, and her friends prepared her body for burial. Someone had heard that Peter was at Lydda, and they sent two men to ask him to come "without delay" (9:38). I rather imagine that they had already sent for Peter before Dorcas died, for it would take at least six hours for the round-trip, and burial usually took place in less time than that. Moreover, there would have been no need for haste if they were either merely asking Peter to come to them in their grief or if they were expecting him to raise Dorcas. But there would be reason for haste if they were hoping that he might heal Dorcas. There is no reason to suppose, however, that they were expecting Peter to raise Dorcas. Once again, we note their reaction when the miracle happened (9:42).

When Peter reached the house in Joppa, he went to the upper room where the body of Dorcas was lying. The widows stood around, weeping, and showing the garments that Dorcas had made for them. If they were not saying the words, they were thinking them: "How can we ever get along without Dorcas?"

Peter put them out of the room. Then he knelt and prayed. And then he pronounced the words, *"Tabitha qumi"*—"Dorcas, get up."

I cannot escape the feeling that Peter's mind went back to a day some years earlier, when he was privileged, along with James and John, to be in the presence of a similar event. The twelve-year-old daughter of Jairus, the ruler of the synagogue, had died. Jesus put the mourners out, and allowed only the girl's father and mother and His three disciples

147

to be in the room with Him. Taking the girl by the hand, He said, *"Talitha qumi"*—"little girl, get up" (Mark 5:41). Only Mark among the evangelists included that story, perhaps because he, as Peter's interpreter, had heard Peter tell it many times. At Joppa, using almost exactly the words that Jesus had used, Peter called Dorcas back to this life. Then he called in the saints and the widows, and gave her back to them—*alive* (Acts 9:41)!

Why did Peter raise Dorcas? So far as the record indicates, they had not asked him to do it. They had simply felt the need of Peter's presence in their hour of deep grief. No member of the First Church had suggested that the apostles should try to bring Stephen back to life. In a little while, James, one of the "inner three" of the apostles, would be taken from them. No one would suggest that they should try to bring him back to life.

It is a vicious heresy that says that death is not the will of God—vicious, because it robs the bereaved of the comfort that only God can give. In this present age, death *is* part of His plan, and has been ever since "sin came into the world through one man" (Rom. 5:12). Death will be the last enemy to be vanquished (1 Cor. 15:26), for as long as there is sin there must be death. But has not Christ overcome sin? Yes—and no. He has begun the process of redemption, and the outcome is certain. In that sense, He has destroyed sin. But the redemption of the world is not yet complete. Sin is still very much present with us—even in the saints. All of creation groans until the completion of the redemption (Rom. 8:22-23), and when that day comes, "then shall come to pass the saying that is written: 'Death is swallowed up in victory'" (1 Cor. 15:54).

*God's Mysterious Ways.* Why was Dorcas brought back to life, and Stephen and James were not? Weren't Stephen and James far more important in the Early Church than Dorcas?

Isn't that a horrible question? But it's the kind of question we often ask. We *do* make such comparisons. We tell ourselves that the vigorous leadership of Stephen is certainly more significant than the making of a few coats and dresses for widows in Joppa.

When a runaway truck crushed a boy and his bicycle under its wheels, leaving his deaf-mute brother as the parents' only surviving child, the mother told me, in her grief, "Everyone in the city is asking, 'Why wasn't this one taken and the other spared?' But I don't feel that way. I loved them both alike." She bowed before the strange will of God in lovely humility that was an example to all who tried to sympathize with her.

God loves all His children alike. His broken heart was revealed in His Son's tears at the grave of Lazarus, and I am certain that Jesus wept also over Stephen and Dorcas. He is touched by all our griefs. Perhaps He feels these things in a way we can never experience, for He knows that sin and death were not in God's original creation.

God's will is done in ways that are mysterious in our sight. But that is because we know such a tiny part of God's will. Stephen's work on earth was finished. So we must conclude, for God took him to Himself. Dorcas was needed here for a little longer —but only for a temporary extension. The day

149

would come when she would be gathered to Him. One is taken and another is left behind. So God wills. But sooner or later, all shall be gathered into His presence, for He has something better for us. This is our hope—and without it, our efforts to understand God's will are hopeless.

*Summation.* Why are these two miracles recorded by Luke? It is his way of reminding us, I think, that the Church is continuing to do and teach in the name of its Lord (cf. Acts 1:1). It is also his way of declaring that one of the principal reasons for the continued growth of the Early Church was the good works which it did.

Before many more years, Christianity would be branded a heresy, and Christians would be persecuted and put to death as evildoers. Luke wanted the record to show that these charges were false. Christianity is truth revealed by God in His Son Jesus Christ and carried to the world by His followers. Christians are doers of good.

May our adherence to the truth and our good works in the Master's name carry conviction to the world of our day!

## Footnotes

1. Our word "church" is derived ultimately from the Greek word *kyriakós* (the Lord's) and can be applied to the Lord's people, the Lord's Day (Rev. 1:10), the Lord's Supper (1 Cor. 11:20), or the Lord's house. The Greek word *ekklēsía* means "assembly, congregation." For a thorough study of the word see *Theological Dictionary of the New Testament*, 3:504-513.

2. Rackham, *Acts,* p. 143.

3. The words translated "make your bed" may possibly mean "prepare your meal." (The same verb is used with this meaning in Mark 14:15.) Bruce observes, "This would accord well with the interest shown by Luke and other New Testament writers in nourishment for convalescents." *Commentary on Acts,* p. 210f.

4. *RSV,* without explanation, omits "which she did." Lots of people are full of good intentions; few actually do them.

# The Conversion of Cornelius

"How did the first Gentile get into the Church? What was the reaction of the Jews?" We can be certain that these questions had been asked, and we can be reasonably certain that Luke was telling the story of the conversion of Cornelius to answer just such questions.

Luke devotes much space and great care to telling the story of Cornelius—including the careful preparation of Peter by God, the preparation of Cornelius, the event itself, and above all, the subsequent investigation of Peter and his staunch defense of his action. Luke treats this event as one of the great crises in the history of the Early Church. We can do no less!

*Cornelius and His Vision.* Caesarea, we have learned, was the seat of the Roman governor of the province of Judea. It was located on the Mediterranean coast, about 60 miles northwest of Jerusalem. Herod the Great had built a large harbor and a splendid city named Caesarea Augusta for Caesar Augustus. At the seat of government we would expect to find sufficient army strength to meet the ordinary needs. According to Josephus, at the time of the First Jewish Revolt (A.D. 66-70) there were five cohorts and a squadron of cavalry at Caesarea.[1] One of the auxiliary cohorts was known as "the Italian Cohort," consisting normally of 1,000 men divided into ten centuries. Cornelius was the centurion of one of these centuries (Acts 10:1).[2]

Luke describes Cornelius as "a devout man who feared God with all his household, gave alms liberally to the people, and prayed constantly to God" (10:2). The term "devout" is used by Luke to describe a man's relation to God, although it can also describe a relationship between men. (The cognate verb is so used in 1 Timothy 5:4.) The expression "who feared God" or "God-fearer" is used by Luke to denote Gentiles who worshiped the God of the Jews, but (usually) not those who had become Proselytes.

That Cornelius was an uncircumcised Gentile is further pointed out by other incidents in the story. Peter was reluctant to go to visit him (10:28-29). Peter recognized that God's action toward Cornelius was the unusual gracious acceptance of a Gentile (10:35). The "circumcision party" criticized Peter, saying, "Why did you go to uncircumcised men and eat with them?" (11:3). And the members of the Jerusalem Church, after hearing the full story, said, "Then to the Gentiles also God has granted repentance unto life" (11:18).

But Cornelius was an extraordinary Gentile, even for a "God-fearer." His prayer life and his deeds of charity are singled out by God as commendable (10:4). But what impresses me even more is the religious character of his home. Some men are pious in a personal way. Cornelius, as soon as he had the vision, called in two of his servants and one of his attending soldiers, and shared the experience with them (10:7-8). Later, while expecting Peter's arrival, he assembled his relatives and close friends, that they all might hear what God had commanded Peter to tell them (10:24,33). Here was a man with a vibrant, vital religion, anxious to share his blessings with all those near and dear to him! It is not hard to understand why one of his aides is called "a devout soldier" (10:7).

One day, at three o'clock in the afternoon (10:3)—which was an hour of prayer for Jews (cf. 3:1)—Cornelius had a vision. He saw "clearly" an angelic visitor coming to him. Just what the nature of the "visions" was that are mentioned several times in Acts, we cannot say.[3] Was the appearance of the visitor visible to others who might have been present, or only to the person experiencing the vision? Was there a person actually standing there, perceived by the eyes, or was this appearance something that occurred (by the action of God, we do not deny) in the mind of the recipient? How shall we decide? And after all, does it really matter?

153

That God was using this means to communicate to the persons who had the visions is never doubted. In the case of Cornelius and Peter there were two visions which supplemented each other.

In the vision which Cornelius saw, the "angel of God" told him to "send men to Joppa, and bring one Simon who is called Peter; he is lodging with Simon, a tanner, whose house is by the seaside" (10:5-6).

After sharing this experience with the two servants and the aide, Cornelius sent them to Joppa, which was a little more than 30 miles to the south.

*Peter and His Vision.* Peter was a Jew and Cornelius was a Gentile. Hence it was unthinkable that Peter would simply start out with three Gentiles to visit the house of yet another Gentile. God knew this, for it was devotion to God's Word that had led Jews to develop their characteristic exclusiveness. They were told to be "holy"—and the very word holy means "set apart."

So God prepared Peter for the event. It was about noon of the following day (10:9), and Peter went on the housetop to pray. He was hungry and had asked someone in the household of Simon the Tanner to prepare food, and while they were doing so, Peter fell into a trance (10:10). In this ecstasy, he saw something like a large sheet or tablecloth coming down from heaven, held by the four corners (10:11). It contained "all kinds of animals and reptiles and birds of the air" (10:12), some of which were prohibited by the laws of clean and unclean foods in Leviticus. A voice said to him, "Rise, Peter; kill and eat" (10:13).

Peter seems to have recognized that voice, for he replied, "No, Lord; for I have never eaten anything that is common or unclean" (10:14).

The voice spoke a second time, "What God has cleansed, you must not call common" (10:15). The event was repeated a second and third time.

In the religious thought of the Old Testament, there are two mutually exclusive categories: that which is "holy" and that which is "profane" or "common." A person or thing that is not "holy" can be "sanctified," or made holy, by some ritual cleansing. Conversely, any person or thing that is "holy" can be "profaned" by contact with that which is not holy. The act of making "holy" is sometimes called "consecration," and the act of profaning is called "desecration."

In Leviticus there are descriptions of various kinds of food that are "unclean" (Lev. 11:1-47). Note the specific warning: "By these you shall become unclean; whoever touches their carcass shall be unclean until the evening" (Lev. 11:24). From these and other laws, Judaism developed the concept of *kashrut,* or "kosher" *(kasher)* and "non-kosher" foods. Moreover, since even the touch was sufficient to profane the person, the Jew was particularly careful not to have table-fellowship with a Gentile, usually not even to enter the home of a Gentile. Peter refers to this taboo when he says to Cornelius, "You yourselves know how unlawful it is for a Jew to associate with or to visit any one of another nation" (Acts 10:28).

The difficulty Peter was having with the unusual command is evident in the fact that the vision was presented three times. In other words, Peter was having an argument with his heavenly Visitor. He wanted to be certain that he fully understood the command and its implications. After reflection he came to see the deeper significance of the words, for he recognized that this was not merely a matter of clean and unclean food; it involved the question of "clean" and "unclean" people. Such is the import of his words in verse 28: "God has shown me that I should not call any man common or unclean."

Years later, after serving as Peter's interpreter, Mark was writing his Gospel, and he recorded the words of Jesus: "Do you not see that whatever goes into a man from outside cannot defile him, since it enters, not his heart but his stomach, and so passes on?" Mark added in parentheses, "(Thus he declared all foods clean)" (Mark 7:18-19). (It is interesting to note that in the parallel account [Matt. 15:15-20], the parenthesis is not added.) We cannot help but wonder whether Peter was not responsible for the parenthesis, and whether he was not thinking of this vision in Joppa.

*Peter Goes to the Home of Cornelius.* While Peter was puzzling over the meaning of the vision, the three men arrived from Caesarea. Since a journey of 30 miles represents a hard day's travel, we must assume that these men, who had started out somewhat later than 3 p.m. on the previous day and arrived in Joppa shortly after noon, had in fact traveled well into the night.

Peter was still thinking about the vision when the Spirit told him to go down and accompany the men (Acts 10:19-20). It was, of course, too late to start out at once, and these messengers needed rest. So Peter, making the first small break in his "holiness," invited the Gentiles in to be his guests (10:23).⁴

The next day Peter took six Jewish members of the church in Joppa (10:23,45; 11:12), and, together with the three sent by Cornelius, they set out for Caesarea. They apparently broke their journey, for they did not arrive in Caesarea until the following day (10:24). "Cornelius was expecting them and had called together his kismen⁵ and close friends" (10:24). When Peter entered, Cornelius prostrated himself at Peter's feet. We should not understand this as "worship" (even though that word is used in 10:25), but as high honor paid to a human being. Even so, Peter refused to accept such honor (10:26). After explaining the restrictions that normally bound a Jew, he added, "So when I was sent for, I came without objection. I ask then why you sent for me" (10:29).

Cornelius told about his vision—Luke carefully repeats the story—and asked Peter to tell them what God had laid upon him (10:30-33). Peter needed no further urging. He preached the gospel of Jesus Christ.

We should note certain things about this sermon of Peter's. There is no quotation of the Old Testament Scriptures. In speaking to a gentile audience, Peter may have felt that there was little to be gained by trying to show the fulfillment of Scripture. On the other hand, the reference to "all the prophets" (10:43) may indicate that Luke has omitted that portion of Peter's message, since it had no significant bearing on the immediate problem.

157

The sermon stresses the life of Jesus Christ (including His preaching and good deeds) (10:36-38), the crucifixion and the resurrection (10:39-40), the appearance to the witnesses, and His command to them to preach the truth about Him (10:41-42). R. B. Rackham notes that Jesus is presented not merely as Christ (Messiah) of the Jews but as Lord of all (10:36) and as Judge of the living and the dead (10:42).[6]

Most of all, however, we note Peter's opening words: "Truly I perceive that God shows no partiality, but in every nation any one who fears him and does what is right is acceptable to him" (10:34-35). This flings the doors of heaven open to Gentiles as well as Jews. Any one in any nation, Jew or Gentile, is acceptable to God if he fears God and does what is right.[7]

*The Gentiles Receive the Holy Spirit.* Peter was still talking when the Holy Spirit fell on all who were present (10:44). The Jewish Christians from Joppa "were amazed, because the gift of the Holy Spirit had been poured out even on the Gentiles" (10:45). The Gentiles were "speaking in tongues and extolling God" (10:46).

Peter made no further resistance. All his Jewish exclusiveness was swept aside, and he declared, "Can any one forbid water for baptizing these people who have received the Holy Spirit just as we have?" (10:47), and he commanded them to be baptized.

*The Apostolic Investigation.* This was an event of extremely great significance, and news of it got back to Jerusalem before Peter did (11:1). In fact, not only did the report get back, but the "circumcision party" was able to marshal its forces for an attack on Peter.

The term "circumcision party" refers to Jews who were zealous for the Law. Actually, the translation is a bit too formal, for the Greeks says simply, "those of the circumcision." In 10:45 there can be no doubt that the term is used with reference to Christians, "the believers from among the circumcised." In 11:2 it is not clear that Christian Jews are meant, but I believe the total context (i.e., the passage through 11:18) supports this view.

We shall meet those of the circumcision again—and again. They are the instigators of the problem which faced the Church in Antioch (15:1), and which in turn led to the Jerusalem Conference. They are responsible for the problem that led Paul to write his Epistle to the Galatians (note Gal. 2:12). They are sometimes referred to as "Judaizers," for they sought to make Jews of Gentiles who came into the Church. We shall return to the problem at greater length when we come to the story of the Jerusalem Conference in Acts 15.

In the present situation, the "circumcision party" criticized Peter, asking, "Why did you go to uncircumcised men and eat with them?" (11:3). Peter replied by telling the story which we have already heard. The very fact that Luke repeats so much of it in Peter's words is an indication that Luke put great importance on the incident. Peter stressed the vision and the divine command (11:5-10), and the fact that the Holy Spirit fell on the Gentiles while he was speaking (11:15). "If then God gave the

159

same gift to them [the Gentiles] as he gave to us [the Jews] when we believed," argued Peter, "who was I that I could withstand God?" (11:17).

The power of this argument is overwhelming. Peter did not set out to convert Gentiles; over his protests (11:8) he was practically forced into it by God through a series of visions and divine commands. Peter did not decide that the Gentiles were converted, baptize them, and then learn that the Spirit had come on them. In fact, even before he finished what he had planned to say, the Spirit fell on them as they began to speak in tongues. Clearly, this was an act of God from beginning to end. As an obedient servant, Peter could only confirm what God had done.

The "apostles and the brethren" (11:1) who were present in Jerusalem were moved by this inexorable logic. "They were silenced. And they glorified God, saying, 'Then to the Gentiles also God has granted repentance unto life' " (11:18).

So the first Gentiles came into the Christian Church. And it all started because one man, a Roman centurion and hence a soldier, was faithful in his own religious life!

*Summation.* Some men say, "My religion is good enough—why do I need to accept Christ?" Cornelius stands as one of the great biblical answers to this question. He was a good man—an exceptionally good man. But his religion was not good enough! God sent an angel to him to tell him that it was not good enough. His prayers and good works were well known to God, and God honored them. But it was still necessary for him to believe in Jesus

Christ, to be baptized, and to receive the Holy Spirit.

Some men ask, "What about the people who have never heard of Christ, and who are trying their best to please God, according to the light they have?" Cornelius stands also as one of the great biblical answers to this question. The prayers and good works even of an unbeliever are recognized by God, who sends His rain on the just and on the unjust. God willed to save Cornelius, even if it was going to take a few minor miracles and the change of a few basic heart-attitudes to get the gospel to him.

Do I believe that this is still true today? Most certainly I do! But let's not overlook the fact that even God's will to save this Gentile and his household required the preaching of the gospel of Jesus Christ. It would have been much easier for God to have "saved" these people without getting Peter into the act. That would have spared the Early Church many of its problems. God could have set apart a special cloud in heaven, or a special room in the heavenly mansions, and sent all the saved pagans there, and never have disturbed the Jewish Church at all!

But that was not God's will.

God willed that men should come to salvation through knowledge of Jesus Christ, that there should be one Church which is His body, and that this should be accomplished through us who believe—even if we have to sacrifice some of our theories of racial or social superiority in the process!

It wasn't easy for Peter to go to the home of Cornelius. It wasn't easy for the Jewish Christian Church to admit Gentiles. And it won't be easy for us to welcome as brothers and sisters in Christ some of the people we consider "common" or "unclean."

But that's the way God has willed for men to be saved.

## Footnotes

1. Josephus *Jewish War* 1.21.5, §§408-415; 3.4.2., §66. It is possible that the Caesarean strength was somewhat less in Cornelius' day.

2. Polybius, the Greek historian who lived c. 208-c. 123 B.C., describes the Roman centurion as follows: "They wish the centurions not so much to be venturesome and dare-devil as to be natural leaders, of a steady and sedate spirit. They do not desire them so much to be men who will initiate attacks and open the battle, but men who will hold their ground when worsted and hardpressed and be ready to die at their posts" (*History* 6.24,§9). While this was written 200 years or so before Cornelius' time, there is no reason to believe the standards had changed appreciably.

3. For a full discussion see *Theological Dictionary of the New Testament* 5:350-352, 371-372.

4. Several writers have pointed out that in staying at the home of a tanner Peter was already taking a step in this direction, for tanning was an "unclean" occupation inasmuch as it required the tanner to touch dead carcasses and these defiled him.

5. The word "kinsmen" may mean simply fellow countrymen, i.e., Italians.

6. R. B. Rackham, *The Acts of the Apostles*, p. 154 f.

7. This does not imply salvation by works. To be "acceptable to God" does not exempt a man from the need of salvation—as the case of Cornelius clearly shows—and salvation is only by God's grace revealed in Jesus Christ.

# The Church in Antioch

An era is drawing to a close. Jerusalem has been the center of the Church, but soon that would no longer be true. Yet, as I suppose so often happens, those who lived through the passing of an era were probably not aware of it. Antioch would become the new center and from it the Church would spread eastward and westward. (Luke will only concern himself with the westward progress.) Instead of "Peter and John" we shall be hearing about "Barnabas and Saul," and then "Paul." A little later the name "Rome" will be mentioned, perhaps with a bit more anticipation than the name "Jerusalem."

163

A sentimentalist would hold on to the old. After all, the Church began at Jerusalem—let's keep that as the center of the Church through the ages! Peter and the apostles were the ones to whom Jesus entrusted His Church. Let's keep them in as the leaders of the Church! So the sentimentalist would speak. But Luke is no sentimentalist—and neither is God. The forward, outward progress of the gospel and the salvation of men of all nations is the first consideration. If a new center is needed, and new leadership, then so be it!

Loving memory of the old will remain. Paul will start his missionary journeys from Antioch, the new center—but he will always return to Jerusalem to participate in worship and to report to the church there. Paul will lead the fight for admitting uncircumcised Gentiles into the Church, but Peter's word will still carry weight. But, let's not run ahead of our story.

*Continued Effects of the Persecution.* Luke takes us back once more to the persecution that arose when Stephen was martyred (Acts 11:19; cf. 8:4). The Hellenist Christians that were scattered traveled northward along the Mediterranean coast "as far as Phoenicia," westward by sea to the island of Cyprus, and either by sea from Cyprus or by land from the Phoenician cities to Syrian Antioch (11:19). About twenty years later Paul will visit the Christians in Ptolemais, Tyre, and Sidon (21:3,7; 27:3): some of these doubtless were converted through this Hellenist Dispersion.

Luke specifies that these Hellenists limited their preaching to Jews (11:19). We assume that for the most part they were Hellenist Jews, but that does not alter the situation. The Church was not yet deliberately evangelizing Gentiles. But something new was happening at Antioch. Men of Cyprus and Cyrene, doubtless Hellenist Christians, began to preach the Lord Jesus to "the Greeks" in Antioch (11:20).

There is a textual problem at this point, for the oldest manuscripts read "Hellenists" instead of "Hellenes." Now it would make no sense whatever, after Luke has already told us about the large Hellenist segment in the church at Jerusalem, the preaching of the Hellenists Stephen and Philip, and other references to Hellenists, for him to record at this point that some men came to Antioch and preached to the Hellenists. Therefore, in spite of the manuscript evidence, we must accept the reading "Hellenes" or "Greeks."[1]

Paul started out on a program that seems to have been aimed at the synagogues across the empire. Then he was led by circumstances to alter this and make it a deliberate effort to evangelize the gentile world. It is entirely possible that Paul's original strategy was to bring his Jewish brethren to Christ and let them evangelize their cities. Certainly hundreds of synagogues and thousands of Jewish believers could evangelize the world far more rapidly than could a handful of apostles! And certainly this was in line with the Scriptures that declared that the reason for Israel's existence was that she be a "light to the Gentiles" (Isa. 42:6, KJV, etc.).

Well, whether the preaching in Antioch was to Gentiles in general or only to those that feared God, the "hand of the Lord" was on this new evangelistic effort, "and a great number that believed turned to the Lord" (Acts 11:21). Barnabas and Saul taught for "a whole year" and the new church developed to such a point that it was possible for the two leaders to undertake an extensive program of evangelization—but Luke does not tell us about that until we come to chapter 13.

*Antioch-on-the-Orontes.* After Rome and Alexandria, Antioch was the third city of the empire, and was thought of as the capital of the East. Founded in 300 B.C. by Seleucus Nicator, it was one of sixteen cities which he built and named for his father. To distinguish this city from the others of the same name, it is usually referred to as "Syrian Antioch" or "Antioch-on-the-Orontes." It became the most important of the many Antiochs because it was the capital of the Seleucid rulers. Then Pompey conquered it for Rome in 64 B.C. and made it a free city; subsequently it became the capital of the Roman province of Syria.

Syrian Antioch was called "Antioch the Beautiful." Herod the Great paved the main street for four-and-a-half miles and lined it with colonnades.[2] The city was renowned for its many public and private baths, its central heating, plumbing, and sanitary facilities, and especially for its illumination, being described as "a city where the brightness of the lights at night commonly equals the resplendence of the day."[3] Cicero refers to Antioch as "a renowned and populous city, the seat of brilliant scholarship and artistic refinement."[4]

Antioch was also a city noted for its sensual

pleasure, for its dancers and actors, and for its chariot races. Libanius looked upon its "extravagant lighting" as an "indication of idle luxury, that hangs over the entrances to our baths."[5] Its morals were proverbially low. About five miles south of Antioch was the pleasure-garden of Daphne, with groves of laurels and a sanctuary to Apollo that included ritual prostitution. "Daphnic customs" became a proverbial expression, and Juvenal satirically makes the statement: "The Syrian Orontes has long since poured into the Tiber, bringing with it its lingo and its manners, its flutes and its slanting harp-strings; bringing too the timbrels of the breed, and the trulls who are bidden ply their trade at the Circus."[6]

Antioch was also an important mercantile city. The river Orontes, which flowed through the city, was navigable as far as Antioch. The seaport, however, was Seleucia, fifteen miles to the west, on an excellent bay which is now silted up. This seaport will become a familiar place in the Church's westward expansion.[7]

The city was divided into "quarters," and had a large Jewish population, as well as Syrian, Greek and Roman communities.

In Christian times, Antioch became noted for its school of biblical interpretation and for its theology. Its bishop was one of the four great patriarchs, and among its many saints and martyrs were Ignatius and Chrysostom. One of the Seven, let us not forget, was Nicolaus "a proselyte of Antioch" (Acts 6:5).

*Barnabas Is Sent to Antioch.* When news of the

evangelization of Greeks by the church in Antioch reached Jerusalem, the "church in Jerusalem" sent Barnabas to Antioch (11:22). He did not return immediately to Jerusalem, but rather settled down in Antioch for at least a year and became a leader in the evangelistic effort. We should not, therefore, look upon this as some kind of investigation; rather, we should probably see it as further evidence of the *koinōnía* of the Early Church, an effort to express the oneness of the Church. There is no evidence that Barnabas went to Antioch for the "laying on of hands" or to "confer the Spirit."

Barnabas, whom we have already met (4:36-37; 9:27), is described here as "a good man, full of the Holy Spirit and of faith" (11:24). He saw the outworking of the grace of God in the new church and "he was glad" (11:23). True to his name ("son of exhortation") he "exhorted them all to remain faithful to the Lord with steadfast purpose" (11:23). And then he did something more: he recognized that the size and nature of this new work were beyond the abilities of the available leadership. What was needed was a man who could give a powerful testimony of his own conversion and positive leadership in establishing new churches. Who was that man?

Barnabas thought of Saul of Tarsus. So he went to Tarsus to look for Saul, and after some difficulty he found him and talked him into joining him in Antioch[8] (11:25-26).

From the time-indications in Paul's letter to the Galatians, and in Acts, it appears that there had been an interval—perhaps as much as ten years—

since Saul had returned to Tarsus (9:30; cf. Gal. 1:18; 2:1). What had Saul been doing all that time?

According to one scholar, he had been weaving goat-hair tent-cloth and doing nothing else.[9] I don't believe it! If Saul had been weaving, Barnabas would have gone to the street of the weavers in Tarsus, and in five or ten minutes he would have found him. But Barnabas wasn't looking for someone who could weave goat-hair. He wanted someone to help found the churches that would result from the evangelization of the Gentiles.

A better clue is the reference to "strengthening the churches" in "Syria and Cilicia" in Acts 15:41. Syria-and-Cilicia was the name of the Roman province where Tarsus was situated (Antioch was its capital). Where did those churches in Syria-and-Cilicia come from? Nothing is said about them previously in Acts. Yet Paul knew about them and wanted to give them additional strength. They may have resulted from the evangelistic efforts of the church of Antioch. But I cannot escape the feeling that Saul had been responsible for founding them,[10] and I feel that Barnabas knew this and therefore thought of Saul as the man for the work in Antioch. At any rate, Barnabas brought Saul back to Antioch and for a year they met with the church and taught the people (Acts 11:26).

*The Name "Christian."* Luke gives us two hints that we are entering a new era in the history of the Early Church. First, he speaks of "the church" in Antioch (11:26). Previously he has used the term "church" of the believers in Jerusalem (5:11; 8:1,3; 11:22) or of those scattered from Jerusalem (9:31).

Moreover, the wording here is quite remarkable, for Luke does not refer to "the church at Antioch," as though that were merely an extension of "the Church." Rather, he specifically says, "they were gathered in the church," as though the church in Antioch is now considered a separate entity.[11] "The church" at Antioch is mentioned again in 14:27 and 15:3.

Luke particularly signals the new era by the introduction of the new name, "Christians." Henceforth, this will be the name by which the Church and the followers of the Lord Jesus Christ will be known.

Did the church in Antioch give itself the name, or did those outside confer it? Scholars divide on the question. Since the word usually translated "were called" may literally be taken to mean "transacted business as" it may be argued that the believers themselves took this as their corporate name. Not all scholars, however, accept this derivation of the word, and prefer to translate the word "bore the name, were called." Further, because of the confusion between *Christus* (Christ) and *Chrestus* (worthy), which sound almost identical, in a text from Suetonius,[12] some scholars think that the name was given to the believers by those outside the believing community, perhaps as a mark of respect or possibly as a mocking term. King Agrippa used it (26:28), as did Peter (1 Pet. 4:16). Outside the New Testament we find it in Josephus,[13] as well as in the Roman writers Pliny the Younger,[14] Tacitus,[15] Suetonius,[16] and others. As an adjective built from the name "Christ" it is particularly well suited to its purpose: Christ's followers are *Christ*-ians.

*The Famine.* Among the gifts of the Spirit in the Early Church was the gift of prophecy, which included the foretelling of future events. Certain prophets, including Agabus, came to Antioch from Jerusalem (Acts 11:27-28), predicting a widespread famine. Luke tells us that this famine occurred "in the days of Claudius" (11:28). The reign of Claudius (A.D. 41-54) was marked by drought and famine," which would indicate a series of local famines rather than a single empire-wide famine. Josephus reports a famine in Judea, when Queen Helena of Adiabene distributed grain and dried figs in Jerusalem." If this is the famine spoken of by Luke, we must assume that, although the prophecy was given prior to the death of Herod Agrippa in A.D. 44 (12:23), the famine (and by inference, the famine-visit) occurred after he died.

The prophecy gave the church at Antioch an opportunity to demonstrate its oneness with the "brethren who lived in Judea." They decided to send relief—"Everyone according to his ability"—to the Christians in Judea, by the hands of Barnabas and Saul (11:29-30).

The question concerning the visits of Saul (Paul) to Jerusalem in Acts and the synchronizing of these visits with his statements in Galatians we shall leave until later. Here we simply point out that there are three possible solutions: (1) Paul's "second" visit to Jerusalem (Gal. 2:1) is to be identified with the famine-visit in Acts (11:29-30); or (2) Paul omits any reference to the famine-visit, his "second" visit in Galatians being identified with the

171

Conference-visit of Acts 15:2; or (3) the famine-visit (11:29-30) is the same as the Conference-visit (15:2).

*Summation.* There are times when it is necessary to forget those things which are behind and to press on to the goal. This is true of movements and of persons. We have seen that the Christian Church has come to one of these times of crisis, when "Jerusalem Christianity" must be replaced with a bigger concept. The gospel of Christ is for the whole world.

Each of us, in our own way, must go through a similar crisis. After coming to know the Lord Jesus, we all tend to settle down and enjoy the personal blessings that we find in Him. But His word to us is still expressed in the words, "You shall be my witnesses . . . to the end of the earth." The old places, the old forms of worship, even the old names, may prove to be obstacles. We must be willing to make whatever break with the past that is necessary to achieve His purpose!

# Footnotes

1. Bruce is willing to accept the reading "Hellenists" with the meaning of "Greek speakers." He derives from the context that Gentiles are intended here. *The Acts of the Apostles*, p. 235 f.

2. Josephus, *Antiquities* 16.5.3, §148.

3. Ammianus Marcellinus, *Constantius et Gallus* 14.1.9 (dated c. A.D. 353). Other references to the night illumination are found in Libanius, *Orations* 11.267, 16.41, 22.6, 33.35f. Libanius is also a fourth-century writer.

4. Cicero, *Pro Archia Poeta* 3.2. Literally he says "most erudite men and most liberal studies." Cicero's dates are 106-43 B.C.

5. Libanius, *Orations* 16.41.

6. Juvenal, *Satire* 3.62-66. Juvenal's dates are A.D. 60-140.

7. For a fascinating description of Antioch, unfortunately without any documentation of his statements, see H. V. Morton, *In the Steps of St. Paul* (1936), pp. 96-98.

8. Luke's wording indicates difficulty in locating Saul. The "Western" text suggests that persuasion was necessary.

9. Lenski, *Acts*, p. 373, "Saul did no work in Tarsus."

10. Phil. 3:8 suggests that Saul was driven from his home and family because of his faith in Jesus. It is impossible to believe that he was silent about the Lord he had so recently come to know.

11. Rackham, indeed, thinks that the Antiochenes "were the first Christians to possess a proper *ecclesia* or church of their own," since there is no mention of the synagogue at Antioch—Acts, p. 169, n.4.

12. Suetonius, *The Deified Claudius* 25.4. In my opinion, the use of *Christiani* elsewhere in Suetonius *(Nero* 16.2) and of *Christus* and of *Christianos* in Tacitus *(Annals* 15.44) indicates that *Chrestus* should also have been *Christus*.

13. Josephus, *Antiquities* 18.3.3, §64.

14. Pliny the Younger, *Letters* 10.96.

15. Tacitus, *Annals* 15.44.

16. Suetonius, *Life of Nero* 16.2.

17. Suetonius, *Life of Claudius* 18.2.

18. Josephus, *Antiquities* 20.2.5 §§51-52. This has to be dated between A.D. 44 and 48.

# The Herodian Persecution of the Church

We come now to the end of the "transition period," which began with the persecution by Saul and the scattering of the Jerusalem fellowship. The scattering, we have seen, was probably limited to the Hellenists, for the apostles remained in Jerusalem, and the Hebrew-speaking Christians seem also to have stayed in Jerusalem. At least, a Christian church continued there, and from the indications given in Acts we may assume that for a period there was no great degree of open hostility toward it on the part of the Jews who did not accept Jesus as their Messiah.

We might conclude that Saul had really been the only one concerned with the extermination of the Church, and when he was converted, that effort ceased. But the Sadducees, especially the chief priests, had strongly opposed the new movement before Saul ever became the leader of the persecution. Moreover, as we shall see, Herod's action against James "pleased the Jews" (Acts 12:3), hence we must conclude that strong feelings against the Church still were present.

*Herod Agrippa.* The king at that time was Herod Agrippa I, son of Aristobulus and grandson of Herod the Great. In Acts he is called "Herod the king" (12:1), but in secular history he is usually called "Agrippa." Aristobulus and his brother Alexander were descended from the Hasmoneans (the Maccabees) through their mother Mariamne. Because of the suspicious nature of Herod the Great and his constant fear of losing his throne, he had Mariamne put to death in 29 B.C., and brought about the execution of her sons, accusing them of plotting against him, in 7 B.C. Agrippa, who was then about four years old, was taken to Rome for his own protection, and there he grew up in close connection with the imperial family. He and Gaius, the grand-nephew of the emperor Tiberius, were close friends.

When Gaius, generally known as Caligula, became emperor (A.D. 37), he made Agrippa king over the tetrarchies that had belonged to Philip and Lysanias (Luke 3:1). Then, when Herod Antipas (Luke 3:19; 23:7ff.) was banished, because of charges that Agrippa had made to Caligula, his territories of Galilee and Perea were added to Agrippa's kingdom (A.D. 39). Finally, when Claudius became emperor in A.D. 41, he added Judea and Samaria, so that the territory ruled over by Herod Agrippa was approximately the same as that which had belonged to Herod the Great.

Of all the Herodian kings, Agrippa was possibly the most popular with the Jews, due to the fact that he was descended from the Hasmonean line. He was careful to preserve and enhance that good will. It is quite likely that the persecution of the Church was part of Agrippa's effort to maintain his favored position.

*The Death of James.* We can only surmise what brought about the Herodian persecution. It may have been that the accumulation of resentment because of Peter's report concerning Cornelius, followed by reports of the actions of the church in Antioch, fanned the embers of hatred. At any rate, "Herod the king laid violent hands upon some who belonged to the church" (Acts 12:1).

One of these was James the brother of John. James was one of the Twelve, but Luke has not told us anything of his work. We may be certain that James was doing significant evangelization, for otherwise there would have been no reason to make him the number-one target, nor could it have been said that his death pleased the Jews.

In youthful exuberance, James and John, the sons of Zebedee, had desired the chief seats in Jesus' kingdom (Matt. 20:20-22; Mark 10:35-37). In the ensuing conversation, Jesus had asked, "Are you able to drink the cup that I [am to] drink?"—which is taken to be a reference to His death (cf. Matt. 26:39). James has now been given that cup to drink. The mode of execution ("with the sword") is generally understood to have been by beheading.

In the early Christian calendar of martyrs, the death of John is marked on the same day as that of James, namely December 27. This fact, plus the words of Jesus in Mark 10:39, have led some scholars to assume that both James and John were killed by Herod Agrippa. However, there is not the slightest evidence, in the New Testament or elsewhere, that John died at this time. If Paul's visit to Jerusalem recorded in Galatians 2 is to be equated with the Jerusalem Conference, John was still alive at that time (cf. Gal. 2:9).[1]

*The Imprisonment of Peter.* Because of the favorable reaction to the death of James, Agrippa "proceeded to arrest Peter also" (Acts 12:3). However, since it was Passover season ("during the days of Unleavened Bread"), Agrippa did not put Peter to death at once, but rather had him held under heavy guard. Peter had been imprisoned before, and there was a remarkable record of those experiences (4:3; 5:18), including an unexplained escape (5:22-23). So this time, he had sixteen guards. Two of them were chained to Peter's arms even while he slept (12:4,6), the others at the prison door and at two guard stations (12:6,10).

Peter had probably been in prison for the entire week, for it was now "the very night when Herod was about to bring him out" (12:6); in other words, the days of Unleavened Bread were over. That Peter could sleep—in fact, sleep so soundly that he had to be slapped awake (12:7), on the very night before he was scheduled for execution—is a testimony to his faith!

177

Meanwhile, the church in Jerusalem was praying "constantly" on his behalf (12:5). Many were praying at the house of Mary, the mother of John Mark (12:12). Are we to understand that the church in Jerusalem regularly met in her house? Probably not, unless the church had been severely decimated by the persecution under Saul. Nor is it necessary to suppose that the entire church met there for the entire period. It is reasonable to assume that each one had other duties and responsibilities, and that members of the believing fellowship came to pray and went out to work. The prayer was still continuing, probably with a renewed fervor, as the Passover was drawing to a close.

*The Deliverance of Peter.* There is an undercurrent of something like humor in this story. Peter was sound asleep, and had to be awakened by his night visitor. There was light in his cell, and the chains fell from his wrists (12:7), but his guards continued to sleep. The "angel"—the word simply means "messenger," whether angelic or human—had to remind Peter to dress and put on his sandals and his mantle (12:8). Peter thought it was all a dream or a vision, until they came to the iron gate leading into the city. This was closed and bolted at night, but it opened automatically, and when they reached a certain street, the angel left him (12:10). Peter finally realized that he was awake and free. The Lord had delivered him from Herod!

Peter thought first of the group that was praying for him at Mary's house. Why? Was it because the believers had often gathered there to pray whenever there was special need? Or was it because they had somehow sent word to Peter, "We're praying for you"? In either event, Peter turned his steps in that direction.

Once again, we are forced to smile. Peter knocked at the gate in the wall that surrounded the house and grounds. A maid named Rhoda answered the knock, and when she recognized Peter's voice, she rushed back to the house to tell the praying band—leaving Peter standing in the street! (12:14).

"Peter's here!" she said, somewhat out of breath.

"You're crazy!" they told her. She insisted that it was Peter, and they replied, "It's his ghost!" But when Peter continued to beat on the door, they all went, and saw him, and were amazed (12:16).

Peter quickly told them how the Lord had delivered him, and then said, "Tell this to James [Jesus' brother] and to the brethren" (12:17). Then Peter left quietly and secretly. Luke does not tell us where he went.

We must note certain things in this story. First, although they prayed earnestly, this group didn't really believe that God was going to release Peter. When Rhoda came in and said, "Peter's here!" they did not say, "Of course, he is; we've been praying for his deliverance." No; they said, "You're crazy!" This is normal human faith—the kind we all have most of the time. But God honors even this kind of unbelieving faith.

Second, James and the brethren were not there. Perhaps they were hiding, lest Herod Agrippa seize them too. Or perhaps they were keeping the Passover and holding a prayer meeting at another home. Peter had no time to go to see them, for his life was now in more danger than ever, but he wanted them to know of his deliverance.³

Two persons have been introduced by Luke in this story: James (to be distinguished, of course, from the James who was martyred) and John Mark. James will move into a prominent place in the Jerusalem church in the next part of Acts (15:13)—but he has already become an important leader. Peter singles him out (12:17), as does Paul, who refers to him as "James the Lord's brother" (Gal. 1:19). John Mark will accompany Barnabas and Saul to Antioch and start out with them on their "first missionary journey" (Acts 12:25; 13:5).

*The Death of Herod Agrippa.* When day came, "there was no small stir among the soldiers over what had become of Peter" (12:18). Agrippa, of course, ordered an investigation, and had the sentries put to death (12:19). Then he went to Caesarea.

The cities of Tyre and Sidon depended upon Galilee for their food supply, and because of some offense they had committed, Agrippa had either cut off that supply or had threatened to do so. The people decided to ask for peace (12:20). So Herod granted them an audience.

On the appointed day, he dressed in his kingly robes—Josephus describes him as "clad in a garment woven completely of silver so that its texture was indeed wondrous."⁴ Luke tells us that Agrippa made a speech, and the people, probably in insincere flattery, cried out, "The voice of a god, and not of man!" (12:22). Josephus tells us that the first rays of the sun fell on his silver robe, "its glitter inspired fear and awe," and the people addressed him as a god.[5]

At once, Agrippa was smitten by "an angel of the Lord," because he did not give God the glory, "and he was eaten by worms and died" (12:23). Josephus reports that Agrippa lingered in severe abdominal pain for five days, confessing that although he had been called immortal by the people he was under sentence of death.[6]

Herod Agrippa died, according to Josephus, "in the fifty-fourth year of his life and the seventh of his reign,"[7] in A.D. 44. We therefore have the first firm synchronism in Acts, for we can date the martyrdom of James prior to Passover (May 1) of 44, and the release of Peter a week or so later. The death of Agrippa may have occurred in connection with a festival honoring the emperor's birthday on August 1.[8]

Luke adds this short epilogue, "But the word of God grew and multiplied" (12:24). His use of such statements, as we have often seen, is an indication that he is about to turn to another subject.

*Summation.* The little band of believers that once could meet in the Upper Room (1:13) has become countless thousands, and in order to maintain the *koinōnia* the church in Jerusalem has to send Barnabas to Antioch and the church in Antioch has to send Barnabas and Saul to Jerusalem. Those who were nameless, sometimes called "followers of the way," or "those who believed" or simply "disciples," now have a name: Christians.

When we turn to the next part of our study in Acts, we clearly find ourselves in a different setting.

The one dominant person throughout Acts 13–28 is Saul of Tarsus, who is better known to us as "Paul."

In this second part of Acts, evangelization will proceed, not from Jerusalem but from Antioch. There will still be difficulties with the Jewish leaders and the Judaizing Christians at Jerusalem, but we shall find ourselves more frequently concerned with Roman proconsuls, gentile town-clerks, and pagan throngs who feel that their pagan gods and goddesses are being threatened. Paul's longing to be in Jerusalem "in time for the Feast" fades before the determination that he expresses in the words, "I must also see Rome." And the book which began in Jerusalem ends with Paul's preaching of the gospel in his own house in Rome.

Yet Acts is not two books, but one. It is false to speak of "the Acts of Peter" and "the Acts of Paul," as some do. Peter's significance is certainly of first importance in the Jerusalem Conference. Paul's gospel is certainly the same as that presented by Peter in the first part of Acts. Paul's first concern, even to the end, is for his fellow-countrymen the Jews. And let us not forget that it will be Paul's presence in the Temple in Jerusalem, participating as a Jew in a religious act, that starts the chain of circumstances that take him to Rome, and even though the trial is properly the Roman governor's responsibility, both the Sanhedrin and the king of Judea will be brought into the account.

But that is getting us into the next part of our story.

# Footnotes

1. Even if we follow Bruce's theory that the visit in Galatians 2 is the famine-visit (which Bruce dates after the persecution of Acts 12—*Commentary on Acts,* p. 247, n. 5), we would still need different dates for the deaths of James and John.

2. Literally "angel," but the implication seems to be that they thought Peter was already dead.

3. Where did Peter go? According to one theory, this was Luke's way of saying that he died. But this completely distorts Luke's clear style. Moreover, Peter is very much alive at the Jerusalem Conference (15:7). According to another theory, Peter went to Rome and founded the church there. But Paul, who refused to build on another man's foundations, makes no reference at all to Peter in Rome. Nor does it seem likely that a visit to Rome of the length required for founding a church could be fit into the chronology at this point.

4. Josephus, *Antiquities* 19.8.2 §344.

5. *Ibid.* §345.

6. *Ibid.* §§347-350.

7. *Ibid.* §350. Josephus obviously dates the reign from Agrippa's appointment over the tetrarchies of Philip and Lysanias.

8. So Bruce, *Commentary on Acts,* p. 255, n.24.

**PART III**

**The Church
in the Gentile World**

# The Antioch Church
# Commissions Barnabas and Saul

Luke now undertakes to answer the question, "How did the Church become a catholic or universal Church?" It had started in Jerusalem as a fellowship of Jews who believed that Jesus was their Messiah. Through a special revelation from God Peter was directed to Caesarea, where the household of Cornelius received the Spirit, and thus the door was opened to the Gentiles. The church in Antioch, established by refugees from Jerusalem, openly sought to evangelize Gentiles.

But so far the Christian church was a Jewish fellowship—a Jewish fellowship that to an extent welcomed Gentiles, it is true, but Jewish nonetheless. So long as this ethnic quality remained, the church could never become truly catholic.

The word "catholic" needs a word of explanation, since we often speak of "the Catholic Church" when we mean the Roman Catholic Church. "Catholic" is an adjective which means "universal in extent, all-encompassing." It comes to us from a compound Greek word,[1] the elements of which mean "according to (the) whole." The English dictionary carefully distinguishes *catholic* from *Catholic*, but we cannot rely upon a difference based on the use of a capital letter, especially since the difference disappears when we are speaking. We must learn to think in terms of basic and derived meanings. The basic meaning of "catholic" is "universal." This is the meaning in the expression "Holy Catholic Church," found in the Apostles' Creed.

Why not use the word "universal" instead of "catholic"? We could. But "universal" often suggests the idea of "for everybody *without exception*." Thus "Universalism" is the teaching that God will ultimately save everyone without exception. This is not a New Testament doctrine—in fact the New Testament clearly opposes this kind of universalism. What we mean by "catholic" is "for everybody *without distinction*." The gospel—the good news of salvation in Christ—is for all men without distinction: for Jew and Gentile, for male and female, for slave and freeman. Salvation, however, is only for those who accept God's offer by faith in Christ. Luke would add, in the words of Peter, "And there is salvation in no one else, for there is no other name under heaven given among men by which we must be saved" (Acts 4:12).

Luke now begins the section of Acts that tells us how the Church became catholic—for everyone, Jew and Gentile, without distinction.

*Prophets and Teachers.* There were in the church at Antioch "prophets and teachers" (13:1). Do these terms imply two distinct offices? Could we say, "Prophets prophesy and teachers teach"? It would take us too far afield in this work to discuss the nature of "prophet" in the Bible.[2] Doubtless the prophet is a teacher. But Paul distinguishes prophets from teachers (1 Cor. 12:28), and prophecy in the sense of foretelling future events (contrasted to prophecy in the sense of setting forth truth from God) is clearly included in Luke's account of the Early Church (e.g. Agabus in Acts 11:28).

Luke lists five "prophets and teachers": Barnabas, Simeon (the one called Black), Lucius the Cyrenean, Manaen the foster-brother[3] of Herod Antipas, and Saul (13:1). Two of these we already know: Barnabas and Saul. It is possible that Simeon is to be identified with "Simon of Cyrene" who carried Jesus' cross (Mark 15:21)—but, then, why was he not identified also as a Cyrenean? As for Lucius, it may be that he was Paul's "kinsman," mentioned in Romans 16:21. Manaen, the prophet, had grown up together with Herod Antipas, who beheaded John the Baptist and shared in the trial of Jesus. Bruce sees here an illustration of the "mystery and sovereignty of divine grace."[4]

These five were "worshiping the Lord and fasting" when the Holy Spirit made known His will.

The word translated "worshiping" is the word from which we get "liturgy." In the Greek Old Testament the word is used of the service rendered by Priests and Levites (Exod. 29:30; Num. 16:9). Therefore our word "worship," as many of us use it, is probably a bit too weak. Whatever we may think of liturgy, we probably agree that a "liturgical service" requires more of the worshiper than a "low-church worship service." On the other hand, the modern concept of "liturgical" is not exactly what is meant by the Greek word, for the service of God is often lacking. These five were serving the Lord in their worship.

They were also fasting. In Western Christianity we know very little of religious fasting. It might be well if we were to make a special study of the place of fasting in the New Testament. Bruce says, "There are indications that New Testament Christians were specially sensitive to the Spirit's communications during fasting."[5]

*The Spirit's Commission.* The Holy Spirit said, "Set apart for me Barnabas and Saul for the work to which I have called them" (13:2). Saul, we have seen, was already aware of his call. Was Barnabas also? We have to be so careful "reading between the lines." It is possible to read in something that God did not put there. But it is also possible to overlook what God clearly intended. When the church in Jerusalem heard about the gentile ministry of the church in Antioch, it sent Barnabas to Antioch (11:22). Why? When Barnabas saw the demonstration of the grace of God among the "Greeks" he rejoiced (11:23), and as the number of converts grew, he went to Tarsus to look for Saul (11:25).

*The Commissioning Ceremony.* Luke says, "Then after fasting and prayer they laid their hands on them and sent them off" (13:3). Who are "they"? The other three? Possibly. These five men apparently had been making a special effort through worship and fasting to get closer to the mind of God. The Holy Spirit spoke to them. We might therefore conclude that the commissioning came from this smaller group.

On the other hand, Barnabas and Saul felt that they had been commissioned by the church in Antioch, and when they returned from this first extensive journey "they gathered the church together"— not merely the other three of the smaller group— "and declared all that God had done with them, and how he had opened a door of faith to the Gentiles" (14:27). One ancient manuscript adds "all" in 13:3, which would confirm the conclusion that Barnabas and Saul were sent out by the entire Antioch Church.

Luke's wording in verse 3 suggests that it was after the Spirit had made known His will that they fasted and prayed. The church was very much aware that they were embarking on a new course that would have grave consequences. They needed to be sure that they were in tune with the will of God.

"They laid their hands on them"—why? All sorts of theories about the "laying on of hands" have sprung up in the church. In this case, the two men were already recognized apostles and had demonstrated the gifts of the Spirit. We must therefore

191

rule out any "ordination" to the apostolate or any "conferring" of the Spirit. We may interpret the act as a "commissioning" to the immediate task, or perhaps it was a way of invoking the divine blessing on the "missionaries."

The word "missionary" comes to us from Latin, just as the word "apostle" comes to us from Greek. Both words mean the same thing, "one who has been sent out, sent on a mission." We use the same Latin root when we say that Barnabas and Saul were "com*missioned*" by the church in Antioch.

*The Three Missionary Journeys.* It is customary to speak of three "missionary journeys" of Paul. For want of a better term, we may continue to use the expression, for Paul was certainly sent forth, first by God and then by the church. This was his apostolate.

The first of these missions is recorded in Acts 13:4–14:28. The second followed the Jerusalem Conference and is recorded in Acts 15:36–18:22. The third "journey" begins at Acts 18:23, but the ending depends on where we think the trip ended: at Tyre (21:3), or Ptolemais (21:7), or Caesarea (21:8), or Jerusalem (21:17).

Each of the three missions began at Antioch. In a sense we might say that each ended in Jerusalem. The first time, this was because of the need for the Jerusalem Conference. The visit to Jerusalem at the close of the second mission seems to have been incidental ("He went up [to Jerusalem] and greeted the church, and then went down to Antioch"). Only at the close of the third journey, it seems, Paul clearly planned to return to Jerusalem (20:16), and that was at least in part because he was traveling with representatives of the gentile churches who were carrying a gift to the Jerusalem Church.

But should we think in terms of *three* missionary journeys? Paul had only one mission: to preach the gospel to the Gentiles. God called him for that task and the church in Antioch sent him out. We do not read of Paul "returning home" or even "returning to Antioch." He thought of his life as a single "course" which he at the end had run.

Yet, not only for convenience' sake but even as a matter of historical record, we may speak of three distinct trips, each starting from Antioch. The first was in the nature of an exploratory venture, a new departure, setting out into the gentile world to convert Gentiles. So, when that venture was concluded, a full report was given to the church in Antioch. Backlash from the venture brought on the Jerusalem Conference with its debate over the question of what to do about gentile converts. In a sense, there could have been no second missionary journey until that problem was decided.

The second journey started out as a revisiting of the cities covered on the first journey (15:36), but developed into a longer and more extended trip that carried the gospel into Europe.

The third mission seems to have been primarily directed at Ephesus (18:21), and Paul seems to have been laying the ground-work for this mission by leaving Priscilla and Aquila there while he returned to Caesarea (19:18-19). During his Ephesus period, however, Paul seems to have set his sights on Rome, planning first to visit Jerusalem (19:22).

From Corinth, later on that trip, he wrote his great letter to the Romans, expressing his fervent hope to visit them (Rom. 1:9-15). As he had left Priscilla and Aquila at Ephesus to prepare for his intended visit, so, it would seem, he had sent them on to Rome (Rom. 16:3-5).

Should we think of the Journey to Rome as a "fourth missionary journey"? In effect, that is what it turned out to be. But in all other details, it certainly was of a much different nature. Paul did not leave from Antioch. He did not go at his own will. No plans were made to revisit any of the churches previously established. Rather, he went from Caesarea as a prisoner under guard, having appealed his case to Caesar. Evangelization done along the way was incidental to the trip. The only church that could be said to have been revisited was at Sidon (Acts 27:3). And his preaching of the gospel in Rome, while "unhindered" (28:31), was limited to what could be done by a man under house arrest (cf. Eph. 6:20; Col. 4:10; Philem. 1).

*Summation.* The words of Jesus' commission, "unto the ends of the earth" (Acts 1:8) are at last about to be realized. That is to say, they are to be understood in their real meaning, and not as some vague ideal. But this will mean once again, as is true whenever a revolutionary idea is undertaken, that there will be a period of difficult adjustment.

If you and I were to put the teachings of Jesus fully into effect in our lives—fully, I said, and not just in vague generalizations, so that "love your enemy," for example, didn't just mean "pretend he's not there" or "tolerate him"—think of some of the complications we would face! Business men have told me that if they tried to carry out Christian teaching literally they would have to go out of business. Maybe they see the issues more clearly than some of the rest of us, or maybe they're just being more honest.

What would it mean if we took seriously only the one commandment of Jesus, to preach the gospel to the whole world? If we did that in the spirit implied by Jesus, we would have to do it by an example so convincing, in love so compelling, in understanding so profound, in truth so complete and yet so simple, that we would never cause anyone to stumble, we would give no unnecessary offense, we would fully understand the mental and moral obstacles to the gospel, and we would patiently love and woo each one for the Lord. I can't speak for you, but that would cause all sorts of difficulties and problems in my life. Friends would oppose, enemies would take advantage, fellow-Christians would argue points of theology, and soon I would be seriously tempted to go back to what I'm doing now.

Well, the Church has set out to win the world to Jesus Christ. It, too, will be opposed by its friends, and hated by its enemies. Times will come when it, too, will be tempted to return to the good old *status quo ante*—which is the path of least resistance. Luke will picture for us many of the trials and struggles of the Church as it sets its face to this task.

# Footnotes

1. *Katholikós* comes from *katá* "according to" and *hólos* "whole."

2. For a good dicussion, cf. "Prophecy, Prophets" in *New Bible Dictionary*, pp. 1036-1046, especially 1045. See also E. Earle Ellis, "The Role of the Christian Prophet in Acts," in W. W. Gasque and R. P. Martin, eds., *Apostolic History and the Gospel* (1970), pp. 55-67.

3. *RSV* "a member of the court" is not precise. The word *syntrophos* means literally 'nourished with,' and was used of children who were brought up together. *TEV* reads 'who had been brought up with.'

4. Bruce, *Commentary on Acts*, p. 261.

5. *Commentary on Acts*, p. 261

# First Journey:
# The Mission to Cyprus

The apostles began the "First Missionary Journey" by sailing from Seleucia to Salamis on the island of Cyprus. They moved through the island to Paphos, then sailed to the mainland of Asia Minor, probably landing at Attalia (modern Antalya), in the coastal province of Pamphylia. Then the apostles moved northeastward to Pisidian Antioch, eastward to Iconium, then to Lystra and Derbe. From Derbe they retraced their steps to Attalia and sailed back to Antioch.[1]

The apostles (or missionaries) of the First Journey were Barnabas and Saul (Acts 13:4). John, better known as Mark, was with them for the first portion of the mission (13:5). It is well to have in mind a general outline of each mission, both as to the places visited and the persons on the mission. It is also important to work with reliable maps.

*Salamis.* Barnabas and Saul had been sent on this mission by the Holy Spirit and by the church in Antioch (13:2,3). From Antioch-on-the-Orontes they journeyed down the Orontes valley to the seaport of Seleucia, about sixteen miles to the west, and sailed to Cyprus.

Cyprus is an island about sixty miles west of the Syrian coast. Its importance can be traced far back in the history of the Mediterranean world, but the name "Cyprus," meaning "copper," dates from the exploitation of the copper mines in the Roman period. Cyprus became part of the province of Cilicia in 55 B.C., and in 27 B.C. it became a separate province governed by a legate. Five years later it became a senatorial province governed by a pro-consul.

Salamis was then an important seaport at the eastern end of the central plain, lying south of the long finger of eastern Cyprus. Its splendid harbor is now silted up and Famagusta, six miles to the southwest, has taken its place. Apparently there was a sizable Jewish community in Salamis, for Luke mentions an unspecified number of "synagogues" (13:5).

Barnabas and Saul applied the principle of preaching first in the synagogue—a principle that was natural enough in Judea and Syria for the "Jewish Church," meaning the church that was up to that time concentrating on evangelizing its Jewish brethren. We shall notice, however, that this principle was continued throughout Paul's life.

The two missioners took Mark with them as an "attendant" or "minister." Just what kind of ministry he performed is not exactly clear, but one attractive suggestion is that he served as a "catechist," rehearsing new converts in the outline facts of the life of Jesus. Luke uses the same word when referring to the early traditions that "were delivered to us by those who from the beginning were eyewitnesses and ministers of the word" (Luke 1:2).[2]

How long the three stayed in Salamis is not recorded. They proclaimed the word of God "in the synagogues," which suggests two or more Sabbaths at the very least.

Then they went through "the whole island as far as Paphos" (Acts 13:6). Again, Luke does not give us details. How many cities and villages did they visit? If we may judge from later journeys, we can be certain that Paul aimed at the large centers and left the evangelizing of the surrounding areas to the newly established churches in those centers.

*Paphos.* Old Paphos was a city founded by the Phoenicians, built close to a good harbor. New Paphos developed in Roman times, about seven miles to the northwest, and became the seat of the Roman proconsul.

When Barnabas and Saul reached Paphos, they doubtlessly looked for a synagogue. In cities where there were too few Jews for a synagogue (at least ten adult male Jews were required), the apostles sought out members of the Jewish community. Luke mentions no synagogue at Paphos, but he tells us "they came upon a certain magician, a Jewish false prophet, named Bar-Jesus" (13:6). This man was "with" the proconsul—probably meaning associated with him in some semi-official capacity (13:7). Luke is telling us that it was through the agency of Bar-Jesus that the apostles came into the presence of the Roman proconsul.

*Saul—also known as Paul.* The proconsul was named Sergius Paulus, identified by a number of scholars with the Lucius Sergius Paulus who was one of the curators of the banks of the Tiber during the reign of Claudius, mentioned in a Latin inscription.[3] Luke describes him as "an intelligent man" (13:7).

Whether the visitors had registered when they entered the city and official notice was passed on to the proconsul, or whether Bar-Jesus mentioned to the proconsul that these Jewish travelers were in the city, we are not told. In any case, the proconsul summoned Barnabas and Saul into his presence, seeking "to hear the word of God" (13:7). We cannot help but wonder whether this sagacious man had not already seen through the "false prophet" (who obviously had claimed to have been sent by God) and wanted to learn the truth about this Jewish God. Elymas the magician,[4] however, opposed this, trying to turn the proconsul away from the faith.

At this point Saul seems to have assumed leadership of the mission. Luke indicates as much by two things: he now and henceforth calls him "Paul," and speaks of the group as "those around Paul" (13:13) or "Paul and Barnabas" (13:46).

As a Jew living in the gentile world, Saul would have had two names: the traditional name drawn from Jewish history (in his case, Saul, doubtless after the Benjamite king of Israel), and a gentile name which sometimes was a translation of the Jewish name and sometimes was a name with a similar sound. It has been suggested that Saul took this gentile name from Sergius Paulus—but this is not likely. From this point on, except in the accounts of the conversion (22:7ff; 26:14), Luke uses the name Paul. In his epistles Paul invariably uses the name Paul.

Paul, filled with the Holy Spirit, looked at Bar-Jesus and said, "You son of the Devil! You are the enemy of everything that is good; you are full of all kinds of evil tricks, and you always keep trying to turn the Lord's truths into lies!" (13:10 TEV). Then he pronounced a judgment of God, temporary blindness, on Elymas. At once the judgment fell (13:11): Elymas groped about seeking someone to lead him by the hand.

The proconsul, when he saw this demonstration of the power of Paul's Lord, "believed" (13:12), being astonished at the teaching. What led Sergius Paulus to this faith, the miracle, or the teaching? Was it "saving faith"? Did he repent? Was he baptized? Luke leaves these questions unanswered. He simply says, "he believed."

*Summation.* Thus the mission to Cyprus ended. Why had they chosen Cyprus, in the first place? Barnabas, according to tradition, came from Salamis. He would have had true concern for his kinfolk and friends who lived there. Then, we remember the men from Cyprus who had been instrumental in starting gentile evangelization at Antioch (11:20). It is only natural that they would have created interest in the evangelization of Gentiles in Cyprus (evangelization of Jews in Cyprus had already been started by some of those scattered in the persecution that arose over Stephen. (See 11:19.)

Gathering together all of these facts, we see that Cyprus was a logical "first step." Barnabas knew the people and their ways. Interest had already been generated in the home church. Such interest is the ideal starting point for any mission!

But it is only a starting point.

## Footnotes

1. For the First Journey, see *Westminster Historical Atlas*, pp. 95-96, plate XV; *Macmillan Bible Atlas*, map 245; or Grollenberg's *Atlas of the Bible*, endpaper II.

2. The word *hypērétēs* meant "under rower" hence "servant." It is used of officials of the Sanhedrin (Matt. 26:58) and the synagogue (Luke 4:20). It is also used of ministers of kings (John 18:36).

3. Bastiaan Van Elderen, "Some Archaeological Observations on Paul's First Missionary Journey,' (in W. W. Gasque and R. P. Martin, eds., *Apostolic History and the Gospel* [1970], pp. 151-156), reexamines this evidence and concludes that the inscrption "cannot be confidently cited as a solution to the identification of Sergius Paulus" (p. 155).

4. The meaning of "Elymas" baffles scholars. "Bar-Jesus" is patronymic, "son of Joshua," and the man must have had a name of his own. "Elymas" seems to be the "translation" of his name into some other language or dialect.

CHAPTER 19 / (Acts 13:13-52)

# First Journey:
# The Mission to Galatia

"What's so different about this 'missionary' idea?,"
someone might have asked Luke. "Some Hellenists
had already taken the gospel to Cyprus (Acts
11:19), and all that Barnabas and Saul have done so
far is little more than others had done." True
enough. Except, perhaps, that the opportunity to
proclaim the word of the Lord to a Roman proconsul was something of a landmark. But we must not
be impatient.

Can we date the First Journey? Not exactly.
Scholars have argued for many dates between A.D.
45 and 48 for the beginning of the journey. Its duration is set at between two and four years. Sir William Ramsay thought the journey started in March

of 47 and ended in July or August of 49.[1] He estimates that not less than two months were spent on Cyprus.[2] I find no indication that the apostles spent two winters in Galatia, therefore I am inclined to limit the mission to less than two years, possibly little more than a year, 47-48 or 48-49.

*Perga in Pamphylia.* "Paul and his company [literally, those around Paul] set sail from Paphos, and came to Perga in Pamphylia" (13:13). Pamphylia was the coastal area of Asia Minor west of Cilicia. Prior to A.D. 43 Pamphylia was part of the province of Galatia, and then it was made part of the province of Lycia-Pamphylia. Perga was an important city on the Cestrus river; it was served by the port of Attalia, founded in the second century B.C. There are extensive Greek and Roman ruins at Perga.

Ramsay is convinced, from Luke's wording, that the original plan was to evangelize Pamphylia from Perga. But something happened to cause the apostles to move immediately to the mountainous region of Antioch. Ramsay's reasons are extensive,[3] and we note only two factors. From Paul's letter to the Galatians we learn that his first visit to Galatia was somehow the result of an illness. "You know that it was because of a bodily ailment that I preached the gospel to you at first; and though my condition was a trial to you, you did not scorn or despise me, but received me as an angel of God, as Christ Jesus" (Gal. 4:13-14). If we accept the identification of Pisidian Antioch as part of the area included in Paul's "Galatians," this supports Ramsay's theory. A second factor was Mark's abrupt decision to leave the apostles in Perga and return to Jerusalem (Acts 13:13). This, reasons Ramsay, could only have been precipitated by a sudden change of plans. Ramsay, incidentally, is convinced that Paul suffered an attack of malarial fever.

Luke gives no reason for Mark's sudden departure. He simply says, "John, having separated himself from them, returned to Jerusalem" (13:13). When they were ready to set out on the Second Journey, Barnabas wanted again to take Mark. Paul opposed the idea, because he "thought best not to take with them one who had withdrawn from them in Pamphylia, and had not gone with them to the work" (15:37-38). This suggests that the "work" had something to do with Mark's withdrawal.

Perhaps we should not think of Paul's decision to "turn to the Gentiles" at Pisidian Antioch (13:46) as a spur-of-the-moment action. It is possible that this had been a growing conviction, namely that converting the Jews and letting them evangelize the Gentiles just wasn't working. Paul may have set forth the idea at Paphos, and spelled it out in more detail at Perga. Mark wasn't "buying" the idea. He withdrew from the work and from the apostles.

Am I being severe in my judgment of Mark? When we study the life of Paul in detail we find that he could patiently endure all things except the refusal to treat Gentiles as equal with Jews before the gospel. In this matter he would tolerate no vacillation—not even in the case of Peter or Barnabas! (Gal. 2:11-14). I am unable to think of any other reason sufficient to account for his harsh judgment of Mark.

*Pisidian Antioch.* Paul and Barnabas went from Perga to Antioch. It is not quite accurate to speak of this city as "Antioch of Pisidia," as it is sometimes translated, for Antioch was not in Pisidia. The geographer Strabo described it as in Phrygia, "the Antioch toward Pisidia."[4] Under the Romans it was made part of the province of Galatia, specifically Phrygia Galatica. The very extensive ruins of Antioch can be seen today a few miles from Yalvac. They testify that it was once a great city on the route between Ephesus and Cilicia.[5]

Following their custom, the apostles went to the synagogue on the Sabbath (Acts 13:14). The service consisted of prayers, the reading of the pericope for the day from the Torah and probably a selection also from the prophets, followed by a word of exhortation or preaching. The suggestion that the readings were from Deuteronomy 1 and Isaiah 1 is a conjecture supported by two words which Paul used which are found in these passages.[6]

*Paul's Sermon in Antioch.* A visiting rabbi would certainly be welcome to give the sermon—in fact, urged to do so. There was a large Jewish community in Antioch (Antiochus the Great had moved 2,000 families of Jews to the cities of Lydia and Phrygia[7]), but Luke refers to "the synagogue" as if it were the only one there. How did they know Paul was a rabbi? Possibly by his robe. Possibly he had identified himself as such when he first entered the city. It is even possible that they invited Paul and Barnabas to speak as fellow Jewish worshipers, not knowing that Paul was a rabbi. But then it would soon become obvious.

206

Paul's sermon is given at some length (13:17-41). A careful comparison of this sermon with Peter's sermon on the day of Pentecost, brings out some interesting and important points of difference and similarity.

First, Paul outlines the story of the chosen Israel (13:17), in Egypt, the desert, and Canaan (13:17-19). He refers to the judges and the kings, zeroing in on David (13:20-22). This leads to Jesus, a descendant of David whom God brought to Israel as the promised deliverer (13:22).

Peter likewise started with an Old Testament background, namely the promise given by the prophet Joel (2:14-21), and applied this to Jesus.

Paul then speaks of the crucifixion and resurrection of Jesus (13:27-31). Peter did likewise (2:22-32). Both apostles speak of the ignorance of those who had rejected Jesus and handed Him over to be killed. Both men see the action as fulfillment of Scripture. Both apostles quote Psalm 16:10 with reference to the Resurrection. Both men point out that David died and was buried.

Finally, Paul applies his message to his hearers: "Let it be known to you therefore, brethren, that through this man forgiveness of sins is proclaimed to you" (13:38). Peter said: "Let all the house of Israel therefore know assuredly that God has made him both Lord and Christ, this Jesus whom you crucified" (2:36). In the reaction, when they asked Peter "What shall we do?," Peter told them to repent and be baptized "for the forgiveness of your sins" (2:38).

Thus far there is remarkable similarity—although

207

we should not overlook the individual differences that clearly refute any idea that Luke by composing these "sermons" was simply trying to balance Paul over against Peter.

But Paul makes a statement not found in Peter's first sermon, and this is the heart of Paul's gospel: "and by him [Jesus] every one that believes is freed from everything from which you could not be freed by the law of Moses" (13:39). Here Paul sets the gospel in contrast to the Law. The one can save; the other cannot.

Peter, of course, held the same view, and he stated it forcefully at the Jerusalem Conference: "Now therefore why do you make trial of God by putting a yoke upon the neck of the disciples which neither our fathers nor we have been able to bear? But we believe that we shall be saved through the grace of the Lord Jesus, just as they will" (15:10-11). However Peter did not make this point in his first recorded sermon.

Stephen also had been moving in this direction. He saw that the Law and the Temple were only temporary, while Jesus was the perfect fulfillment. This is only another way of saying that if the Law is temporary it cannot meet the needs of all men. Paul carried the idea through to its logical conclusion. Where the Law fails, Jesus finishes the redemptive task.

*The Reaction to Paul's Sermon.* As the apostles left the synagogue, "the people begged that these things might be told them the next sabbath" (13:42). Moreover, "many Jews and devout converts to Judaism followed Paul and Barnabas" and the apostles "urged them to continue in the grace of God" (13:43).

On the following Sabbath "almost the whole city gathered together to hear the word of God" (13:44). This crowd, of course, included a great many Gentiles.

There were Gentiles present in the synagogue on the first Sabbath. We passed over the verse at the time, but let's go back and look at Paul's opening words: "Men of Israel, and you that fear God, listen" (13:16). "Men of Israel" applied, obviously, to the Jews. "You that fear God" referred to Gentiles, either proselytes (converts to Judaism) or worshipers of the God of Israel who had not become proselytes. Since they were present in the synagogue service we might assume that they were proselytes, and in fact Luke uses this word in verse 43.

But in the crowd that gathered on the following Sabbath, the additional Gentiles were not proselytes; they probably were not even God-fearers. They were pagans. They were defiling the devout Jews who were present and the sanctuary. Naturally the Jews were furious. But Luke singles out another fact: "They were filled with jealousy" (13:45). We should like to think that at last they regretted that they had had such little effect in giving light to the Gentiles! But if so, there is no sign of repentance. They contradicted Paul and reviled him.

That was when Paul made his great pronouncement.

"*We Turn to the Gentiles.*" It was not a unilateral action by Paul. Luke carefully records that "Paul and Barnabas spoke out boldly, saying, 'It was necessary that the word of God should be spoken first to you. Since you thrust it from you, and judge yourselves unworthy of eternal life, behold, *we turn to the Gentiles*' " (13:46).

Paul supported his decision with a well-known quotation from Isaiah: "I have set you to be a light for the Gentiles, that you may bring salvation to the uttermost parts of the earth" (Isa. 49:6; Acts 13:47).

This was the basic reason for the election of Israel. The idea of "chosen people" has been badly distorted. They were not chosen as an end but as a means to an end. They were elect by God in order that the knowledge of God might be spread over all the earth. They were given light that they might give light to the Gentiles. They were a choice vineyard, destined to produce grapes. How many different ways did Isaiah say it? How many different figures of speech did he use? Paul, as a Jew, had felt the thrust of these passages. He knew now, as a result of his conversion, the purpose of his own election. This was also the purpose of Israel's election. He had preached to the Jew first, in synagogues at Damascus, Jerusalem, Syrian Antioch, Salamis, Pisidian Antioch, (and who knows where else?), praying that when Israel was converted Israel would fulfill the purpose of her election.

Israel had failed. This was the judgment pronounced by Jesus in Jerusalem. Paul echoed the judgment in Antioch.

For the rest of his earthly course, Paul would preach "to the Jew first." This was because Paul loved his kinsmen. He would have given up his own hope of eternity if he could have saved them. He believed wholeheartedly that God was not through with them. If their rejection had been the means of bringing blessing to the Gentiles, how much more would their ultimate restoration mean to the world![8]

But meanwhile, there is a lost world to save. There is a Saviour to proclaim. And since Paul cannot count on the earthly Israel to mediate his preaching, he must go directly to the Gentiles with the gospel.

*Results of the Proclamation.* The Gentiles were overjoyed. They could worship the God of the Jews without becoming Jews! Luke adds, "As many as were ordained to eternal life believed" (13:48).

"The word of the Lord spread throughout all the region" (13:49). This was the start of the churches in Galatia. These Galatians would bring Paul much joy and many heartbreaks.

The Jews incited "the devout women of high standing," obviously God-fearing women of the upper strata of the Gentiles and "the leading men of the city," and the resulting persecution drove Paul and Barnabas out of the district (13:50).

The apostles, in biblical fashion, "shook off the dust from their feet" as a witness against those who had rejected the word of life, and went on to Iconium.

The disciples, doubtless meaning the newly converted Christians in Antioch, "were filled with joy and with the Holy Spirit" (13:52).

*Summation.* What's different about these "missionary journeys"? Now we know. Paul has started

211

a new departure: he will henceforth carry a mission directly to the Gentiles. This course will take him to cities where there are no synagogues. Some of his messages will not be based on Old Testament teachings and illustrations. He will even quote pagan poets to get his points across. But he will never preach a different gospel!

Does it sound easy? Well, it's not! When news gets back to Jerusalem, the reaction will nearly tear the church apart. Paul will have to fight alone. Even Peter and Barnabas will fail to see the implications of their own positions. Paul will have to rebuke Peter openly. Paul will write letters, retrace his steps, and wage relentless war against those who would set up a second-class citizenship in the kingdom. He will be maligned, persecuted, beaten, left for dead. But he will stand his ground. There is only one Lord and one faith. There can be no middle wall of separation in the Church of Jesus Christ. In Him we all are one.

But I wonder if we have learned this lesson, even today?

## Footnotes

1. Ramsay, *St. Paul the Traveller and the Roman Citizen*, p. 128.

2. Ramsay, *The Church and the Roman Empire*, p. 61.

3. Ramsay, *St. Paul the Traveller*, pp. 90-97.

4. Strabo, *Geography*, 12.6.4. Luke's term "Antioch the Pisidian" is quite accurate. He knew that Antioch was not in Pisidia, cf. Acts 14:24.

5. "Antioch," Ramsay, *The Cities of St. Paul*, pp. 247-297.

6. Ramsay, *St. Paul the Traveller*, p. 100. The suggestion appears in J. A. Bengel, *Gnomen of the New Testament* (trans. by Charlton T. Lewis and M. R. Vincent, 1862) 1:833.

7. Ramsay, *Galatians*, p. 191.

8. For Paul's own words on this theme read Rom. 9-11.

# First Journey:
# The Mission to Iconium,
# Lystra, Derbe

The pattern has been set, and we shall see it repeated in nearly every place where Paul went. First he sought out the synagogue and preached the gospel. Some of the Jews, and usually an even larger number of Gentiles, believed. This caused opposition to develop among the unbelieving Jews who then sought to stir up the unbelieving Gentiles. The opposition often developed into a riot, and Paul was forced to move on.

A second fact should be noted. Paul almost invariably sought out the large cities, preferably those which had some official Roman status. The modern attempt of many missionaries to evangelize every village in every part of every country does not follow the apostolic pattern. Paul aimed at the large centers, establishing training schools, and left the evangelization of the villages to his disciples in the cities.

*Iconium.* About 100 miles southeast of Antioch was Iconium, modern Konya. Originally a Phrygian settlement, named Kawania, it became the chief city of Lycaonia; later it was included in Galatia. The Roman emperor Claudius gave it the name of Claudiconium. Finally under Hadrian, it was made an honorary Roman colony.[1]

The apocryphal story of Paul and Thecla is laid in Iconium. This story, which may have a historical substratum, contains the well-known description of Paul by Onesiphorus, who, with his wife and children, had gone out to meet Paul on the road from Lystra to Iconium. Here is how Onesiphorus portrays him: ". . . a man small in size, bald-headed, bandy-legged, well-built, with eyebrows meeting, rather long-nosed, full of grace. For sometimes he seemed like a man, and sometimes he had the countenance of an angel."[2]

Paul and Barnabas went to the synagogue in Iconium and "so spoke that a great company believed, both of Jews and of Greeks" (14:1). The "unbelieving Jews" set about to turn the Gentiles against "the brethren," meaning the members of the young church in Iconium (14:2). If we follow the oldest manuscripts, we must assume that the opposition was not strong and not well organized at the outset.

The work of the apostles was a work of preaching ("speaking boldly for the Lord") and of "signs and wonders" (12:3). God was honoring their ministry in a remarkable way.

At last, however, the effect of the opponents began to be seen. The city was divided; "some sided with the Jews, and some with the apostles" (14:4). A plot against the apostles was discovered, and they moved on before it could be carried out (14:5). Luke reports that they "fled to Lystra and Derbe, cities of Lycaonia, and to the surrounding country" (14:6).

*Lystra.* Luke's use of terms has been both challenged and defended. His language here seems to imply that Iconium was not in Lycaonia. Ramsay shows that Luke is precise in his use of terms for that period of time, for Iconium was a Phrygian city when the apostles visited it.[3]

Lystra, like Derbe, seems to have been one of the exceptions to Paul's plan of evangelizing only the large cities. It was neither large nor important. However, it had been selected by Augustus as the site of a Roman colony, since it was located on the military road between Pisidian Antioch to the west and the Cilician Gates to the east. In Latin inscriptions the name is always spelled Lustra.[4]

At Lystra, a man who had been crippled from birth, was listening to Paul as he preached. Paul was "looking intently at him" and saw something in the man indicating "that he had faith to be made well" (14:9). Had this man seen the apostles perform miracles at Lystra? Had he heard reports of their works at Iconium? Luke does not tell us. Perhaps the man was moved, as Paul spoke about Jesus, and thought with faith, "If Jesus had only come here, He could make me walk."

Paul said, "Stand upright on your feet," and the man "sprang up and walked" (14:10).

The healing of the cripple by the apostles had an unexpected effect on the Gentile audience. They began to shout in excitement, "The gods have come down to us, in the likeness of men!" But since they were shouting in Lycaonian, Paul and Barnabas did not understand what they were saying. Then the priest of the temple of Zeus-before-the-city, brought oxen and garlands and wanted to lead the people in sacrifice to these "gods." The people had decided that Barnabas was Zeus, the father of the gods (perhaps he was tall and dignified looking, like the statues of Zeus). Paul, the speaker, they decided was Hermes (the messenger of the gods).

At the signs of the sacrifice, Paul and Barnabas suddenly realized what was happening. Tearing their clothes as a sign of blasphemy, they protested. "Men, why are you doing this? We also are men, of like nature with you . . ." (14:15).

But Paul did not stop there, he went on to preach to them.

*Paul's First Sermon to Pagans.* The message that followed was (so far as we know from the record) Paul's first sermon delivered to a wholly pagan group. It should be compared with the message in the Areopagus when we get to Acts 17, for that also is a message to pagans.

Note the points that Paul covers. (1) "We bring you good news; (2) to turn from these worthless things; (3) to a living God; (4) who made heaven and earth and the sea and all things in them; (5) who in past generations allowed all nations (or Gentiles) to go their own ways; (6) yet he did not leave himself without a witness; (7) but he gave you from heaven rains and fruitful seasons, filling your hearts with food and gladness" (14:15-17).

The apostles are not gods. They are messengers sent by God. They did not come to be served (the basic meaning of "worship"), but to give good news. The purpose of their coming was to turn Gentiles from precisely this worship of "no-gods" which their hearers were even now trying to perform.

The God whom they represented is not one of the "no-gods"; rather, He is a living God, in fact, the God who made heaven and earth and all things. He has permitted pagan nations to wander in their own ways, neither knowing nor worshiping Him. Yet He has given evidence of His providential power, for He gives even to pagans the rain from heaven, the food for man's needs, and good things to make man happy.

This is "natural theology" or knowledge of God drawn from nature. It is to be contrasted with "supernatural" or "special" revelation, which is the knowledge of God that we get from God's special revelation of Himself. Some scholars seem to think that the only kind of revelation is natural revelation. They rule out any special revelation, such as inspired Scripture, incarnation, and miraculous deeds. Other scholars seem to have little if any place in their systems for natural revelation. They hold that we can only learn about God from the Word written and incarnate.

The Bible, particularly in the Psalms, teaches us that there is a revelation of God in nature. His created world bears the marks of the Creator. The heavens declare the glory of God, and the firmament shows His handiwork. (See Ps. 19:1.) Paul likewise uses natural revelation in his teaching (Acts 14:15-17; 17:24-29; Rom. 1:19-23).

But there is an important difference between natural revelation and supernatural revelation, and we wind up with a false theology if we do not observe the difference. Natural revelation tells us of God's wisdom, power, and providential care; it does not declare His redemptive purpose. Nature "red in tooth and claw" tells man nothing about God's will to save. Nor do destructive cyclones, earthquakes, and other "dysteleological surds." Only in His revealed Word, and especially in the Word made flesh in Jesus Christ, do we learn of His redeeming love.

Why, then, did Paul preach only natural theology at Lystra? But who said that this was all he preached? Luke tells us that the apostles "preached the gospel" there (Acts 14:7). Still, there are times when natural men refuse to hear anything but a message from the natural world.

Something in Paul's message struck home. Perhaps it was the reference to the fact that God had in the past overlooked the idolatry of paganism, inferring that now that time is past. Perhaps it was the protest that they were only human beings like the men who would have "worshiped" them. In either event, they were just barely able to keep the crowd from offering the sacrifice (14:18).

*The Stoning of Paul and the Flight to Derbe.* How long Paul and Barnabas were able to continue their evangelizing in Lystra we are not told. If we keep in mind the fact that the entire first mission was bracketed by sea-travel and therefore by the months when the sea-lanes were open, we arrive at a schedule somewhat as follows:

The apostles sailed from Seleucia to Salamis, probably in the spring soon after the shipping season opened. Ramsay suggests that they spent not less than two months in Cyprus, which would seem reasonable. They would then have sailed to Pamphylia in summer—which would be a good time to quit Pamphylia quickly and get up to the higher elevations of Galatia. Evangelizing Antioch may have lasted for several months—which would bring the apostles into fall or possibly early winter. The balance of the first mission, including the "long time" in Iconium (14:3), the indefinite stay in Lystra and in Derbe, the return through Lystra, Iconium, and Antioch (14:21), and the evangelizing of Perga (14:25), could not have been completed before the opening of the sea-lanes in the spring of the following year, not later than the close of the sailing season in the fall of that same year. I find it difficult to stretch this out by another entire year.

If the "long time" in Iconium included most of the winter, then the periods in Lystra and Derbe must have been relatively short. Luke's account suggests the same.

Jews "from Antioch of Pisidia and from Iconium"

came to Lystra and "won the crowds to their side" (14:19 *TEV*). It is not hard to believe that a crowd would hail the apostles as "gods" one day, and a few days later turn against them. Remember Palm Sunday and Good Friday! Paul was stoned and left for dead. He refers to this in 2 Cor. 11:25, "once I was stoned."

Luke does not indicate that Paul was actually dead, nor does he give any hint that a miraculous resuscitation occurred. We must therefore assume that Paul was still alive (but barely so) when they dragged him outside the city gates, that he revived while "the disciples gathered about him," and that he was taken back into town where his friends tended his wounds (14:20). No attempt was made to impress the enemy with the remarkable recovery. Paul and Barnabas left "the next day" for Derbe.[5]

Derbe was on the eastern edge of Lycaonia and Roman Galatia. To the east lay the kingdom of Antiochus. The site of Derbe was identified by Michael Ballance in 1956; it lies thirteen miles north-northeast of Karaman.[6]

Paul and Barnabas, by their preaching, "made many disciples" in Derbe. One of these was doubtless Gaius (Acts 20:4). Another may have been Timothy—although it is more generally held that Timothy came from Lystra. We shall hear much more about Timothy in days to come. Later on, when writing to Timothy, Paul reminded him, "Now you have observed . . . my persecutions, my sufferings, what befell me at Antioch, at Iconium, and at Lystra, what persecutions I endured" (2 Tim. 3:10-11). When Paul reached Derbe and Lystra on his second mission, Timothy and his mother were already believers (Acts 16:1).

*The Return Journey.* Paul and Barnabas, when they reached Derbe, stopped their advance and retraced their steps. But it was not the "end" of the mission. One of the most important points of Paul's missionary strategy comes into view at this time, namely his care of the churches which he founded.

As they returned to each city, the apostles strengthened "the souls of the disciples, exhorting them to continue in the faith" (Acts 14:22). They knew that it is not enough to count "converts." Those who are young in the faith can easily be led into error, fall into sin, or even turn from their new-found faith. They need pastoral care. The New Testament knows nothing of "hit-and-run evangelism." In three years Jesus might have gone through most of the Near East. He chose to concentrate on His few disciples in Galilee. Paul and Barnabas might have gone on to new and unevangelized regions. They were led by the Spirit to retrace their steps, even to spend their brief moments with men and women who were already converted.

In addition, they "appointed elders for them in every church" (14:23). The white, Anglo-Saxon, Protestant missionary for two centuries has been reluctant to let the "natives" run their own churches. Paul and Barnabas, after only a few weeks or months, appointed elders in these pagan areas—and they could only have been very recent converts!—and then "they committed them to the Lord in whom they believed" (14:23). That is faith!

From Luke's account, we assume that there was

some evangelistic effort in Perga, possibly of very short duration. Luke says, "and having spoken the word in Perga, they went down to Attalia" (14:24). We should not, however, assume that this evangelization was indifferent or mere routine. The apostles may have been trying to get back home to Syrian Antioch before the sea-lanes closed.

*Summation.* We can summarize the First Missionary Journey best by looking at the way Luke gave his summary. The apostles arrived in Antioch, where they had been commissioned, gathered the church together, and "declared all that God had done with them, and how he had opened a door of faith to the Gentiles" (14:27).

They were not independent missionaries. They had been sent out by the church and they felt responsible to report back to the church.

They did not boast of what they had done. They simply told all that God had done "with them." This is an interesting expression; it loses some of its force in English. I can drive a nail "with" a hammer—but in Greek that would take a different preposition. Or I can spend an evening "with" my family. This is the word used here. They had gone on the mission and God had gone with them. While He was with them, He performed His wonderful and gracious acts—acts of saving, of healing, of watching over His own, of advancing His redemptive purpose in this world. In particular, He had opened a door of faith to Gentiles—like you and me.

# Footnotes

1. "Iconium," Ramsay, *St. Paul the Traveller*, pp. 107-110; *Cities of St. Paul* pp. 317-382; *Galatians* pp. 214-222.

2. "Acts of Paul and Thecla," in *The Ante-Nicene Fathers* (eds. A. Roberts and J. Donaldson; reprinted 1951), 8:487.

3. Ramsay, *St. Paul the Traveller* pp. 111-112. Antioch and Iconium were in the portion of Galatia which may have been called Phrygia Galatica (cf. Acts 18:23 which reads literally "the Galatic region [which is] also Phrygian"), while Lystra and Derbe were in the portion of Galatia which may have had the corresponding name Galatic Lycaonia.

4. "Lystra," Ramsay, *St. Paul the Traveller* pp. 110-119; *Cities of St. Paul,* pp. 407-419; *Galatians,* pp. 223-227.

5. They did not reach Derbe the next day, as English translations suggest, for Derbe was 60 miles from Lystra—too far for even a healthy man to travel in a day, and Paul was recovering from being nearly stoned to death. "The next day he went out with Barnabas unto Derbe" in Greek is a pregnant expression meaning that they started out for (and subsequently reached) Derbe.

6. "Derbe," M. Ballance, "The Site of Derbe: A New Inscription," *Anatolian Studies* 7 (1957): 147-151.

CHAPTER 21 / (Acts 15:1-35)

# The Jerusalem Conference

Paul and Barnabas on their First Mission carried the gospel into the gentile world, and actually welcomed pagans into the church! These Gentiles were brought directly into fellowship, and were not required first to become proselytes to Judaism! How can I say it that will be meaningful to us today? We fail to see the problem, for we are Gentiles!

A fine family seeks membership in a church in a "high-class" neighborhood. The congregation meets and summarizes their feelings in the words, "They're a fine family—if only they were white!" Or, "—if only they were Americans!"

224

"If only they were Jews!" But they weren't. They were not even converts to Judaism!

*The Problem.* "Some men came down [to Antioch] from Judea and were teaching the brethren, 'Unless you are circumcised according to the custom of Moses, you cannot be saved'" (Acts 15:1). Let's read that over carefully. These men were not merely saying, "Those Gentiles are Christians, all right—but let them go join a church with their own kind!" That would have been bad enough. But these men were saying, "No one can be saved unless he Judaizes. *A Gentile must become a Jew to become a Christian!*"

Lenski says: "All the uncircumcised gentile Christians in Antioch were thus pronounced unsaved. Faith in Jesus Christ was not enough to save, circumcision must be added."[1] This is the full implication of the Judaizing position. The Church, however, did not yet understand the full implication. Only Paul understood.

The Judaizers were talking about the Mosaic convenant, about keeping of the Law. They demanded that all Christians obligate themselves to keep the law of Moses. Unless Gentiles Judaized— became Jews—they could not be saved.

This, of course, is the most extreme position. There were "compromise" positions, such as that taken by Peter, who certainly never would have gone along with the extreme Judaizer position after his experience with Cornelius. Peter surely would have granted that the uncircumcised Gentiles were Christians—but, fearing the "circumcision party," he broke off table fellowship (Gal. 2:12). In other

225

words, he began to divide the Church into two groups: "we who are circumcised, and those who are not." This problem, too, must be faced by the young church. There can be no "second-class citizens" in the kingdom of heaven.

Paul and Barnabas had "no small dissension and debate with them" (Acts 15:2). The expression "no small dissension" means a great dissension, or "fierce argument" (*TEV*). Note that Barnabas was involved as well as Paul. Paul was the prominent figure in the Judaizer controversy, but he was not alone.

The church at Antioch felt that this question had to be settled at the "ecumenical" rather than the local level, so "Paul and Barnabas and some of the others were appointed to go up to Jerusalem to the apostles and the elders about this question" (15:2). On their way, they reported the conversion of the Gentiles to the churches in Phoenicia and Samaria, and the news was joyfully received (15:3).

When they reached Jerusalem "they were welcomed by the church and the apostles and the elders" (15:4). The repeated use of the expression "the apostles and the elders" suggests that this group somehow represented the "official leadership" of the church. The apostles, of course, had been commissioned by Jesus. Their appointment was to the universal church. The elders, if we may judge from other churches in the New Testament, were the men who had been chosen by the local congregation (and probably ordained by the apostles). It can only lead to confusion if we think of the "apostles and elders" as a sort of bicameral leadership of the Jerusalem Church. The apostles, using the term in its larger sense to include Paul and Barnabas, held a roving commission, a commission that extended to the ends of the earth. The elders held a local office. Nor should we think of the Antioch Church as sending a delegation to "find out the official position of the Jerusalem Church." The church in Antioch was every bit as much a part of the Church of Christ as was the church in Jerusalem. Their purpose was to have a bilateral, rather than a unilateral, decision on the question.

The delegation from Antioch—and we are surely right if we assume that Paul and Barnabas were the chief spokesmen, but wrong if we think they were the only spokesmen—"declared all that God had done with them" (15:4).[2]

"But some believers who belonged to the party of the Pharisees"—Christians who, like Saul, had been Pharisees before their conversion—returned to the basic question. They gave their opinion concerning gentile converts: "It is necessary to circumcise them, and to charge them to keep the law of Moses" (15:5).

We make a serious mistake if we suppose the Judaizer problem arose outside the Christian Church, that unconverted Jews were insisting that the church should require Gentiles to become Jews when joining the church. Unconverted Jews "couldn't have cared less" what the church did. Of course, they opposed the church and the preaching of the gospel. Of course they objected to Christian Jews attracting Gentiles into the synagogue. They doubtless objected, too, when Christian Jews broke the fence of the Law to have fellowship with Gentiles. But these things were secondary.

The primary issue arose within the church, and was essentially a church problem. If the Law was not able to save men, and if Jesus Christ came to save men (Jew and Gentile), then what did a Gentile gain by attempting to keep the law of Moses? Peter had long ago declared that the only way of salvation was in Jesus Christ (4:12). Imposing the Law on Gentiles could only be for one of two reasons: it was necessary for salvation, or it made the Gentile a "better" Christian.

The men from Judea who had gone to Antioch and stirred up this problem, were arguing for the first of these reasons: Circumcision (= keeping the Law) is necessary for salvation. The former Pharisees in the Jerusalem Church were probably arguing for the same position, although it is possible that they would have supported the second alternative. All of them would have said that faith in Jesus Christ was necessary for salvation.

*The Conference.* "The apostles and the elders were gathered together to consider this matter" (15:6). Does this suggest a smaller meeting, consisting only of the leaders? Some scholars think so. They believe the problem was first laid before the entire church in Jerusalem (15:4,5), but then the apostles and elders met, perhaps in an executive session, to debate the problem. This would be reasonable—but is it accurate? Luke mentions "all the assembly"—literally the "multitude," a term generally referring in Acts to the entire church (15:12, cf. 4:32; 6:2,5). The apostles and elders had come to a common mind on the subject, Luke specifically says, "with the whole church" (15:22).

At first there was "much debate" (15:7). There usually is, in a meeting of this sort. After many persons have spoken, often in a disorganized manner, the true leaders—those with true leadership ability, and not necessarily those who occupy office (although the latter are often the same as the former) —the true leaders begin to crystallize the problem, state the essential issues, and suggest the approaches to a solution.

Peter was the first in Luke's account to set forth the essential points:

> "Brethren, you know that in the early days God made choice among you, that by my mouth the Gentiles should hear the word of the gospel and believe. And God who knows the heart bore witness to them, giving them the Holy Spirit just as he did to us; and he made no distinction between us and them, but cleansed their hearts by faith. Now therefore why do you make trial of God by putting a yoke upon the neck of the disciples which neither our fathers nor we have been able to bear? But we believe that we shall be saved through the grace of the Lord Jesus, just as they will" (15:7-11).

Peter, of course, was referring to the conversion of Cornelius and his household. It had been brought about not by a decision of Peter nor by any other human being, but by a sovereign act of God.

That fact had been clearly manifested by the outpouring of the Spirit, just as on the day of Pentecost. The opposition might have replied at this point, "Well, if God wants Gentiles in the church, let Him repeat this process each time. But let's not go out trying to convert Gentiles!"

Peter, however, moved on to another point. The salvation of the Gentiles—Peter uses the expression "He cleansed their hearts"—was by faith. Salvation of all men, Jew and Gentile alike, is "through the grace of the Lord Jesus" (15:11). The Law was a "yoke"—an unbearable one (15:10). Jewish writers sometimes referred to the Law as a yoke. Perhaps this is what Jesus had in mind when He said, "Take My yoke upon you and learn from Me . . . For My yoke is easy, and My burden is light" (Matt. 11:29). To "take up the yoke of the kingdom" was an expression used with reference to proselytes. Perhaps Peter was thinking of the contrast between the yoke of the Law and the yoke of his Master. This is speculation. But it is no speculation to say that Peter was setting aside the Law as necessary for salvation.

Now Barnabas and Paul spoke. (Luke returns here to the order in which these apostles would be named at Jerusalem.) Their testimony, like Peter's, was based on what God had done through them in their ministry to Gentiles. To men who believe that God acts, the evidence of His acts is an indication of His will—for God only does what He wills to do. The apostles had not compelled God to show His wonders and mercies to the Gentiles. He had willed to act in that way.

Then James spoke. This, of course, is not James the apostle but the one Paul calls "James, the Lord's brother" (Gal. 1:19). We therefore assume that he was one of Jesus' four brothers (Matt. 13:55), an unbeliever before the Crucifixion (John 7:5). The risen Jesus appeared to him (1 Cor. 15:7). According to tradition, James was the first Bishop of Jerusalem.[3] It is believed by many scholars that he was the author of the Epistle of James.[4] In A.D. 61 he was martyred by stoning, following the death of Festus.[5]

James referred to the testimony of Peter (using his Jewish name, Symeon), and then turned to Scripture for confirmation, quoting from Amos 9:11-12, with some phrases reminiscent of Jeremiah 12:15 and Isaiah 45:21. The point of the quotation is that the time of the re-establishment of the Kingdom promised to David has now come, when "the rest of men may seek the Lord, and all the Gentiles who are called by my name" (Acts 15:17).

James then makes his suggestion. "Therefore, I for my part judge that we should stop crowding in on those of the Gentiles who are turning to God" (15:19, *lit. trans.*). Lenski comments, "Thus in a distinct though mild way James passes an adverse verdict on all Judaistic legalism. . . . He does not mean to compromise with the Judaizers."[6] Efforts to impose any of the Law on Gentiles, which is what all previous efforts of Jewish proselytizing had been, were "crowding in beside,"[7] or "annoying" the Gentiles. James further suggests that they write to the Gentiles to abstain from four things. We shall discuss these further. And he adds, "For from early generations Moses has had in every city those who preach him, for he is read every sabbath in the synagogues" (15:21).

What did he mean by this statement? Did he mean that Moses would still have his followers throughout the world who would continue to make known his Law? Or did he mean that Christians should be careful not to offend Jews who scrupulously observe the Law? I prefer the latter.

*The Apostolic Council.* The apostles and the elders and the whole church decided to send delegates back to Antioch with Paul and Barnabas, and to send a letter that included the four points suggested by James.

These four points are often referred to as the "apostolic decrees," as if they were a binding action. But it would be ludicrous, to set aside legalism by a legalistic decree! We must therefore consider the "decrees" not as a substitute law, but as guidelines in the current controversy. If this is true, it will affect our interpretation of the four points of the decree.

The four points, as set forth in the letter sent to the churches differ only slightly from the points proposed by James. They are: "that you abstain (1) from what has been sacrificed to idols and (2) from blood and (3) from what is strangled and (4) from fornication" (15:28-29).

If we interpret "blood" to mean "murder," and take "fornication" in its most obvious meaning, two of these points refer to the moral law. Indeed they reiterate words of the Decalogue, "Thou shalt not murder" and "Thou shalt not commit adultery"

(Exod. 20:13-14). Then we would have to ask what relationship there is between these moral laws and abstaining from what has been sacrificed to idols and from what is strangled.

In my opinion, all four points should be considered as items that would be commonly found in the every-day life of the gentile world which would be particularly offensive to the religious and moral sensitivities of the Jew.⁸

(1) Eating food which had been placed before an idol is considered at length in Paul's First Letter to the Corinthians (1 Cor. 8:1-13; 11:25-29). Obviously it was a serious problem in the Early Church.

(2) "Blood" I understand to mean the eating of blood or of meat with the blood still in it. I cannot possibly conceive of anyone in the Early Church saying "If you abstain from murder, you do well"!

(3) Abstaining from what is strangled is similar to the preceding, and in James' words, is placed before "blood" (Acts 15:20). If this was the correct order (there is considerable variation in the order of the terms in the older manuscripts), we could possibly group the two points as one, namely, "Abstain from what is strangled or [any meat that contains] blood."

(4) "Fornication" then would refer to pagan attitudes toward sex. Anyone familiar with ancient Greek or Roman customs, or with modern novels based on those customs, is fully aware of the fact that ritual prostitution was a part of several religions, while sex, for the male at least, was looked upon as a bodily appetite little different from

hunger or fatigue. The loose attitude toward sex was particularly prominent in the church in Corinth (cf. 1 Cor. 6:13-20).

Any attempt to interpret these four points consistently, I admit, is difficult. My interpretation is no less free of difficulties than other interpretations, particularly with reference to fornication. I do not mean to imply that the Christian attitude toward sexual morality is the same as the Christian attitude toward meats offered to idols. Certainly the rest of the New Testament would not support such an interpretation. On the other hand I seriously question the interpretation that makes "fornication" here refer to the forbidden degrees of marriage as defined in Leviticus 18. Are we to suppose that the Jerusalem Conference was telling Gentile Christians, "Before you marry, check and see whether the degree of consanguinity is objectionable to Jews"?

The decision of the Council after deliberating the problem, was unanimous, and they felt that the Holy Spirit concurred with their finding (Acts 15:25,28). They chose Judas (called Barsabbas) and Silas, who were leading men among the Christians in the Jerusalem Church, and commissioned them to give a verbal report in addition to the "decree" (15:22,27). This in itself tells us something about the Church's attitude concerning the letter. Just how binding is a "decree" that depends on oral interpretation for support?

The letter clearly disclaimed responsibility for the men who had stirred up the problem at Antioch (15:24). Further, it testified to a cordial acceptance

234

of Barnabas and Paul ("our beloved Barnabas and Paul," 15:25).

*The Delegation to Antioch.* The apostolic delegation, consisting now of Paul, Barnabas, and "the others" who had been appointed by the Antioch Church, plus Judas and Silas from the Jerusalem Church, travelled to Antioch-on-the-Orontes. Reaching that city, they assembled the congregation and delivered the letter (15:30-31).

There was no feeling that the Antioch Church had been "sold short" or compromised. There was no feeling that the Jerusalem Apostles were "throwing their weight around." The Antioch Christians "rejoiced at the exhortation" (15:31). Gentiles could now freely come into the Church without becoming Jews. As Christians, they were to avoid any action that would be offensive to their Jewish brethren in the church, or any action that would be misinterpreted by those outside the church. Paul and Barnabas and the Hellenists and the Antioch Church were vindicated in their gentile evangelization.

Judas and Silas were "prophets," so they took the occasion to "exhort" the brethren "with many words" and to strengthen them (15:32). And then, "after they had spent some time," the two returned to Jerusalem (15:33).[9] Paul and Barnabas, along with many others, remained in Antioch, teaching the word of the Lord and evangelizing (15:35).

*Summation.* The Jerusalem Council and its handling of the Judaizer problem is history. But the problem was not quickly solved. Problems are rarely solved by resolutions!

The more I study the Early Church the more I see it as a Spirit-led human institution, with the strengths of the Spirit and the weaknesses of human beings.

The Church had a problem. It faced the problem honestly and humbly. It came to a common mind and felt that that was also the mind of the Spirit. It moved forward on the basis of the "conclusion" reached.

But "conclusions" hardly ever conclude a problem. New problems arise, as do variations of old problems. The Spirit-led church will seek the Spirit's mind, remembering that even though God is the same, "yesterday, today, and forever," He is not dead. He is living. His actions are dynamic, not static. Solutions to human problems will therefore be dynamic. Eternal principles will remain, but the specific applications will change from generation to generation.

We shall meet the Judaizer problem again. Paul met it often, in various cities and in various forms. Today the question may not be "Does a Gentile have to become a Jew to become a Christian?" Rather, it may take another form. "Does a Catholic have to become a Protestant to become a Christian?" "Does an Oriental have to become a Westerner . . . ?" "Does a Jew have to become a Gentile . . . ?" "Does a Black have to become a White . . . ?" "Does *he* have to become like *me* to become a Christian?"

The essential problem remains: Are we going to have two doors into the kingdom, one for "us" and the other for "them"? Are we going to have two classes of citizens in the kingdom: those who are merely "saved," and our special group composed of the few who are not only saved but who in addition _____ ?

I refuse to fill in that blank. Perhaps it is "don't smoke" or "shave and wear short hair." Or possibly it is "don't have instrumental music in church," or "keep the seventh-day Sabbath." Whatever it is that you and I set up that gives us a feeling of superiority within the church, let's write it in that space.

And then let's face it once and for all. *There are no second class citizens!* The kingdom of heaven has only one door. As someone long ago stated: Salvation is by grace, through faith, plus nothing.

## Footnotes

1. Lenski, *Interpretation of the Acts of the Apostles*, p. 586.
2. See comments on the use of "with" in the summation of chapter 20.
3. Eusebius, *Ecclesiastical History* 7:19.
4. J. B. Mayor finds "remarkable agreements" between the speech of James here and the Epistle of James: *The Epistle of James* (1897), pp. iii-iv.
5. ". . . Ananus (the high priest) thought that he had a favourable opportunity because Festus was dead and Albinus was still on the way. And so he convened the judges of the Sanhedrin and brought before them a man named James, the brother of Jesus who was called the Christ, and certain others. He accused them of having transgressed the law and delivered them up to be stoned." Josephus, *Antiquities* 20.9.1 §200.
6. Lenski, *Interpretation of the Acts*, p. 607.
7. The Greek verb "to annoy" is composed of the elements "besides" plus "in" plus "to crowd," hence my translation. I am not aware that the word was ever used literally.
8. I think that Lenski's treatment at this point is excellent, *Acts*, pp. 606-612
9. Verse 34 is omitted from the oldest manuscripts and is contradicted by the plural forms used in verse 33.

CHAPTER 22 / (Acts 15:36—16:5)

# Second Journey:
# Galatia Revisited

Now that the Church has "settled" the question of what to do with gentile converts, Paul and Barnabas can resume their evangelization of the gentile world. At least, that's the way theory works. We meet a problem. We set up a commission to study it. They bring in their resolutions. We go on from there. But life is never so simple—a fact that theoreticians never seem to learn!

*Paul and Barnabas Split Up.* Where should Paul and Barnabas go? There's a whole world to be saved. But Paul thinks first of the young churches they have established, so he says, "Let us return and visit the brethren in every city where we proclaimed the word of the Lord, and see how they are" (Acts 15:36). That would have been the cities of Cyprus, Pamphylia (if any churches had been established there), and southern Galatia.

Barnabas apparently was in accord, and he said, "Let's take John Mark."

But Paul, perhaps stiffening his lip and getting a stern look in his eyes, said, "I don't think it's good to take anyone who backed out of the work in Pamphylia" (cf. 15:37-38). Luke then reports, in complete candor, "There arose a sharp contention"— "paroxysm" is the word he used, but the word may not have conveyed as much the idea of violent emotion as our word does—"so that they separated from each other" (15:39).

From somewhere I once got the idea that there were no "church fights" in the first century; such things belong to post-Reformation Protestants, particularly to American churches of the nineteenth and twentieth centuries! When I began to study the New Testament, I came to the conclusion that those who teach such ideas have not spent enough time with their Bibles. The men and women of the Early Church were the same kind of human beings that you and I are. If God hadn't been watching over His Church, it would have disappeared quickly!

But perhaps we can even learn a few things from a "sharp contention" in the Early Church.

When Mark had withdrawn from the work, Barnabas obviously backed Paul, for he stuck with Paul and did not return home with Mark. He fought shoulder-to-shoulder with Paul against the Judaizers. But now he breaks with Paul and forms a new partnership with his young cousin Mark. Why? Mark's home was Jerusalem. Did Barnabas and Mark have a long talk sometime during the Jerusalem Conference? Did Barnabas come to a better understanding of why Mark had backed out? Did he comfort, encourage, exhort Mark (4:36)? We do not know. But we do know that Mark was reclaimed for the work of Christ, and we can reasonably infer that Barnabas had much to do with it.

Mark was with Peter when he wrote his First Epistle, for Peter includes greetings from "my son Mark" (1 Pet. 5:13). According to tradition, Mark served as Peter's interpreter, later writing the Gospel called by Mark's name. Mark was also useful to Paul in later years. He was with Paul during Paul's first imprisonment at Rome, when he wrote Colossians (Col. 4:10), and he was wanted and needed by Paul at the end, for Paul wrote to Timothy, "Get Mark and bring him with you, for he is very useful in serving me" (2 Tim. 4:11). The Church's loss would have been grave if Barnabas had not maintained confidence in Mark!

We should note, too, that after the apostolic disagreement, they split up the territory to be covered. In modern times, schismatics build churches on opposite street corners, or form duplicate mission boards to serve the same countries. There have been more than a few cases where the separatists thought they were doing the Lord's will if they gained "converts" from each other's churches. But Barnabas and Mark chose to go to Cyprus, and Paul and Silas went to Galatia.

It would be a mistake to conclude that Barnabas

chose a "dead end street." It is true that he passes from history at this point. However, Paul's reference to him in First Corinthians indicates either that Barnabas was personally known by the church at Corinth or at least that they knew such details about him as the one Paul casually mentions, that he, like Paul, refused to accept support but did secular work for a living (1 Cor. 9:6).

If the events of history give a clue to the mind of God, we can conclude that the split between Barnabas and Paul was providential. If Paul and Barnabas had gone together, they would have gone to Cyprus and Galatia. That might have consumed their energies. By going separately, Paul finished his visitation of the churches in Galatia with enough energy left to look for new worlds to win for Christ. And this time, with unerring instinct, aided and driven by God's Spirit, he set his sights on the great Roman cities. As we shall see, he was obviously planning to evangelize Asia—meaning Ephesus, no doubt, since that was the main city in the province and Paul's goal for the Third Mission. But God had other plans to be carried out first.

*The New Team: Paul and Silas.* Barnabas took Mark with him, and Paul chose Silas to be his fellow evangelist. Mark had been a "minister," the exact meaning not being clear. We have suggested that he helped in the catechetical instruction of new converts. Other scholars have suggested that he handled many of the incidental details of travel for Paul and Barnabas. Silas was possibly a replacement for Mark; more likely he was a replacement for Barnabas.

241

Silas was a member of the Jerusalem Church. There is no indication that he was an apostle. Barnabas was, in the broader meaning of the term (Acts 14:14). Silas was chosen, however, along with Judas Barsabbas, to accompany Paul and Barnabas and the others to Antioch with the letter from the Jerusalem Conference. We may assume that he was held in high esteem by the Jerusalem Church. We may also assume that he gained Paul's confidence by the way he discharged this responsibility and in addition entered into the work at Antioch (Acts 15:32). Silas, we should add, was a Roman citizen.

Silas is certainly to be identified with Silvanus, who is mentioned with Paul and Timothy in the opening sentence of both letters to the Thessalonian church (1 Thess. 1:1; 2 Thess. 1:1)—letters written during the Second Journey. Silvanus is also mentioned as the one by whom Peter wrote his First Epistle (1 Pet. 5:12). He does not appear with Paul after Corinth on the Second Mission. When he joined Peter we do not know. If Peter was in Corinth sometime after that (cf. 1 Cor. 1:12), Silas may have joined him there.

Silas and Judas had returned to Jerusalem after their mission to Antioch. We assume that Mark was also in Jerusalem at the time. It is possible that Barnabas and Paul sent a joint request for Mark and Silas.

*The Mission to Syria and Cilicia.* Paul and Silas started the Second Mission by visiting the churches in Syria and Cilicia (15:41).[1] The origin of these churches is unknown. Personally, I assume they were founded by Paul during the period between his first visit to Jerusalem as a Christian and the time Barnabas came looking for him to help in the work at Antioch. I can't imagine the young convert spending years without doing some evangelizing. Nor can I imagine Barnabas looking for someone to help who had done nothing to indicate his worth for such work.

Again we see an important element of Paul's missionary work: to revisit young churches in order to strengthen them.

*The Mission to the Churches in Galatia.* The journey from Syrian Antioch to "Syria and Cilicia" probably took the missioners across the Amanus mountains by the pass known as the Syrian Gates. They went along the coast past the plain of Issus, where Alexander first waged war with Darius and the Persian forces, and then possibly east- or northward to any of several small towns, or more probably westward directly to Tarsus.

The next part of the journey, to the cities of Galatia, would be much more difficult.[2] First they had to cross the Taurus mountains, doubtless by the ancient pass known as the Cilician Gates.[3] Paul was not concerned about the sailing season on this part of the journey, yet winter would hardly be the time to cross the Taurus range. On the other hand, travel across the barren plain with dust like flour and with little water would not be recommended in midsummer.[4]

Luke records that Paul "came to Derbe and to Lystra" (16:1), naming the cities in reverse order of the first mission, since now Paul was coming from the east. Paul and Silas had traversed the kingdom of Antiochus of Commagene and entered Roman Galatia. We get the impression that not much time was spent at Derbe.

"A disciple was there, named Timothy," writes Luke, "the son of a Jewish woman who was a believer; but his father was a Greek" (16:1). Timothy was to become one of Paul's dearest co-workers throughout the rest of Paul's earthly life. Luke, however, introduces him rather casually. We are not even sure whether Timothy came from Lystra or from Derbe. Timothy "was well spoken of by the brethren at Lystra and Iconium" (16:2). Bruce infers, since Lystra is mentioned twice in two verses, that Timothy came from Lystra. We might possibly reason just the opposite: since Luke refers to Timothy's reputation among the Christians at Lystra and Iconium, Luke is implying that he came from Derbe. One ancient tradition does say that he came from Derbe.

Timothy's mother and his grandmother had a sincere faith (2 Tim. 1:5). Between them they had brought up the child Timothy to know the Scriptures (2 Tim. 3:15)—meaning, of course, the Old Testament. We can safely assume that they were won to the Lord Jesus by the apostles on the First Mission, for Timothy was already a "disciple" when Paul arrived on the Second Mission.

Paul addressed Timothy as "my true child in the faith" (1 Tim. 1:2), and referred to him as "my son" (1 Tim. 1:18; 2 Tim. 2:1), "my beloved and faithful child in the Lord" (1 Cor. 4:17), and "my beloved child" (2 Tim. 1:2). Therefore it is often assumed that Timothy was brought to Christian faith by

Paul on the First Mission. This is not necessarily so. Paul, speaking of Timothy's faith, says it was "a faith that dwelt first in your grandmother Lois and your mother Eunice, and now, I am sure, dwells in you" (2 Tim. 1:5). This may imply that Timothy's faith came later than that of his mother and his grandmother—in other words, that they led the youth to their Lord after Paul and Barnabas had gone on.

Why, then, would Paul call Timothy his "son"? Let's look at a few more facts. Timothy's father was dead (the force of the verb tense in Acts 16:1 requires this interpretation: "his father *was* a Greek"). His mother had been enough of a Jewess to bring up Timothy with a knowledge of the Scriptures. She had not been enough of a Jewess, however, either to marry a Jew or to insist that her son be circumcised a Jew. (In Judaism the child of a mixed marriage is considered a Jew only if his mother was a Jew or a convert.) Paul took Timothy and had him circumcised (Acts 16:3). Paul seems to have been taking on himself the responsibility of bringing up Timothy as a Jew. Possibly this is why Paul calls him, "my son."

This action on Paul's part has led to much criticism. He has been charged with inconsistency, because he refused to have Titus circumcised and yet had Timothy circumcised. But there was a major difference between the two young helpers. Titus was a Gentile. Timothy as the son of a Jewess was born a Jew. To submit Titus to circumcision would clearly have been to yield to the demands of the Judaizers. Paul refused. There was no reason to circumcise a Gentile. Not to circumcise Timothy, on the other hand, would have been to restrict Timothy's sphere of usefulness. Neither he nor Titus could have been of any significant use in Paul's ministry to Jews, Titus because he was a Gentile, Timothy because he was a Jew who had repudiated the law of Moses.

Paul set up a principle that controlled his actions: "all things to all men" (1 Cor. 9:22). To the Jew he was as a Jew; to those under the Law as one under the Law; to those outside the Law as one outside the Law—for one dominating purpose: "that I might by all means save some" (1 Cor. 9:19-23). This principle was being carried out when Paul circumcised Timothy.

How old was Timothy when Paul took him along on the Second Mission? We can work backwards from Paul's First Letter to Timothy, written about A.D. 63. At that time Paul charged Timothy, "Let no one despise your youth" (1 Tim. 4:12). The statement could have been used for a man of forty or for a man of twenty. Timothy was fifteen years younger when he started out with Paul on this mission. Thus the disciple who joined Paul's party could have been as young as 16 or all of 25 years old.

We assume that Paul and his fellow workers also visited Iconium and Antioch; Luke is content to report, "As they went on their way through the cities, they delivered to them for observance the decisions which had been reached by the apostles and elders who were at Jerusalem" (Acts 16:4).

*The "Apostolic Decrees" Once More.* The letter from the Jerusalem Conference had been addressed

246

"To the brethren who are of the Gentiles in Antioch and Syria and Cilicia" (15:23). Luke does not tell us that Paul read the letter to the churches in Syria and Cilicia, but we may assume that he did. Strictly speaking, it was not necessary for Paul to read the letter to the churches in Galatia, since the letter was not addressed to them. But he did. Can we assume that he did so because he was cordially consenting to the action?

Some—among them Ramsay—say Paul was never too happy about the decision of the Jerusalem Conference. The problem has grown all out of proportion because we have failed to understand the nature and purpose of the letter which the apostles and elders sent from Jerusalem. This was not a neo-legalism to replace the old Law. It was a declaration of freedom from the Law, and the placing of limits on freedom in the form of consideration of the convictions of the other people. Paul had a part in shaping the decision, and Paul makes clear his own position in his letters. Nothing else would have been acceptable to him.

*The Aborted Plan to Evangelize Asia.* From Galatia Paul planned to move west to proconsular Asia. This was probably the finest Roman province in Asia Minor, with many important cities. Its capital was Ephesus, sometimes looked upon as "little Rome" and "more Roman than Rome itself." Paul's strategy was excellent. But his timing was off. It was not God's time. So the Holy Spirit said *no!* (Acts 16:6).

The three missioners therefore turned northward, passing through "the Phrygian and Galatic region," or that part of Galatia which was Phrygian. Obviously Luke is not referring to the portion of Galatic Phrygia that included Iconium and Antioch, for the missioners had already covered that part and were about to go to Asia.

Paul, apparently, next set his sights on Bithynia, a province that lay on the Black Sea, which had a number of important cities. Again the Spirit said *no!*

It is interesting to note Luke's careful wording. Paul and his party actually had to cut through a portion of Asia on this journey. Luke reports that they were "forbidden by the Holy Spirit *to speak the word in Asia*" (16:6). It was not necessary to pass through Bithynia to get where God wanted them to go. Luke records that "they attempted *to go into Bithynia*, but the Spirit of Jesus did not allow them" (16:7).

Two choices were left: to turn westward once more, or to turn back. They turned to the west, "passing by Mysia"—which means they went through it but that's all. They did not evangelize as they went. God wanted them to get to Troas, where they would receive further orders.

*Summation.* The Second Mission, which began with Paul and Silas, is now composed of Paul, Silas, and Timothy. It was preceded by a quarrel and the splitting up of the old team of Paul and Barnabas. How God kept Paul from preaching in Asia or setting foot in Bithynia we are not told, but to Paul at the time it must have been frustrating. There is no indication that God gave any positive instructions—just negative commands. You or I might have asked, more than once, "Was I ever supposed to make this trip?"

But apostles are made of sterner stuff—at least, Paul was. Apostles say, "If God doesn't want me here, He must want me there. If He wants me to be silent here, it must be for a good reason. If He doesn't want me to take Barnabas, He must have some other work for Barnabas, and He must have someone else to go along with me."

That is why God uses apostles.

## Footnotes

1. For the Second Journey, see *Macmillan Bible Atlas,* map 246; *Westminster Historical Atlas,* pp. 96-97, Pl. XV.

2. For a full description, see Ramsay, *Pauline and Other Studies* (1906), pp. 273-298.

3. See *Atlas of the Bible,* photos 398-399.

4. If Barnabas left at the same time as Paul, it must have been during the sailing season, since he went to Cyprus. I suggest the middle part of A.D. 49 as a reasonable starting date, and a crossing of the Taurus range before the winter of 49-50 set in.

CHAPTER 23 / (Acts 16:6—17:15)

# Second Journey:
# The Mission to Macedonia

We often speak of the Second Missionary Journey as the mission that took the church into
Europe. Aside from the strong possibility that
Christianity had already reached Rome—to which
we shall return later—it is not quite accurate to
think of the journey from Troas to Neapolis as moving from Asia to Europe. Oh, yes, I know that all
maps and modern geographies make this distinction. But in Paul's day, this was hardly so. I doubt if
Paul or Luke ever thought of "Asia" and "Europe"
as two "continents." (They really aren't, are they?)
To the Greeks, there was the Aegean Sea, its adja-
cent lands, and its islands.[1] The eastern shore of the

Aegean was Ionia, and it was every bit as Greek as Greece itself. Alexander the Great set out to liberate this part of Greece from Persian domination. Many of the great names in Greek life and culture belong to the eastern shore of the Aegean: Helen of Troy and the heroes of the Trojan War, Homer, Permenides, Pythagoras, Hippocrates, Galen, Thales, Heraclitus—the list seems endless.

What we often refer to as "Greece" in the New Testament times was in fact two Roman provinces: Macedonia and Achaia.[2] Paul refers to the area in these terms (1 Thess. 1:7). Accordingly we might better speak of the Second Journey as the Mission to Macedonia and Achaia.

*"Come Over to Macedonia."* Troas is not ancient Troy (or Ilium), but rather Alexandria Troas about ten miles farther south, a city founded by Antigonus, one of the successors of Alexander. Under Augustus, a Roman colony was planted here.

At Troas Paul had a vision in the night. A man of Macedonia was standing, beseeching Paul, saying, "Come over to Macedonia and help us" (Acts 16:9). Some scholars have suggested that the man in the vision was Luke, that Paul had just met Luke who (they tell us) was a Macedonian from Philippi, and Luke had told Paul something about Macedonia. That night, Paul dreamed about Luke, and the things he had told Paul appeared as a message from God. Perhaps. But we have no proof whatever that Luke was a Macedonian. God wanted Paul in Macedonia, and God used a vision to convey this message.

Paul wasted no time. "When he had seen the vision, immediately we sought to go on into Macedonia" (16:10). I understand that to mean that they took the first available boat, and God saw to it that a boat was available and that the winds were favorable.

Notice that little word "we." This begins the first of the "we-sections" in Acts. The best explanation of these portions of Acts is that whenever Luke the author joined the group he reported in the first person. Since "we" is first used at Troas, we assume that Paul met Luke there.

Was Luke already a Christian? We do not know. No account of his conversion is given, either by himself or by Paul. Since he joined Paul at once in the work, it is reasonable to suppose that he was already a Christian and perhaps had even had some experience as an evangelist when Paul met him. The suggestion that he came from Antioch in Syria, and that he had been with Paul and Silas for the entire journey, in my opinion, breaks down just at the point where Luke's presence is established. If he was with Paul and did not use the first-person pronoun, then we can no longer use that as a criterion for his presence. In that case we do not know that he was with Paul at all.

Well, assuming that he was not already with Paul, how did he happen to meet him in Troas? One thing is perfectly clear: the meeting was, humanly speaking, not pre-arranged. Paul hadn't the slightest idea that he was going to Troas. The Holy Spirit led him and his party there, we might say, blindly.

One suggestion has more to commend it than

most of the others: Paul may have had a return of his illness—his "stake in the flesh"—and he may have had to find a physician in Troas. God may have led him to Luke through any one of many possible circumstances. The eastern Aegean was the home of medicine. Hippocrates and Erasistratus came from Chios,[3] Herophilus from Chalcedon, and Galen was from Pergamum.[4] It has even been suggested that Luke may have studied medicine somewhere in this area.

Paul, Silas, Timothy and Luke sailed to Samothrace and then to Neapolis. The journey took two days. Some years later, when Paul made the trip in the opposite direction, it took five days (20:6), hence we conclude that the wind was favorable on this occasion.

Neapolis is now Kavalla, a pretty seaport with two harbors, and remains of the Roman city are readily visible. It was the eastern end of the famous Egnatian Road, a military thoroughfare 490 miles long built in 146 B.C. The western end of the road branched, with termini at Dyrrachium and Appollonia (modern Durazzo and Valona respectively, both in Albania). Across the Adriatic Sea, the road continued to Rome, but in Italy it was known as the Appian Way.

From Neapolis it was a journey of about ten miles on the Egnatian Road to Philippi. The Roman road can easily be seen today, just after crossing the ridge and descending to the Plain of Drama in which Philippi is located. Another portion has been uncovered near the agora in Philippi.

*Philippi.* The city had been rebuilt about 356 B.C.

and named by Philip of Macedon, father of Alexander the Great. Alexander, who began his famous march at Amphipolis, passed through Philippi in 335 B.C. When the Romans established the province of Macedonia (148 B.C.), they united the four "districts" which had existed from the Roman conquest in 167, and made Thessalonica the provincial capital. However, the concept of the four districts remained. Philippi was in the first district, with its capital at Amphipolis. The other district capitals were Thessalonica, Pella, and Pelagonia. Luke describes Philippi as "the leading city of the district of Macedonia" (16:12), a statement that would doubtless have been strongly challenged by residents of Amphipolis. Ramsay's comment may just be right: "Amphipolis was ranked first by general consent, Philippi first by its own consent."[5]

In 42 B.C. the Roman Republic died on the Plain of Drama, when Brutus and Cassius (who were responsible for the assassination of Julius Caesar) took their own lives and Antony and Octavian won the battle. Octavian later was known as the emperor Augustus. Veterans of the battle were settled in a Roman colony at Philippi. A colony enjoyed three things: *libertas* or self-government, *immunitas* or freedom from paying tribute to the emperor, and *ius italicum* or the rights of those who lived in Italy. Six Roman colonies are named in Acts, but only Philippi is indentified as such.[6] The city rulers of Philippi called themselves praetors (translated "magistrates," 16:20-22), and were accompanied by lictors (officials who carried rods to beat offenders, cf. 16:22), imitating the Roman pattern.

It would seem that the church in Philippi was Paul's favorite church. Only from Philippi was he willing to receive support (Phil. 4:10,15; 2 Cor. 1:8,9), and only in his letter to the Philippians does Paul express such great joy. There is no indication that Judaizers ever became a serious problem in the church in Philippi.

*Lydia, First Convert in Macedonia.* Paul, Silas, Timothy, and Luke made their way, on the Sabbath, to a place beside the Gangites River, outside the city. They had probably asked where the synagogue was located, and were told that there was only a "place of prayer" by the river. In order to form a synagogue, there must be ten adult, male Jews (a "minyan"). No mention is made of any men at this meeting, other than the evangelists, and men's names are relatively rare in the letter to the Philippians. There seems to have been a strong anti-Jewish feeling at Philippi.

The missioners "sat down and spoke to the women who had come together" (16:13). One of these women was a Gentile, a "worshiper of God" from Thyatira in Asia, named Lydia.[7] No husband is mentioned, so we assume that she was a widow, a business woman (probably conducting the business established by her husband), who sold "purple goods," cloth or garments dyed with the colorful dye known as madder red or Turkey red, for which Thyatira was noted. Lydia was a woman of some means, with a house large enough to serve the church that was established in Philippi.

The Lord opened her heart. It may have been on that first Sabbath or some time later. She "and her household" were baptized (16:15), and then she insisted that the four missioners stay in her house. Luke's statement, "And she prevailed upon us" suggests that the evangelistic team was somewhat reluctant to accept her hospitality.

Lydia, so far as we know, was the first of Paul's converts in Europe. I am not sure however that we should call her "the first Christian convert in Europe." When Claudius drove out the Jews from Rome (A.D. 49), it was, according to Suetonius, because "the Jews constantly made disturbances at the instigation of Chrestus."[3] Many scholars are convinced that the word should be "Christus," and that the disturbances were due to Jewish-Christian animosities. Among those driven from Rome were Priscilla and Aquila (18:2). Since Paul nowhere hints that he had any part in the conversion of these two, we conclude that they were Christians when he met them soon after their arrival from Rome, which suggests that they were already Christians in Rome. Moreover, when Paul wrote to the Romans (about A.D. 56), he greeted a number of fellow-Christians there, among them Andronicus and Junias. Paul calls them "my kinsmen . . . men of note among the apostles," and says "they were in Christ before me" (Rom. 16:7). That means that they were converted before Paul was, probably in Jerusalem, since they were known to the apostles. They may have been among the converts on the day of Pentecost, some of whom were "visitors from Rome" (Acts 2:10). I have no theory to defend; I am simply pointing out the possibility—probability is not too strong a word—that Christians were in

Rome, therefore in Europe, before Paul brought Lydia to Christ at Philippi. But Paul paid little attention to such things. I doubt if he even thought to say to Luke, "Write that down; Lydia's our first convert in Europe!"

*The Demon-Possessed Slave Girl.* One day as Paul and his companions were going to the place of prayer, they were met "by a certain slave girl who had a spirit of divination" (16:16). She followed Paul and his little group, crying out, "These men are servants of the Most High God, who proclaim to you the way of salvation" (16:17). She kept this up "for many days" (16:18).

Paul was annoyed by this behavior, for it probably brought derision on the group and therefore on the message that they proclaimed. Moreover, Paul recognized it as demon possession. According to Luke's language, the girl had "a spirit, a Python" in her. (The Greeks used the word "ventriloquist" to describe the "Python," thinking that such a person spoke what someone else put in his or her mouth.) Her owners used this strange gift as a way to make money possibly through "fortune-telling." But demon possession to Paul was spiritual slavery, and he exorcised the demon with the words, "I charge you in the name of Jesus Christ to come out of her" (16:18). The demon went out of her.

With the demon also went the financial gain of her owners. Humanitarian deeds often run into trouble when they affect men's profits! So the owners seized Paul and Silas and dragged them to the agora (the market-place) before the rulers (16:19).

"These men are Jews!" they said, "and they are disturbing our city. They advocate customs which it is not lawful for us Romans to accept or practice" (16:20-21).

The charge is noteworthy. It begins with a clearly anti-Jewish attitude. If news of the Claudian edict of expulsion of all Jews from Rome had already reached Philippi—which is not impossible—a wave of anti-Semitism may have come with it. At any rate, we must note that the opposition to Paul at Philippi is not from Jews, and it does not accuse Paul of denigrating the laws and customs of Moses. Quite the opposite. The foes claim that Paul and Silas are Jews and are advocating un-Roman customs.

The crowd joined the attack, whether on the basis of the anti-Jewish expression or the pro-Roman. The magistrates "tore the garments off them and gave orders [to the lictors] to beat them with rods" (16:22). And after they had "inflicted many blows upon them, they threw them into prison" (16:23).[9]

*The Philippian Jailer.* The jailer put his new prisoners in the inner prison and fastened their feet in the stocks (16:24). Then he turned in for the night, probably in his quarters above the prison. About midnight "Paul and Silas were praying and singing hymns to God, and the [other] prisoners were listening to them" (16:25). Possibly the two couldn't sleep, because of the painful welts on their backs and the uncomfortable position forced on them by the stocks.

Suddenly a great earthquake shook the foundations of the prison and sprung open the doors, "and every one's fetters were unfastened" (16:26). Doubtless the prisoners were cowering in fear from the earthquake. The jailer was awakened by the shock, saw the prison doors open, and concluded that the prisoners had escaped. Since his life was the guarantee of their security, he was about to kill himself, but Paul cried loudly, "Don't do that! We're all here!" (16:28).

The jailer called for torches, rushed in, and fell down before Paul and Silas. We have to read between the lines for Luke expects us to. That's the way he writes. We can assume that the prisoners, at first thoroughly frightened by the earthquake, had become calm and had gathered around Paul and Silas, trying to learn why these men were praising God instead of cursing their ill fortune. We can also assume, perhaps, that the jailer had heard the hymns of praise. At any rate, the jailer was well aware that there was a connection between the fact that the prisoners had not escaped and the behavior of the two new prisoners.

"Men, what must I do to be saved?" he asked. Was he merely talking about safety from punishment? Or was he talking about some kind of theological salvation? Scholars who have no desire to defend Christianity tell us that the mystery religions of the Roman Empire were full of the idea of salvation. It is reasonable to assume that the jailer was talking about theological salvation. But he probably did not expect the kind of answer he got from Paul.

"Believe in the Lord Jesus, and you will be saved,

259

you and your household," Paul told him (16:31). And in that brief sentence, Paul expressed the gospel in a nutshell.

That was not all that Paul told him. Gospel preaching must have more content than that—even though it adds nothing to the principle stated. Paul and Silas "spoke the word of the Lord to him and to all that were in his house" (16:32). That was the detailed proclamation of the gospel.

The jailer took Paul and Silas into his quarters and washed their wounds. Thereupon they baptized him "at once with all his family" (16:33). He was not required to wait until he had attended catechetical class. He was baptized at once. Were there small children in his family? I suppose that depends on whether we believe in "infant baptism" or "believer baptism."

But we must not pass over the fact, repeated for the second time at Philippi, that the Christian faith is not just a religion for individuals. It is a family matter. The Bible treats faith as a family matter. Lydia and her household were baptized (16:15). The jailer and all his family were baptized (16:33). If we who insist so ardently for "individual salvation" have members of our family who have not accepted the Lord Jesus, it is time we ask ourselves, Why not? The household of Lydia was present when the message was proclaimed. The family of the jailer was present when the word of the Lord was spoken. They were baptized because they were present and believed. They were present because the head of the family saw to it that they were present. If we are going to insist on "believer baptism," at least let's get our children where they can hear the word and become believers!

Then, after the jailer washed the wounds and was baptized with the new believers, he set food before his guests (16:34). And finally Paul, Silas, and the prisoners all went quietly back to jail.

I know it doesn't say that. But the rest of the story clearly implies it. Read it over again.

*The Apology.* For some reason which Luke does not explain, the praetors sent the lictors to the jail with the message, "Let these men go" (16:35). Perhaps the praetors had gotten more details about the disturbance. Perhaps it had come to their attention that the prisoners were Roman citizens, and the rulers wanted to drop the matter before it kicked back on them. Perhaps they associated the earthquake with the unjust beatings.

The jailer told Paul, "The magistrates have sent to let you go; now therefore come out [of the jail] and go in peace" (16:36).

But Paul replied, "They have beaten us publicly, without due process of investigation, men who are Roman citizens, and have thrown us into prison. . . . Now are they going to put us out secretly? No! Let them come themselves and take us out" (16:37). Strong words! But Paul knew the rights of a Roman citizen. Under no condition, whether innocent or guilty, could a Roman citizen be beaten. On the other hand, to claim Roman citizenship falsely was punishable by death.

The words of Paul were reported back to the praetors. They knew Roman law, too, "and they were afraid when they heard that they were Roman citizens." So they came to the jail, apologized, took the prisoners out, and "asked them to leave the city" (16:39). So Paul and Silas "went out of the prison," visited their first converts, exhorted the Christians, and departed (16:40).

Luke stayed in Philippi, as we learn from the personal pronouns. He will not resume the use of "we" until Paul reaches Philippi on his return from the Third Mission (20:5). We may conclude that Luke spent the intervening years in Philippi, possibly evangelizing the surrounding area. Timothy also may have stayed for a short time.[10]

*Thessalonica.* Paul and Silas traveled westward by the Egnatian road. A normal day's travel of about thirty miles would bring them to Amphipolis, a second day would bring them to Apollonia,[11] and a third, to Thessalonica, capital of the province of Macedonia.[12] There is no indication that they evangelized any of the cities on the way; Luke says "they passed through" (17:1). Thessalonica is located on the Gulf of Salonica (the Thermaic Gulf), with a magnificent view. The surrounding plain is formed from the confluence of several valleys, and by these valleys roads radiate to cities to the north, east, and west. The sea lanes connect it not only with the cities of the Aegean but with all the Mediterranean world. Paul could realistically say to the Thessalonians, "Not only has the word of the Lord sounded forth from you in Macedonia and Achaia, but your faith in God has gone forth everywhere" (1 Thess. 1:8).

There was a synagogue in Thessalonica, and Paul preached there for three weeks (Acts 17:2). It is obvious, when we read the Thessalonian epistles, (which were written shortly after this mission), that Paul must have stayed in the city much longer; hence the "three weeks" must refer only to the period in which he carried on his arguments in the synagogue over the interpretation of the Scriptures (17:2,3). Luke does not need to tell us that Paul finally had to withdraw from the synagogue and carry on his teaching at another location.

Paul and Silas probably stayed with Jason. At least this is inferred from the statement in verse 5. They persuaded "some" of the Jews, "a great many" of the gentile God-fearers, and "not a few" of the leading women (17:4). This stirred up jealousy among the Jews who did not accept Paul's message, and by means of some rabble-rousing, they gathered a crowd and "set the city in an uproar" (17:5).[13] The mob turned toward the house of Jason, "seeking to bring them [the evangelists] out to the people." But Paul and his companions were not there. However, Jason and some other Christians were dragged before the "politarchs."[14]

The charge, in this case, was different from that made at Philippi. "These men," who are vaguely accused of having "turned the world upside down," "are all acting against the decrees of Caesar, saying that there is another king, Jesus" (17:7). Jason is implicated because he "has received them."

We can see the truth showing through the charge. From Paul's letters to the Thessalonians, it is clear that he must have done considerable teaching about the Kingdom of God and the Second Coming of Jesus Christ. Some statement to the effect that "Jesus is coming to set up His Kingdom," could easily be distorted to form the charge made to the politarchs. The gravity of the charge disturbed the people and the politarchs.

What they did, however, turned out to be a serious blow to the evangelists. The city-rulers put "Jason and the rest" under some kind of bond—Paul's inability to return to Thessalonica suggests that the bond was to be forfeited if Paul showed up again in the city. You can go back to preaching after a beating or stoning, but it's a different matter if your friends and your host are made to suffer for your "boldness." So Paul had to leave Thessalonica.

The Christians spirited Paul and Silas (and probably Timothy as well) out of the city by night, and they went to Beroea, about forty miles to the west (17:10). The city lay south of the Egnatian Road.

The Jews at Beroea "were more noble than those in Thessalonica" (17:11). Rackham takes this to mean that they belonged to the nobility or aristocracy of the city,[15] but this certainly does not seem to fit Luke's sentence structure. Their nobility lies in the fact that "they received the word with all eagerness, examining the scriptures daily to see if these things were so" (17:11). Luke reports that "Many of them therefore believed, with not a few Greek women of high standing as well as men" (17:12). Among them probably was Sopater (20:4).

Jews of Thessalonica heard that Paul was preaching at Beroea so they followed him there and proceeded to stir up trouble and incite the crowd. Again the Christians "sent Paul off on his way to the sea," some of them going with him "as far as Athens" (17:14,15). Silas and Timothy, however, were left in Beroea.

From Athens Paul sent back orders for Silas and Timothy to join him "as soon as possible" (Acts 17:15).

*Summation.* The gospel—meaning deliberate evangelization—has moved across Asia Minor and penetrated Europe. Perhaps it had already reached Rome and other places. But that was the result of individual believers telling others of their Saviour. I do not belittle this "lay" witness, for I believe all Christians are called to be witnesses. Yet, in this present day, with its peculiar attitudes, I think we need to stress the biblical truth that some men are called by God to preach the gospel, to establish and pastor churches, and in this way to extend the Kingdom of God. So far as we know, three thousand witnesses spreading over the Empire after Pentecost did not do as much to establish the Church of Jesus Christ as Paul did even before he finished the Second Mission.

The Church uncovered a new enemy: "anti-Semitism," by which we mean, of course, the anti-Jewish set of mind. The Christians were persecuted in the Empire because they were Jews. The time would come when they would be persecuted because they were Christians. But Christianity at this time in our story is still a Jewish sect.

# Footnotes

1. Cf. *Atlas of the Classical World* maps 1 and 3. Most atlases fail to illustrate this fact.

2. *Macmillan Bible Atlas* map 246; *Westminster Historical Atlas*, plate XV. For some periods of its history, there was only one Roman province, Macedonia-and-Achaia.

3. *Encyclopedia Britannica* (1970) 11:518f. Another authority says it was Cos.

4. Art. "Medicine," *Encyclopedia Britannica* (1970) 15:94B-95.

5. Ramsay *St. Paul the Traveller*, pp. 206f. I think that Ramsay overplays the idea of Luke's local pride in Philippi.

6. The others are Pisidian Antioch, Lystra, Troas, Corinth, and Ptolemais.

7. Some scholars take this as a gentilic, "the Lydian" (i.e. from Lydia). At that time, however, Thyatira was considered to be in Mysia, not in Lydia.

8. Suetonius, *Claudius*, 25.4.

9. This was one of the three occasions mentioned in his letter to Corinth (2 Cor. 11:25) when Paul was beaten by rods.

10. If Timothy stayed behind, he probably carried the gifts from the church in Philippi to Paul—see Phil. 4:16.

11. This to be distinguished from another Apollonia at the western end of the Egnatian Road.

12. "Thessalonica," *Atlas of the Bible* map 32 and endpaper II; *Westminster Historical Atlas* plate XV. Many books, some recent, tell us that the modern name is Saloniki. I can testify that the road signs (in Greek, hence not for tourists), business letterheads, airline tickets, etc., all read "Thessaloniki."

13. For the seriousness of the riot, cf. 1 Thess. 2:14-16.

14. This unusual name of the city-rulers of Thessalonica has been substantiated by an inscribed stone from a first-century arch, listing the names of several "politarchs." The stone can be seen in The British Museum.

15. Rackham, *Acts*, 298-299.

# Second Journey:
# The Mission to Achaia (Athens)

"You've told us what the gospel can do with Jews and gentile proselytes, and you've told us what the gospel can do with ignorant and superstitious pagans," someone might have said to Luke, "but what can the gospel do with highly educated, cultured people?"

Of course, this is an overstated question. There were highly educated Jews, and some of them did accept the gospel. Saul of Tarsus would be the first to come to mind. And there were cultured Gentiles, both proselytes and pagans, and some of them also had become believers. But Luke would understand the intent of the question, and now he tells us what happened in the city that above all cities epitomized Greek culture.

*Athens.* To mention the name "Athens" is to think of classical Greek architecture and sculpture, of the great philosophers, of the logical human mind that thought of the atom long before the atom was ever discovered scientifically, that thought of the shape and size of the earth long before argonauts or astronauts ever were able to measure the earth or see it from space, that thought out mathematical and geometric principles that, centuries later, would make possible the rise of the modern scientific age. If we were to put it all into a single statement, I suppose we could call Athenian thought the glorification of the human mind. Its products are numerous and varied, including music, the theater, grammar, ethics, medicine, and many, many other areas of human thought.[1]

In a sense, all of that was in the past. In the first century A.D. there were no great philosophers or artists in Athens. Logic had so dominated philsophy, replacing the empirical method, that science and medicine had been strangled. The death of scientific method, so often attributed to Christianity, rightly should be laid at the door of the speculative thinkers whose principle might be summarized in the words, "My mind is made up; don't confuse me with facts!"

Politically, Athens had fallen into second place. Corinth was the capital of the province of Achaia. We think of Athens as the place where democracy was born—but democracy had long since become moribund in Athens!

It is not clear that Paul planned a mission to Athens. Many scholars believe it was incidental to his

268

presence in that city. Luke suggests something like this when he introduces the account: "Now while he was waiting for them [Silas and Timothy] in Athens . . ." (17:16). We probably cannot reconstruct Paul's plans at this particular juncture. He had gone to Macedonia with a divine revelation. The events at Philippi had forced him to move to Thessalonica, leaving Luke and Timothy behind. Perhaps he hoped to be able to return to Philippi. As it turned out, he had to leave Thessalonica and moved to Beroea.

Then he had to leave Beroea and went to Athens. Silas and Timothy were left behind. The evangelistic team was broken up and scattered. The opposition in Macedonia was so strong that it might be years before Paul could return. I strongly suppose that Paul was seeking the Lord's answer to questions that kept arising in his mind: Where was he to go next? What was to happen to the young churches in Macedonia? What of his fellow-workers, Luke and Silas and Timothy?

*Paul's Impression of Athens.* Whenever I visit Athens, I marvel at the physical beauty of the ancient temples, the monuments, the sculpture, and the fascinating artifacts in the archeological museum. Dominating all of Athens is the acropolis with its magnificent Parthenon.[2] When I look at the Parthenon, I say to myself, "If that building is so beautiful today, even after the bombing and explosion in 1687, what must it have been like when Paul was in Athens? What must it have been like six centuries earlier when Pericles built the buildings that even today in ruins sit so majestically atop the acropolis?" Paul never mentions the beauty of Athens. Not a word! Did he see the sculptures? Of course he did! But his reaction was akin to anger. "His spirit was provoked within him as he saw that the city was full of idols" (17:16).

"Therefore"—note the connection! Paul saw the great amount of idolatry in Athens, therefore he began to speak up. "He argued in the synagogue with the Jews and the devout persons, and in the market place every day with those who chanced to be there" (17:17). The reason he undertook this two-pronged attack was because of the number of idols in the city.

In the synagogue (was there only one in Athens?), probably on the Sabbath days, and in the agora every day, Paul carried on this ministry. The agora was more than a "market place." It was a large area, usually rectangular, with colonnades at the sides that provided covered walks lined with various shops. Temples, public buildings with the inscriptions of wealthy citizens who erected them, statues, fountains, and other gifts of public-spirited citizens or monuments of invaders, were built in and around the agora. In the mornings, on "market days" if not daily, farmers brought their cattle and produce to the agora for sale. The rest of the time the agora was given over to peripatetic teachers, schools of philosophers, sleight-of-hand artists and others with various means of catching and holding the attention of the passers-by. Zeno taught his pupils in a part of the porch or *stoa* of the agora; from that they derived their name, "Stoics." Often a raised stone or dais served as the place where a teacher or speaker might stand in order better to be heard by the group he was addressing.

Paul took his place daily in the agora, doubtless competing with other wandering teachers. What did he talk about? Well, the Epicurean and Stoic philosophers' who chanced to meet him, said "He seems to be a preacher of foreign divinities"—Luke adds, "Because he preached Jesus and the resurrection." Obviously Paul was referring again to his favorite subject: the risen Lord Jesus.

*Paul before the Areopagus.* It is no longer fully clear just what happened next. We know that there was a council of learned men that met on the Areopagus (Mars' Hill), southwest of the agora. We know that at one time it was the custom for this council to examine the subject and the credentials of visiting teachers. We also know that at one time a larger council met to try seditious teachers and other criminals. And we know that some Epicurean and Stoic philosophers "took hold of him and brought him to the Areopagus, saying, 'May we know what this new teaching is which you present?' " (17:19). But we do not know precisely how the Areopagus functioned at that time.

The incident almost certainly was not a trial. No charges are introduced against Paul. None of the characteristics of other trials in Acts are included here in Luke's account. It was in the nature of an investigation, but was it official or merely done out of curiosity? Likely the latter, but we cannot be certain.

Although from a sentimental viewpoint we could wish that it might have been, it probably was not on Mars' Hill. It would have been a "good theatre" if Paul had stood on the top of the great outcropping of rock, with the acropolis and magnificent Parthenon to the southeast, the busy and beautiful agora to the northeast, under a brilliant Athenian sky. I like to think it was that way. But Luke seems to treat the name "Areopagus" as the name of a group of councilmen rather than the name of a place. Moreover, at that period, the Areopagus no longer met on Mars' Hill, but in the Royal Portico of the agora.[4] Putting sentiment aside, then, we conclude that Paul was taken to the council meeting in an area of the agora.

*The Address to the Areopagus.* With a striking beginning, Paul said: "Men of Athens, I perceive that in every way you are very religious. For as I passed along and observed the objects of your worship, I found also an altar with this inscription, 'To an unknown god.' What therefore you worship as unknown, this I proclaim to you" (17:22-23).

Paul might have condemned them for their excessive idolatry. This was proverbial, and one writer of antiquity said, "In Athens it is easier to find a god than a man."[5] Or Paul might have taken an Old Testament text against idolatry. Those who criticize his approach at Athens probably would have done so. But Paul wanted to hold the audience at least until he had gotten his central point across to them.

Was there actually an altar to an unknown god? I have seen and photographed an altar in Rome from the same period inscribed "To either a god or a goddess." If altars could be erected to some deity whose gender was unknown, I do not find it hard to believe that an altar could have been dedicated to an unknown god. But far stronger proof, in my mind, is the fact that Paul would not have made such a statement to the Athenian learned council unless it had been true. He would immediately have lost his audience.

The "unknown God" that Paul proclaimed is creator of "the world and all things therein." He is the governor of all nations, determining the length of their existence and the extent of their boundaries. As such, He does not need a temple to live in—in fact no man-made temple could contain Him—and He does not need anything from man. We do not give to Him; He gives to us, life, breath, and all things. He has made "of one" every nation of men (17:24-26).

We could spend pages on just these few statements. Paul is undercutting the pagan doctrines of polytheism (many gods) and atheism (no gods). He is stabbing at the heart of Athenian pride and Greek racial superiority. He is putting God at the center of the universe, in place of man's wisdom. Those familiar with the Epicurean and Stoic philosophies will see at once that Paul, without mentioning any names, is carrying out a devastating attack on the foundations of these systems. Then, as though to clinch that part, he quotes from two of their own poets, Epimenides of Crete, and Aratus of Cilicia: "For in him we live and move and have our being," and "For we are indeed his offspring" (17:28).*

Paul then turns to the next point. If we are the offspring of God, then it is not only an offense to the

Creator, but even a despoiling of our own nature to represent God by man-made idols of gold or silver or stone. But God has up until now "overlooked" these insulting offenses, these "times of ignorance." Now, however, "he commands all men everywhere to repent." He will no longer overlook pagan idolatry and sin. "He has fixed a day on which he will judge the world in righteousness."

This judging will be "by a man whom he has appointed." The credentials of this human judge of all men are confirmed by the fact that God raised him from the dead (17:31). Paul is clearly referring to Jesus Christ, but he does not mention His name.

As in the case of the message at Pisidian Antioch (14:15-17), Paul was preaching natural theology, to which he had added just a speck of truth from revealed theology, namely concerning judgment by Jesus Christ. It is purely a message to Greeks by one who was obviously at home in Greek thought.[1]

*The Reaction.* When Paul mentioned the resurrection of the dead, he lost his hearers. It was curiosity over his "strange things" (17:19)—which included his "foreign divinities," Jesus and "Resurrection"—that led to this hearing before the Areopagus (17:18-20). But now they had heard enough. "Some mocked; but others said, 'We will hear you again about this'" (17:32).

Perhaps we should not make too much of the point, but after all, Luke is careful in his use of language. He has given us the customary formula of an approximately equal division. He does not say, "Some mocked, but a few said . . .", nor does he say, "A few mocked, but many said. . . ." Perhaps also we should not read openness of mind in those who said, "We'll hear you again." That may have been their way of dismissing the matter. However we must again note Luke's great care in his choice of expressions. I gather that he intended to divide the listeners into three groups, the first two being about equally divided, and the third rather small.

There were those who mocked. The wisdom of this world has little time for revelations from God. There were those who were interested in hearing more, whether from curiosity or from a sincere desire to know more about Paul's God. But there were "certain men" who "joined him and believed" (17:32-34). Included in this group were Dionysius, a member of the Areopagus, a woman named Damaris, and others, including possibly Stephanas (1 Cor. 16:15).

Much has been written about Paul's speech on Mars' Hill. It has even been given a special name, the *Areopagitica*.[8] Scholars have taken many and varied positions. Ignoring those who think the whole scene was invented by Luke, we may divide the opinions into two general categories: those who think Paul was "right on," and those who think he "struck out."

Ramsay, who is the "last word" to some scholars, thinks Paul came to Athens merely to wait for news that he could return to Macedonia. His stay was no more than six weeks, probably less than four. He was "disappointed and perhaps disillusioned by his experience in Athens," and went on to Corinth, probably having been forced to leave Athens. He no longer attempted to speak as a philosopher. In fact, his reaction shows up in his First Letter to the Corinthians (2:2). As Ramsay puts it, "Nowhere throughout his writings is he so hard on the wise, the philosophers, and the dialecticians, as when he defends the way in which he had presented Christianity at Corinth."[9] Others add to this evaluation the facts that Paul founded no church at Athens and wrote no letters to Athens. "As for Dionysius and the others who 'believed,' they were not really converted," they say, "there is no mention that they were baptized, and they probably drifted back into paganism. The woman Damaris must have been a *hetaira*—an educated courtesan."

On the other side are those scholars who believe that Athens was the measure of Paul, and he stood as a giant. Lenski's treatment is representative of this group.[10] Paul moved easily among the Greek thinkers and writers, showing his familiarity with their systems. He presented the scriptural position without referring to Scripture. (Of what value is a quotation of Scripture to worldly-minded philosophers?) He cut away the foundations of pagan philosophy and religion. And, in a situation where the number of converts would predictably be extremely small, he succeeded in converting one of the council of twelve learned men.

It is in keeping with Luke's method not to dwell on regular details once they have been set forth. Luke assumes that his reader will know that Paul baptized (or rather, had someone baptize) those who "believed," that he stayed until the young church was organized and standing, even if unsteadily, on its own feet, and then he moved on to

Corinth. There is no indication whatever that he was "run out of Athens."

Is it possible to decide between these two opposing schools of thought? For myself, I believe so.

First, although I think we make a serious mistake if we assume that "Paul could do no wrong" (he was just as much a human being as was Peter, who likewise was not infallible), I believe we can sense that Luke is telling the story here with a positive reaction. The negative feelings have been drawn not from Acts but from First Corinthians. We must remember that First Corinthians was written three or four years later. Paul was not presenting his feelings as of his arrival from Athens. He was reacting to the divisions in the Corinthian Church, partly due to two types of preaching that they had experienced. It is a serious error to read into this a sense of failure in Athens. I am convinced that Luke intended to show that Paul's work in Athens was a success, not a failure, and Luke's climax was his reference to the conversion of Dionysius, Damaris, and the others.

Second, we must believe that the Holy Spirit was leading Paul, and that the Holy Spirit is leading us as we read the Scriptures. If Paul was wrong, the Holy Spirit would have corrected him by one means or another, just as He had corrected Peter and Barnabas through Paul, just as He had opened and shut doors when they planned to journey into Asia or Bithynia. If Paul was wrong, the Holy Spirit would have made that clear to us, for the things which have been recorded in Scripture have been written for our instruction (1 Cor. 10:11).

The Holy Spirit is not the spirit of ignorance. He puts no premium on human ignorance. He did not choose Paul for a ministry of ignorance. The Holy Spirit is the spirit of wisdom and understanding, the spirit of knowledge (Isa. 11:2). God went to unusual lengths to bring Saul of Tarsus into the kingdom. He committed to Paul the ministry to the Gentiles. I believe this action was taken because Paul was equipped by his secular education, as well as by his knowledge of Scripture, for his ministry to the Gentiles. If we rule out the use of natural theology and wisdom in the Church, then we must rule out most of the Psalms, Proverbs, and other Wisdom Literature in the Old Testament.

Paul was "all things to all men." He was as a Jew to the Jews, and he was as an Athenian to the Athenians. I believe God so willed it.

## Footnotes

1. Cf. *Atlas of the Classical World*, pp. 39-66.
2. *Atlas of the Bible*, photo 404; *Atlas of the Classical World*, map 13, photos 53-59.
3. *Atlas of the Classical World*, p. 89.
4. The original name was "the Council of (or in) the Areopagus." This was shortened in common speech to "the Areopagus," as we know from several ancient writers. See Bruce, *Commentary on Acts*, p. 352, n. 23.
5. Attributed to Petronius.
6. Bruce gives the references, and for Epimenides' quotation the context; *Commentary on Acts*, pp. 359-360, nn. 49, 50. For full discussion, cf. *Beginnings of Christianity* 5:246-251.
7. Bruce's statement is well taken: "In general, it is true to say that those classical students who have studied this speech and its setting are prominent among the scholars who have defended its authenticity"— *Commentary on Acts*, p. 354. H. J. Cadbury (*Beginnings of Christianity* 5:406 n. 1), similarly states, "The classicists are among the most inclined to plead for the historicity of the scene of Paul at Athens."
8. For a list of references to outstanding discussions, see Bruce, *Commentary on Acts*, p. 353f., n. 31. For a recent conservative work, see N. B. Stonehouse, *The Areopagus Address* (1950).
9. Ramsay, *St. Paul the Traveller*, p. 252.
10. Lenski, *Acts*, pp. 702-737

278

# Second Journey:
# The Mission to Corinth

We have seen what the gospel can do (or can't do) in an intellectual center. Now, what can it do in Sin City? Where is Sin City? In Paul's day it was Corinth, for even the name "Corinthian" meant profligate, and "Corinthian woman" meant harlot, while "to Corinthianize" meant to go a-whoring.

*Corinth.* The Peloponnesus of Greece is connected to the mainland by a narrow isthmus (about four miles wide). The Saronic Gulf on the east and the Gulf of Corinth on the west serve to separate the Peloponnesus from the mainland.

Corinth was a port city. Ships from the east unloaded at Cenchreae and those from the west ot Lechaeum. Small boats were hauled across the isthmus on rollers, but larger ships had to be unloaded. The sailors considered Corinth a good liberty port. On top of Acrocorinth there was a temple to Aphrodite, with a thousand cult prostitutes free to any "worshiper."

Corinth was a cosmopolitan city, because of its location and its commerce. It has been called the least Greek of all Greek cities. In a sense, then, we can look upon Corinth as the representative of any worldly city, and we can apply the lessons we learn from Corinth to the evangelization of any wicked metropolis. Paul wrote at least four letters to the church in Corinth,[1] two of which remain (possibly three, if Second Corinthians is a combination of two letters). From Corinth, on the first visit, he wrote both letters to the Thessalonians and, on the second visit, the letter to the Romans. Thanks to this quantity of material we have a rather full knowledge of Corinth as Paul saw it.

The sin of Corinth seeps into the church in Corinth, as is readily apparent in Paul's letters to the Corinthians. Note 1 Corinthians 5 and 7.

An interesting sidelight on the accuracy of Luke is shown by the following facts. From A.D. 15 to A.D. 44 Corinth was governed by an imperial legate[2] but Luke does not use this title. In 44 Claudius made the territory a senatorial province and placed it under a proconsul and this is the word Luke uses.[3]

Gallio became proconsul of Corinth in July of A.D. 51 (possibly 52, according to some scholars). It appears that Paul had already been in Corinth for some time, hence we can date his arrival in Corinth at 50 (or 51). He stayed there eighteen months

(Acts 18:11), to which we should perhaps add the "many days longer" of 18:18.

*Aquila and Priscilla.*[4] A Jewish tentmaker,[5] Aquila, who was born in Pontus on the Black Sea had migrated to Rome. He and his wife, who was probably a Gentile, had been forced to leave Rome by the edict of Claudius expelling all Jews. They moved to Corinth. Luke calls Aquila's wife Priscilla, but Paul calls her Prisca.[6] Not long after they came Paul arrived in Corinth, all alone. Somehow, whether in a synagogue or in the agora, Paul met Aquila, "and because he was of the same trade, he stayed with them, and they worked" (18:3).

Were Priscilla and Aquila Christians when Paul met them? We do not know. Since neither Luke nor Paul says anything about their conversion, we assume that they were—possibly having heard the gospel in Rome. But scholars are divided on this point. From Aquila Paul seems to have gotten the desire to see Rome (for Luke soon introduces this goal, Acts 19:21), and possibly also much information about the church in Rome. When Paul wrote his letter to the Romans, five years later, Priscilla and Aquila were back in Rome and a church was meeting in their house (Rom. 16:3-5).

*Paul's Ministry in Corinth.* Paul worked with his hands to support himself. On Sabbath days he went to the synagogue, and "sought to persuade Jews and Greeks." (See 18:4.) I find nothing in the record to substantiate the view that Paul was despondent or that he had no plans for a ministry in Corinth. He was waiting for his "team" and for divine guidance.

281

What had happened to Paul's evangelistic team? Luke, of course, had stayed in Phillippi.[7] Silas and Timothy, who had been left in Beroea (17:14), received word from Paul from Athens to come to him as soon as they could (17:15).

One possible reconstruction of events is as follows: Silas and Timothy joined Paul in Athens, although Luke makes no mention of the fact. Paul, concerned about the young church in Thessalonica, sent Timothy to establish them in the faith (1 Thess. 3:2). He probably sent Silas to Philippi for a similar reason. Meanwhile, Paul went on to Corinth (Acts 18:1).

Silas and Timothy returned from Macedonia to Corinth (18:5). Paul was so delighted with the news that Timothy brought from Thessalonica (and a bit disturbed, too, by certain developments), that he sat down and wrote First Thessalonians. Silas and Timothy were with him when he wrote the letter (1 Thess. 1:1; 3:6). It is likely that Timothy carried this letter back to Thessalonica, returned with a report and many questions, to which Paul replied by writing Second Thessalonians. Timothy also carried this letter to Thessalonica, and remained there. Neither he nor Silas is mentioned again as being in Corinth.[8] Paul speaks of the ministry in Corinth in these words, "For the Son of God, Jesus Christ, whom we preached among you, Silvanus and Timothy and I . . ." indicating that while the three were together they had carried out an active campaign (2 Cor. 1:19).

When Silas and Timothy first came to Corinth, according to a statement which may be translated either way, "Paul was occupied with preaching" (Acts 18:5, RSV), or "Paul *began* devoting himself completely to the word" (*NASB*). If we accept the second rendering, we may assume that this was one of the occasions when the Philippian church sent gifts to Paul (Phil. 4:15), and that he was able for a while to ease up on tentmaking and devote himself to preaching.

The main theme of Paul's preaching in the synagogue was "the Messiah is Jesus" (Acts 18:5). This stirred up opposition—although it does not seem to have become violent at first—but finally Paul "shook out his garments" and left the synagogue (18:6,7).[9] He relocated next door in the house of a "God-fearer" named Titius Justus (18:7).[10] Some of the Jews moved with Paul, including Crispus the ruler of the synagogue (18:8).

Opposition continued to build up, and Paul may have begun to feel concern for his work in Corinth. God gave him a vision one night, telling him, "Do not be afraid, but speak and do not be silent; for I am with you, and no man shall attack you to harm you; for I have many people in this city," and he stayed a year and six months (18:9-11). But it is not clear whether this is the total length of his stay in Corinth, or whether the "many days longer" of 18:18 are to be added.

Gallio became proconsul of Achaia and it would seem that this was a signal for the Jews to make "a united attack upon Paul" (18:12). Perhaps they felt that such action at the very beginning of a proconsul's customary year in office had a better chance of success. Their charge is somewhat vague: "This man is persuading men to worship God contrary to the law" (18:13). Did they mean the Jewish law or the Roman law? Christianity, officially viewed as a sect of Judaism, came under the Roman category of *religio licita*—a permitted religion. Were the Jews in Corinth attempting to have Gallio name Christianity a *religio illicita*? Possibly so, but it seems unlikely. Lenski thinks the charge was rather "that [Paul] contravened Roman law in the way he practiced the Jewish religion."[11]

Paul was about to answer the charge when Gallio himself spoke up. Interpreting the charge to be a matter of Jewish law, he refused to be drawn into the argument and drove them from the tribunal (18:14-16).

"They all seized Sosthenes, the ruler of the synagogue, and beat him in front of the tribunal" (18:17). Who seized him? The Jews, angry because their spokesman had "blown" this responsibility? Or Gentiles in the crowd who had been attracted to the scene, and who were venting anti-Jewish sentiments? Probably the latter, since Luke says "they all," but the point is uncertain.[12] Lenski thinks "they all" refers to Gallio's lictors, who had to drive the Jews away from the tribunal. Gallio chose to ignore this breach of peace (18:17).

The decision was a landmark, and would serve as a precedent for other Roman courts for the next ten years. This official attitude, accepting Christianity as a sect of Judaism (or a *religio licita*)—and so permitting the Christian movement to grow—changed, especially after the Great Fire at Rome in A.D. 64.

*The Close of the Mission to Corinth.* When Paul

"took leave" of the church in Corinth, Priscilla and Aquila went with him (18:18). Since he left them in Ephesus (18:19), promising to return there himself "if God wills" (18:21), I assume that he expected this couple to lay groundwork for his mission to Ephesus. He seems to have done the same thing with regard to his plan to visit Rome (Rom. 16:3-5, cf. Rom. 1:10,11).

At Cenchreae, the port of Corinth on the Gulf of Saronica, "he cut his hair, for he had a vow" (18:18). The grammatical antecedent of "he" is Aquila. Lenski strongly insists that Luke intended us to understand that Aquila was the one who made the vow. But Luke's story is entirely about Paul; Aquila is only incidentally a part of it. Most scholars therefore interpret this to mean that Paul had taken a vow. But in either event, Luke tells us no more about it, and anything we might add would be speculation.

At Ephesus, Paul "went into the synagogue and argued with the Jews" (18:19). They asked him to stay longer, but he was anxious to move on, so he declined their invitation, promising to return if God so willed, and he sailed for Caesarea.

*Summation.* We have seen the power of the gospel in Athens and in Corinth. Since "God chose what is foolish in the world to shame the wise" (1 Cor. 1:27), there were far more converts in Corinth than in Athens. But we dare not overlook the fact that *some* of the wise, the noble, and the strong in the world are chosen by God.

Certainly it's more difficult to preach to the educated, the cultured, the leaders. The preacher must be educated at least enough to command their respect. But even more, he must be willing to work long and hard for a very few converts.

On the other hand, it's more pleasant to preach to the "nice" people than to sinners. How the sin in the Corinthian church must have galled Paul! But what a triumph when the foolishness of the Cross turns a sinner into a saint! The church must never make the mistake of excluding either group from its evangelistic effort.

In his account of the First Journey, Luke has given us the story of the apostles' determination to evangelize Gentiles and the great cleavage that threatened the Church because of that program. In his account of the Second Journey, Luke has shown us the various types of problem that arose in the gentile world when the gospel was preached.

The account of the Third Journey, it seems to me, serves to set forth Paul's method in considerable detail. If we take the principles that are seen at work in Ephesus and carry them back to the First and Second Journeys, we find that they were even then at work. But we are running ahead of our story.

# Footnotes

1. He had already written a letter before "First" Corinthians. See 1 Cor. 5:9.

2. Tacitus, *Annals* 1:76.

3. Suetonius, *Claudius* 25.

4. For a fuller study, see my *Great Personalities of the New Testament*, pp. 138-146.

5. According to Lake and Cadbury the word originally meant "tent-maker," but in Paul's day it meant "leather-worker" (BC 4:223). In his novel, *God's Warrior* (1967), Frank G. Slaughter describes Paul and his father as sail-makers.

6. Priscilla is the diminutive of Prisca. Ramsay points out that Paul regularly uses the more formal names, Prisca, Sosipatros, and Silvanus, whereas Luke uses "the language of conversation," Priscilla, Sopatros, and Silas (Ramsay, *St. Paul the Traveller*, p. 268).

7. Frank G. Slaughter, *God's Warrior*, has Luke with Paul in Athens and Corinth. The biblical student must use historical novels with caution.

8. Silas is not mentioned again in Acts.

9. There is no reason to interpret this to mean that he moved out from the home of Aquila and lodged with Titius Justus.

10. Ramsay suggests that the full name was Gaius Titius Justus, and that he is the Gaius of Rom. 16:23 and 1 Cor. 1:14. *Pictures of the Apostolic Church* (1910), p. 205, n. 2.)

11. Lenski, *Acts*, p. 752.

12. It is also uncertain whether this Sosthenes is the same as Paul's associate in writing First Corinthians (1 Cor. 1:1).

# Third Journey:
# The Mission to Ephesus

After landing at Caesarea at the close of the Second Journey, Paul "went up and greeted the church" (18:22). That is, Paul went up to Jerusalem, the only place to which you always "go up," and the only place where "the church" could need no qualifying term. Then Paul "went down to Antioch," meaning of course Antioch-on-the-Orontes, where he spent "some time" (18:23).

*Paul Revisits the Galatian Churches.* Then Paul set out again, with Ephesus in Asia as his destination (18:21), and this time the Spirit did not turn him away from that objective. So far as we know, he started out alone, although some scholars say that Timothy was with him. His Third Journey, like the Second Journey, took him through Syria and Cilicia, by way of the Cilician Gates, to the "Galatic and Phrygian region" where he "went from place to place . . . strengthening all the disciples" (18:23).

This is one of the main points in Paul's evangelistic strategy, namely to revisit the churches he had already founded and to strengthen the believers. One famous missionary preacher used to insist that "No man has the right to hear the gospel twice until every man has heard it once." Well, Paul did not agree with this principle.

*Apollos.* While Paul was on his way to Ephesus, a Jew named Apollos had already reached that city from Alexandria. "He was an eloquent man, well versed in the scriptures," meaning, of course, the Old Testament. "He had been instructed in the way of the Lord" and "spoke and taught accurately the things concerning Jesus" (18:24,25).

How he had gotten this instruction is one of the gaps in our knowledge of early Christianity. Because the Bible records only the spread of the gospel westward to Rome, we sometimes erroneously believe that it did not spread in other directions. But there was a church in Egypt. Moreover the oldest known fragments of the New Testament, dating to the first half of the second century, were found in Egypt. Great Christian writers, such as Clement of Alexandria and Origen, were active in Egypt in the late second and early third centuries. Apollos probably was in touch with some of the earliest members of the Egyptian church.

But his Christian teaching was deficient. "He knew only the baptism of John" (18:25). Just what this means is a matter of debate. Since he knew the "things concerning Jesus," we must assume that he had a rather complete knowledge of the life and teachings of Jesus, probably including His death and resurrection. I see no reason to assume that he taught some kind of "Gnostic" philosophy, and little reason to think that he made use of an allegorical interpretation of Scripture.[1] Rather, I incline to the view that he was deficient in his knowledge of the Holy Spirit and the spiritual gifts in the Church. The "baptism of John" was a baptism of repentance, yet even John had promised that One was coming who would baptize with the Spirit.

Apollos was speaking in the synagogue in Ephesus and Priscilla and Aquila heard him. They saw that his preaching, fervent in spirit and bold, had a serious deficiency. "They took him and expounded to him the way of God more accurately" (18:26). Some Christians would have branded Apollos a heretic, and would have had nothing to do with him, but not Priscilla and her husband. Some great preachers would resent it if a lay couple were to attempt to straighten them out doctrinally. Not Apollos.

Apollos wanted to go to Achaia. Luke does not tell us why, but we can guess. Aquila and Priscilla had told him of the work in Corinth, and he wanted to have some part in it—and he did. "When he arrived, he greatly helped those who through grace had believed, for he powerfully confuted the Jews in public, showing by the scriptures that the Christ was Jesus" (18:27,28). Later, Paul wrote to Corinth, "I planted, Apollos watered, but God gave the growth" (1 Cor. 3:6).

*The Disciples of John at Ephesus.* "While Apollos was at Corinth, Paul passed through the upper country and came to Ephesus" (Acts 19:1). Some scholars hold that this refers to the cities of north Galatia. More likely, it refers to the direct route from Phrygia to Ephesus.[2]

At Ephesus, Paul found "some disciples," a term generally meaning "Christians" in Acts. What strikes us as unusual is Paul's question, "Did you receive the Holy Spirit when you believed?"[3] They replied that they hadn't even heard there was a Holy Spirit. After a bit of questioning, Paul said, "John baptized with the baptism of repentance, telling the people to believe in the one who was to come after him, that is, Jesus" (19:4). The disciples then were baptized in the name of the Lord Jesus; Paul laid his hands on them, the Holy Spirit came on them, and they spoke with tongues and prophesied (19:5,6).

Luke leaves us with a number of questions. Where did these disciples get their teaching? If from Apollos, why did not Apollos or Priscilla and Aquila straighten them out? Why were they rebaptized, whereas Apollos was not (at least, no mention is made of any baptism of Apollos at Ephesus)? Was the laying on of hands necessary? Why was it not done for Apollos? Another problem concerns the small group of Christians Paul first met at Ephesus (18:27). There seems to be no fellowship between these "brethren" and the "disciples" he now met. Why?

Of various treatments I have studied of this portion of Acts the most satisfactory is Lenski's.[4] He

291

says Paul was not conducting a test; he was merely interested in the particular experience of these Christians. Some new converts received the charismatic gifts of the Spirit, some did not. If anyone insists that all believers must be exactly alike, let him study 1 Corinthians 12, especially verses 7-11, and 28-30. Paul was interested in knowing whether these believers had received the Spirit. The question turned up an unexpected but very serious fact: they knew nothing about the Spirit. Lenski says, "Here is the salient point in this entire account— people who know nothing about the Holy Spirit cannot have received the genuine and valid Baptism."⁵ They were baptized—or thought they were —into John's baptism, but since this had not led them to the Coming One that John preached, they had not really received John's baptism. Therefore they were not truly baptized. By inference we might add that Apollos was truly baptized in John's baptism. If this strikes us as strange teaching, let us remind ourselves that all of the original disciples of Jesus were baptized in John's baptism, and no second water baptism was necessary.

As for the laying on of hands, we must notice carefully that it did not always result in speaking with tongues or other charismatic gifts. These gifts are from God, not from apostolic action, and God confers them where and when He wills.

Lenski does not answer all our questions, and perhaps his answers will not satisfy everyone. This is a very difficult passage of Scripture. We might ask why these disciples at Ephesus received the Spirit and spoke with tongues. Speaking with tongues had occurred (in Acts) only on Pentecost (by the Apostles, we should note, not by those who were converted) and at the time of the conversion of Cornelius (by the converts). One marked the beginning of the conversion of Jews, the other the beginning of the conversion of Gentiles. But what does this event at Ephesus mark? Bruce takes a suggestion from Lampe: "Ephesus was to be a new center of the gentile mission . . . and these twelve disciples were to be the nucleus of the Ephesian church."[6]

*Extraordinary Miracles.* To those who have not thought about the problem, all miracles are "extraordinary." But miracles in the Bible are never performed merely for the sake of the miracle. There is a humanitarian or a didactic purpose: the miracle serves to meet some need or to teach a lesson. In the case of humanitarian miracles, which also have a didactic purpose in nearly every case, there is usually personal contact between the one working the miracle and the one on whom it is worked. Moreover, there is usually some demand of faith, by which I mean that the person who receives the benefit is expected to demonstrate some evidence of faith either before or after the miracle.

In the case of Paul's miracles in Ephesus, Luke tells us that they were "extraordinary," and he describes them in these words: "so that handkerchiefs or aprons were carried away from his body to the sick, and diseases left them and the evil spirits came out of them" (19:12).[7]

The fame of Paul's miracle-working power seems to have spread over the area to such an extent that there was not only a demand for healing beyond his ability to give personal ministry, but there was also an attempt to imitate this power. "Some of the itinerant Jewish exorcists undertook to pronounce the name of the Lord Jesus over those who had evil spirits" (19:13).

Luke gives one example of this, which at the same time is an example of his keen sense of humor. Seven sons of Sceva were attempting exorcism by using the formula, "I adjure you by the Jesus whom Paul preaches." On one occasion, "the evil spirit answered them, 'Jesus I know, and Paul I know; but who are you?'" (19:15). And the demoniac jumped on the exorcists and beat them.

The power of Paul's Lord and the story of the false exorcists became known "to all the residents of Ephesus, both Jews and Greeks" (19:17). Believers began to confess their former (and apparently even their continued) use of magical practices. A number of those who had engaged in such magic brought their secret books and burned them publicly (19:19). "So the word of the Lord grew and prevailed mightily" (19:20).

To understand these unusual events, we have to understand Ephesus. It was the seat of magic, of exorcism, of belief in the powers of darkness. A few years ago, the Western mind was unable to believe in demons and satanic powers. Now, with the rise of the "church of Satan" and with the increasing popularity of witchcraft and other occult practices, the Westerner is more willing to believe some of the stories that missionaries have brought back about the African spirit cults, Haitian voodoo, and Korean shamanism. According to the New Testament there is such a person as Satan (the Devil); he has his demons, and he concentrates his satanic works in certain areas of his "kingdom." Ephesus was one of Satan's strongholds. Paul was given the power to work extraordinary miracles in order to demonstrate that the Jesus whom he proclaimed was greater than the prince of the powers of darkness. Against this background, many statements in Paul's letter to the Ephesians take on a new clarity (for example, Eph. 1:19-23; 3:20; 5:11,12; 6:11,12).

*Paul's Plans.* After this, "Paul made up his mind to travel through Macedonia and Greece and go on to Jerusalem" (19:21 *TEV*).[8] "After I go there," he added, "I must also see Rome." Here Luke uses his favorite technique of preparing us for an important future event by mentioning it casually before it takes place. He is reaching the part of his story where Rome becomes the primary objective.

But "man proposes, God disposes," and Paul's plans are temporarily changed. This change of plans can perhaps be seen in Paul's remarks in 2 Corinthians 1:15-17.

In keeping with his plan to leave Ephesus for Macedonia and Achaia, Paul sent Timothy and Erastus on ahead. Who this Erastus was we do not know. I find it difficult to identify him with the city treasurer of Corinth mentioned in Romans 16:23. Nor have we heard much of Timothy in Ephesus. Paul had sent him to Corinth (1 Cor. 4:17); Timothy returned and now, with Erastus, was to be sent on another mission.

*The Riot at Ephesus.* Paul's plans were changed, as we said, by a riot that broke out in Ephesus.[9]

Demetrius, who was possibly the head of the guild of silversmiths, gathered together his fellow craftsmen and pointed out that Paul was ruining their business. He combined the economic argument with one that would make a better popular appeal, namely that even the worship of the goddess Artemis (*KJV* Diana) was in danger (19:24-27).

This charge gives us a very clear idea of Paul's approach. As Demetrius put it, Paul was convincing the people "that gods made with hands are not gods" (19:26). By driving home this one simple thought, Paul was undercutting the religion of the great Earth-Mother Cybele or Artemis.

Demetrius inflamed the silversmiths, who in turn stirred up the city. The crowd rushed to the theater —a magnificent building even today—that held about 25,000 persons. Paul was not at hand, but they dragged two of his fellow missioners into the theater: Gaius and Aristarchus.[10]

When Paul heard what was happening, he wanted to go, but was dissuaded by some of the Asiarchs (19:31) or chief citizens, who obviously recognized that an ugly situation was developing and Paul's life would be in danger. This regard for Paul by leading citizens of the provincial capital throws an interesting sidelight on how highly Paul was regarded by the "upper crust"—a point frequently overlooked.

Most of the crowd had no idea what they were demonstrating about (19:32)—which is too often true of pure "democracy." The Jews, most of whom were engaged in some kind of business and therefore unwilling to be found in opposition to the silversmiths, put forth a spokesman named Alexander.[11] He attempted to speak, but when the crowd recognized that he was a Jew, their anti-Jewish feelings broke out, and they shouted, "Great is Artemis of the Ephesians" and kept shouting like this "for about two hours" (19:34).

At last the town clerk, who was the chief official of the democratic form of government and the liaison officer with the Roman government in Asia, got control of the crowd. His words deserve careful study, for they throw a brilliant searchlight upon Paul. After pointing out that the religion of Artemis was not really in danger (the town clerk could hardly say otherwise!), he continued, "You have brought these men here who are neither sacrilegious nor blasphemers of our goddess" (19:37).

Think of it! Paul had been in Ephesus for more than two years. He was driving many silversmiths out of business—those who lived by making little shrines with images of the goddess Artemis. Yet he was never sacrilegious nor blasphemed their goddess. He simply taught that "gods made with hands are not gods."

The town clerk went on to point out that the courts were open, if there were any charges to be brought; that there were proconsuls to handle legitimate complaints; that there was the regular assembly. The present manner of rioting could only get them in serious trouble (19:38-40). And he dismissed the assembly.

Soon after this, Paul started on his delayed trip to Macedonia, Corinth, and Jerusalem.

*Summation.* Ephesus was Rome in Asia. Paul's

strategy was to plant churches in the great centers of the empire. Ephesus was the center of the Artemis-cult. Of the thirty-three centers of Artemis-worship in the world of that day, Ephesus was first. Here was located the great temple of Artemis, greatest of the seven wonders of the ancient world. As at Athens, Paul did not attack by naming names. He drove home principles that undercut the foundations of false religions and philosophies. Ephesus was the center of magic and satanic powers of darkness. Paul demonstrated the power of God, the God who is Light.

Paul had started, as was his custom, in the synagogue. When that door closed, he moved into the Hall of Tyrannus. There is no indication that he attempted to evangelize the surrounding regions. He taught daily in the Hall and visited house to house (20:20). Yet at the end of two years, "all the residents of Asia heard the word of the Lord, both Jews and Greeks" (19:10). Those whom he trained evangelized the surrounding cities. Among these cities we must list Colossae and Laodicea, "who have not seen my face" (Col. 2:1). It seems most reasonable to assume that it was by this means that churches were established in other cities such as Smyrna, Pergamum, Thyatira, Sardis, Philadelphia, Hierapolis, and perhaps Magnesia, Tralles, and other cities where strong churches appeared by the end of the first century.

Thus we see the man and his method. The dangers he faced are hardly mentioned in Acts and only briefly referred to in his letters. Did he actually fight "with the wild beasts at Ephesus" (1 Cor.

15:32), or was this a figure of speech? Probably the latter. Was he imprisoned and did he write Philippians from an Ephesian prison? I find no compelling reasons to accept this theory. He certainly wrote First Corinthians from Ephesus, and quite possibly wrote Galatians also from there. He always tried to keep in close touch with the churches he founded.

## Footnotes

1. So Macgregor in *Interpreter's Bible*, 9:247.
2. Ramsay, *St. Paul the Traveller*, p. 265.
3. The *KJV* ". . . since ye believed" is an incorrect translation.
4. Lenski, *Acts*, pp. 776-781.
5. *Ibid.*, p. 777.
6. Bruce, *Commentary on Acts*, p. 387, citing G. W. H. Lampe, *The Seal of the Spirit* (1951), p. 76.
7. The word translated "handkerchiefs" means "sweat bands"—rags tied around the head while working.
8. It is impossible to tell whether Luke meant "spirit" or "Spirit," the phrase being capable of translation either as "in the spirit" or "by the Spirit." "Resolved in the spirit" equals *TEV's* "made up his mind."
9. Possibly this was not the only reason, for 1 Cor. 16:8-9 tells of a "wide door for effective work" which had opened.
10. Luke calls them Macedonians in Acts 19:29. In 20:4 Aristarchus is identified as a Thessalonian, and, as usually punctuated, Gaius a Derbean.
11. Possibly the coppersmith of the same name mentioned by Paul in 2 Tim. 4:14, but we cannot be certain.

# Third Journey:
# The Collection for the
# Church in Jerusalem

One of the characteristics of the Early Church—
as indeed of the Church in every generation—was
her works of charity. "There was not a needy person" in the first church at Jerusalem, for the "haves"
shared with the "have-nots" (Acts 4:34,35). Dorcas
was "full of good works and acts of charity" which
she did (9:36). When the church at Antioch heard
about the severe famine in Judea, they "determined, every one according to his ability, to send
relief to the brethren who lived in Judea" (11:29).

Charity was not an invention of the Christian
church. The Old Testament puts great stress on

charitable deeds, especially care of widows and orphans (the "fatherless"). Judaism likewise cultivated the doctrine of deeds of righteousness. Perhaps the characteristic of Christian charity is that it is done in Christ's name.

Paul, on his Third Journey, put into action a plan which he believed would not only benefit the Christians at Jerusalem in their poverty, but would also develop a deeper sense of unity between the Jewish and gentile Christians.

*Macedonia and Greece Revisited.* After the riot in Ephesus had died down, Paul gathered together the Christians, spoke words of encouragement to them, and said good-bye (20:1). It was probably toward the end of summer, and the sailing season was nearly over. Paul journeyed overland to Troas, where he expected to meet Titus who was coming from the church in Corinth with news. At Troas "a door opened" for Paul, but because Titus was not there (possibly the sailing season had already closed at Athens), Paul's mind "could not rest" so he went on to Macedonia (2 Cor. 2:12,13). We assume that through most of the fall and winter it was possible to cross the narrow body of water that separated Europe from Asia at Troas. Paul probably went at once to Philippi, and soon Titus joined him there with good news from Corinth (2 Cor. 7:5-7).

Luke gives us only the barest hints about this portion of the Third Journey. Paul must have traveled overland to Thessalonica and perhaps to Beroea. Luke says simply, "He went through those regions and encouraged the people with many messages" (Acts 20:2, *TEV*).

To the Romans Paul wrote that he preached the gospel "as far round as Illyricum" (Rom. 15:19).[1] He may simply be using that term as the limit of his work. If we assume that he actually carried out evangelistic work in Illyria, he must have done it at this time, for it will fit in no other place in Paul's life prior to the writing of Romans.

Then Paul "came to Greece" where he spent three months (Acts 20:2,3). Luke here uses the familiar term for "Greece," and not the provincial name "Achaia"; he almost certainly means Corinth. During the three months in Corinth Paul wrote his great Epistle to the Romans and sent it with Phoebe, a deaconess of the church at Cenchreae (Rom. 16:1). Paul was staying with Gaius (Rom. 16:23) for Aquila and Priscilla had already gone on to Rome (Rom. 16:3). According to his plans at that time, Paul was going to Jerusalem "with aid for the saints," and then he hoped to visit the church in Rome "in passing as I go to Spain" (Rom. 15:24,25).

*The Offering for Jerusalem.* Paul had planned to sail from Corinth (actually from the port of Cenchreae) for Syria as soon as the season opened. But somehow he learned that the Jews were making a plot against him, so he changed his plans. He returned by land to Macedonia, accompanied[2] by men who apparently joined him in Corinth for the voyage to Caesarea: Sopater the son of Pyrrhus a Berean;[3] the Thessalonians Aristarchus and Secundus, and some would add here Gaius; Gaius a Derbean and Timothy; and the Asians Tychicus[4] and Trophimus[5] (Acts 20:4).

Analyzing the list we find one Berean, two Thessalonians, two Galatians, and two Asians. Why no representative from Corinth and none from Philippi? At this point in the narrative Luke again shifts into first person ("These went on and were waiting for *us* at Troas"). Thus it is clear that Luke is representing the church in Philippi, for he apparently spent most of the time between Paul's visit on the Second Journey (16:40) and the present occasion, in Philippi (judging from the "we sections"). Timothy or perhaps Paul himself may have represented the church in Corinth.

First Corinthians, we have seen, was written from Ephesus. In it Paul makes the first reference to the collection for Jerusalem, but he had already set in motion the same plan in Galatia. To Corinth he wrote:

"Now concerning the contribution for the saints: as I directed the churches of Galatia, so you also are to do. On the first day of every week, each of you is to put something aside and store it up, as he may prosper, so that contributions need not be made when I come. And when I arrive, I will send those whom you accredit by letter to carry your gift to Jerusalem. If it seems advisable that I should go also, they will accompany me" (1 Cor. 16:1-4).

Second Corinthians was written from Macedonia, after Paul had left Ephesus. In it Paul set forth in some detail his plan (2 Cor. chs. 8-9): he cited the example of the churches of Macedonia, who, in spite of their own "extreme poverty have overflowed in a wealth of liberality" (2 Cor. 8:2), even "begging us earnestly for the favor of taking part in

303

the relief of the saints" (2 Cor. 8:4). Paul urged
Titus, who was to return to Corinth with this letter,
to complete this benevolent project among the Corinthian church, and Paul added, "see that you
excel in this gracious work also" (2 Cor. 8:7). Some
of Paul's finest statements about giving are found in
these chapters: "He who sows sparingly will also
reap sparingly, and he who sows bountifully will
also reap bountifully" (2 Cor. 9:6). "God loves a
cheerful giver" (2 Cor. 9:7). "He who supplies seed
to the sower and bread for food will supply and
multiply your resources and increase the harvest of
your righteousness" (2 Cor. 9:10).

Romans was written from Corinth. He obviously
was not appealing to the Christians in Rome for this
gift, since the church in Rome was not founded by
him. But he did mention the offering.

> "At present, however, I am going to Jerusalem
> with aid for the saints. For Macedonia and
> Achaia have been pleased to make some contri-
> bution for the poor among the saints at Jerusa-
> lem; they were pleased to do it, and indeed
> they are in debt to them, for if the Gentiles
> have come to share in their spiritual blessings,
> they ought also to be of service to them in ma-
> terial blessings" (Rom. 15:25-27).

In this last statement we see the basis of Paul's
plan. It was part of his philosophy expressed at the
beginning of the letter to the Romans, "I am under
obligation both to Greeks and to barbarians" (Rom.
1:14). But more specifically, it was a way of showing the unity of the Church. "The gentile churches

were to be made to feel the essential unity of the Church by realizing their debt to, and their unity with, the Mother Church; and the Mother Church was to recognize the gentile communities as true daughters of Israel."[6]

*The Farewell Visit to Troas.* The seven men named in verse 4 went ahead to Troas (Acts 20:5). Paul and Luke, for reasons not given, remained at Philippi until "after the days of Unleavened Bread" (20:6). Ramsay believes he can precisely date the events right up to the arrival in Caesarea.[7] In A.D. 57, Passover fell on Thursday, April 7; Paul and Luke sailed on Friday and arrived in Troas on the following Tuesday. But can we derive this accuracy from Luke? When he wants to say "on the next day" he does so. Here he simply says "after" Passover. It is enough that we can place the voyage between Passover and Pentecost.

The party, at least nine in number, spent seven days in Troas. Why? Probably waiting for a ship. The suggestion that Paul chartered his own ship for this journey has little to commend it.

On "the first of the Sabbaths," which could mean after sundown Saturday (if they were following the Jewish reckoning) or Sunday (following the Roman reckoning), the Christians met "to break bread" (20:7). There can be no doubt that the First Day was already established in the New Testament as a particular day for Christians. At Troas and at Corinth (1 Cor. 16:2) the day is specifically named. John refers to "the Lord's day" (Rev. 1:10), and it seems reasonable to conclude that he was referring to a day by that name.[8] But what is the meaning of

305

the expression "to break bread"? Were they observing the Lord's Supper, or was this a common meal? Possibly it was both. If we can judge from Paul's admonition to the church in Corinth (1 Cor. 11:20-34), Christians met for a fellowship meal, sometimes called the Agapē (cf. Jude 12), which concluded with the Lord's Supper.[9]

Luke is not interested in describing the service. He tells us of another event. Paul used the occasion for a long farewell speech that extended into the middle of the night. In the poorly ventilated room, lighted by oil lamps, a young man named Eutychus got sleepy. While sitting in a window, he fell asleep, and tumbled from the third story to the ground. Luke reports that he "was taken up dead" Acts (20:8,9). Paul went down, bent over him, and announced that he was alive (20:10). Are we to understand that a miraculous resuscitation took place? Luke does not say that Eutychus was taken up "as dead" but "dead." It would seem to call for a miracle but Luke makes nothing whatever of it. They returned to the third-floor room, ate, and Paul went on talking until dawn. They took Eutychus home alive. Paul's party went to the dock to board the ship; Paul went by land to Assos (20:12,13).

*The Farewell at Miletus.* "Paul had decided to sail past Ephesus" (20:16). This does not necessarily mean that Paul had chartered the ship and therefore could decide where it would land. It could mean that he decided in Troas to take a ship that docked at Miletus. His reason is clear: he did not want to spend time in Ephesus; he wanted to get to Jerusalem by Pentecost (20:16).

The farewell to the elders is one of the most emotion-charged accounts in Acts. At the same time, it adds important details about Paul's work in Ephesus and about the organizational structure of the church there. Furthermore, it shows that Paul sensed the true danger that the Church faced, namely internal apostasy more than external persecution.

Paul reminds the elders that he had taught publicly (in the Hall of Tyrannus) and from house to house (20:20), preaching to Jews and to Greeks. He had experienced trials and Jewish plots (20:19). He had declared "the whole counsel of God" (20:27) for three years, day and night (20:31). Moreover he had supported himself and his assistants and given help to the weak (20:34,35).

These elders or overseers were "guardians" of the flock by the action of the Holy Spirit, responsible "to feed the church of the Lord" (20:28). Paul's prediction that "fierce wolves" would enter and harm the flock (20:29,30) is borne out historically. In the Apocalypse the Spirit says to the church in Ephesus, "You have abandoned the love you had at first" (Rev. 2:4). Paul also knew that "imprisonment and afflictions" of an unspecified nature lay ahead for him (20:22,23). As a result he believed that his dear friends in Ephesus would never see him again (20:25).[10]

Paul then committed them to God, "knelt down and prayed with them all" (20:32,36). They wept, kissed and embraced him, and went with him to the ship.

*Summation.* In our portrayal of Paul as the great

champion of truth, we sometimes forget that he was also the pastor. He loved the people he brought to salvation, and they loved him. Even in the heat of his letter to the Galatians or in the censure of the Corinthian correspondence, we see ever and again his loving heart. It would be well if every pastor would read over and over Paul's farewell to the Ephesian elders. Let us ask ourselves, Do I care for God's flock as this man cared?

## Footnotes

1. Illyricum (Illyria) was a Roman province on the Adriatic coast. Its boundaries changed from time to time and we cannot positively locate the southern and eastern boundaries at this time. Bruce thinks that if we put the visit to Illyricum here, Acts 20:2 covers "as much as a year" (*The Acts of the Apostles*, p. 369). But if Paul only went "as far as Illyricum" and did not attempt to evangelize the area, I see no reason to require anything like a year.

2. The words "into Asia" in *KJV* must be rejected. They are not found in the oldest manuscripts and they make no sense.

3. This is Sosipater in Rom. 16:21, who was with Paul when he wrote Romans.

4. Tychicus was one of Paul's trusted co-workers, cf. Eph. 6:21,22; Col. 4:7-9; Tit. 3:12; 2 Tim. 4:12.

5. Trophimus was the indirect cause of Paul's arrest in Jerusalem at the end of this trip, cf. Acts 21:27ff.

6. B. H. Streeter, *The Primitive Church* (1929), pp. 52f.

7. Ramsay, *St. Paul the Traveller*, pp. 289-295.

8. The term is so used early in the second century by Ignatius, *Epistle to the Magnesians* 1.67.

9. The Passover celebration included a meal. Since Jesus took one of the *matsoth* (breads) and one of the cups of wine from the Passover to institute the Lord's Supper, as the Gospels indicate, it is easy to see how the Church might have developed a "love feast" (Agapē) which concluded with the Communion.

10. But see 1 Tim. 1:3 and 4:13.

# PART IV

## The Gospel
## Takes Paul to Rome

CHAPTER 28 / (Acts 21:1-17)

# The Last Visit to Jerusalem

When Paul left Corinth with the delegates of the churches that were sending offerings to the poor in Jerusalem, he was really traveling to Rome. Geographically, of course, this is nonsense. But when Paul wrote the epistle to the Romans, just before he left Corinth, his mind was set on Rome and the West. Jerusalem was just a side trip (Rom. 15:23-25).

In the cities where Paul stopped, en route to Jerusalem, he heard repeated warnings of events that would happen in Jerusalem that would be of grave consequence to him. The next two years would be years of frustration, and if God hadn't given Paul the promise that he would reach Rome

(Acts 23:11), I suppose Paul would have lost all hope of fulfilling that aspiration.

*The Journey to Caesarea.* In the Aegean Sea at that time of the year, the wind comes up some time between midnight and dawn, blowing from the north, and continues until the next afternoon. We suppose, then, that Paul and his party boarded the ship in Miletus around midnight. With a following wind they sailed straight to Cos (about 45 miles). The next day brought them to Rhodes (about 70 miles), and the third day to Patara (about 70 miles).[1] For this part of the journey they sailed in a small coasting vessel that did not venture out of sight of land (Acts 21:1).

At Patara they found a larger ship that sailed directly to Phoenicia, a distance of about 400 miles. The route took them under the lee of Cyprus (it was "on the left"), straight to Tyre, where the ship was to unload cargo (21:3).

At Tyre, after a bit of searching, they found some fellow-Christians and spent seven days with them. Lenski comments on the fact that though Paul was almost a complete stranger and his companions had never been to Tyre, "yet during this one week the bond of attachment became so strong that men, women, and children turned out to a person to bid farewell to Paul and his company."[2] I have found it even so, in China, in Korea, in Ghana, in Taiwan, and many other places. Christian fellowship is unlike anything in this world!

From Tyre the ship sailed to Ptolemais (modern Acco or Acre), where Paul and his party spent a day with the "brethren" (21:7), and then continued

314

on to Caesarea. At Caesarea Paul and his group were put up at the home of Philip the Evangelist, one of the Seven (21:8, cf. 6:5; 8:5ff.). Philip had four daughters who were "prophetesses," which probably means that they proclaimed the word of God. They are not the ones who predicted to Paul what was going to happen in Jerusalem.

*The Prophecy of Agabus.* Already at Tyre, the believers "kept telling Paul through the Spirit not to set foot in Jerusalem" (21:4 *NASB*). At Caesarea something more striking happened. Since the travelers were apparently ahead of schedule they stayed with Philip "some days." A prophet named Agabus, doubtless the same one who had predicted the famine some years earlier (11:27,28), came down from Judea and went to Philip's house. Taking Paul's belt he bound his own hands and feet and said, "Thus says the Holy Spirit, 'So shall the Jews at Jerusalem bind the man who owns this girdle and deliver him into the hands of the Gentiles'" (21:11).

Luke reports, "When we heard this, we and the people there begged him not to go up to Jerusalem" (21:12). Luke and the other delegates joined in urging Paul not to go.

Paul's reply was, "What are you doing, weeping and breaking my heart? For I am ready not only to be imprisoned but even to die at Jerusalem for the name of the Lord Jesus" (21:13).

When they saw that they could not persuade Paul, they gave up the attempt and said, "The will of the Lord be done" (21:14).

Was Paul wrong to ignore all these warnings—

warnings which had been given by the Holy Spirit? Many scholars think so. They tell us that because of Paul's headstrong refusal to listen to God's prophets, he lost at least four years of his life: two in custody in Caesarea and two in house arrest in Rome. He accomplished nothing by going to Jerusalem. His plan to bring about unity of the Jewish Christians and the gentile churches was lost in the riot that broke out. Some even suggest that he had to use all the money he brought to pay the expenses of trials and travel (which is why Luke, embarrassed, never mentions the fund!).

I find myself unconvinced by these arguments. Paul, too, was a prophet (13:1). He, too, sought the Spirit's leading. He seems to have understood that imprisonment, but not death, awaited him in Jerusalem (cf. 21:13), and he was content that it was in the will of God. It is false theology that assumes that success results from doing the will of God, while every calamity and failure indicates that God's will has not been done. Go back over the prophecies. The Christians at Tyre warned Paul not to go, but did they say that this was the revelation of God's will? Agabus said his prophecy was a revelation from God, but did he tell Paul not to go to Jerusalem? The Spirit was making known to Paul— and to his fellow Christians, to prepare them— something of what lay ahead of him. This had been going on for some time, even before Miletus (20:23). Paul apparently never felt that God's will had barred the way to Jerusalem. If Paul did not think that it was contrary to the will of God for him to go to Jerusalem, who am I to say otherwise?

*Paul in Jerusalem.* So the little group of travelers packed up and started for Jerusalem. Some of the Christians from Caesarea went along with them. (See 21:15,16.) The trip, nearly seventy miles, took at least two full days, probably three, since it was uphill much of the way.

To find a place in Jerusalem where eight Gentiles could lodge, and particularly where Paul, who was supposed to be the enemy of the Jewish Law, could find hospitality, was not easy. If the Christians in Caesarea had not made arrangements with Mnason, who knows what might have happened to this mission?

The older manuscripts are certainly right in reading, "bringing us to Mnason, a Cypriote, with whom we should lodge" (21:16). Mnason is described as "an early disciple," which probably means that he was a believer from the earliest days. Perhaps he was one of those converted on the first Pentecost.

*A Good Idea that Went Wrong.* The day after their arrival in Jerusalem, the delegation went to visit James and the elders (21:18) to deliver the offering. James, we remember, was the one who presided at the Jerusalem Conference (15:13-21). Paul set forth in detail the work that God had done through his ministry among the Gentiles. The Jerusalem leaders seem to have been pleased with this news of Paul's gentile ministry, and they glorified God (21:20).

But there was a very serious problem that had to be faced, and it is always best to bring such problems into the open. Speaking directly to Paul, they said, "There are myriads (tens of thousands)

317

among the Jews of those who have believed; they are all zealous for the law, and they have been told about you that you teach all the Jews who are among the Gentiles to forsake Moses, telling them not to circumcise their children or observe the customs" (21:20,21). This was not true, of course, and Paul had circumcised Timothy just to forestall any such mistaken notions. James indicated that it was a false report (21:24). But people get upset more easily over false rumors than they do over the truth.

The news of Paul's presence in the city would spread like wildfire. There are several indications that the church at Jerusalem at that time was largely Jewish and maintained good relations with the non-Christian Jewish community. James, we know, stood in high regard among the Jews.[3] Paul and his party would have to face the hostility not only of the Christians but also that of the Jews.

So James came up with a suggestion. There were four men who had taken on a vow. Why, we are not told. It would seem that there was a seven-day period that concluded the vow, during which time the men had certain obligations in the Temple. The details are obscure, and we are merely speculating when we try to fit them into the pattern set forth in Numbers 6.[4] James suggested that Paul act as the men's sponsor, that he appear with them in the Temple, pay the cost of their sacrificial offerings, and so demonstrate that "there is nothing in what they have been told" about him (21:24).

Paul accepted the suggestion. The next day he went to the Temple with the men, to give notice of the fulfillment of the vows, and continued to sponsor them for a week. Then the whole idea blew up. On the seventh day, Jews from Asia, probably from Ephesus, who were in Jerusalem for Pentecost, saw Paul in the Temple with some unknown persons. Earlier they had seen him in the city with Trophimus of Ephesus, whom they recognized (21:27,28). So they jumped to a conclusion, and began to scream, "Help!"

They passed the word that Paul had brought Gentiles into the Temple—for which there was a death penalty. The word spread quickly, and "all the city was aroused." They seized Paul, dragged him from the Temple, and were about to kill him. The uprising was promptly reported to the Roman tribune.[5] He took soldiers and centurions, who were stationed in the Fortress Antonia adjoining the Temple, and ran down into the area around the Temple (possibly the Court of the Gentiles).

When the mob saw the Roman soldiers, they stopped beating Paul; the tribune at once took Paul into custody, putting him in chains (21:31-33).

It was the chiliarch's responsibility to find out what was going on, who was responsible, etc. But he could make little sense of what the mob was shouting, so he ordered his soldiers to take Paul to the barracks. But the mob was so violent that Paul had to be carried, perhaps, as one scholar suggests, above the heads of the soldiers while the mob kept shouting, "Kill him!" (21:34-36).

So the prophecies of Agabus and the others were fulfilled. Paul was bound with two chains, hand and feet. The plan that James suggested had failed.

*Was Paul Wrong?* According to some scholars, Paul had no business adopting James' suggestion in the first place. He was going against his own principles. He was in fact a hypocrite. He was trying to appear to the Jews as something which both they and he knew he was not. At least, he was guilty of attempting to compromise on an issue that would bear no compromise.

Once again let us remind ourselves that Paul was not infallible. It is an error to carry over the doctrine of infallibility in Scripture to infallibility in all matters. Apostles could err and did err. Peter stands as one of the primary exhibits of this fact. Paul was no more infallible than Peter.

But Paul himself said he lived according to the principle of "all things to all men" in order to win some. To the Jews he was as one under the law, even though he was not under the law. He did these things for the sake of the gospel. Read 1 Corinthians 9:19-23. In my opinion, Paul was simply putting this rule into practice when he accepted the suggestion of James.

*Summation.* To discover the will of God is never easy. God's will is not simple. After all, He is not just dealing with me! There are other men and women in His will, and that portion of His will that includes me must be harmonious with that portion which includes you. Sometimes it may seem that God is moving me in the wrong direction.

If a microscopic Lilliputian got into a watch case, he would have difficulty understanding how the watch runs. And if he spent a long time studying the escapement, he might finally exclaim, "Oho! Here's something that doesn't belong here! It actually stops the works five times every second!" But without the escapement there could be no watch.

It's a poor illustration, I know. God's will is not just a watch that He wound up and left to run down. But maybe I've made my point.

## Footnotes

1. For these distances I am using the more familiar statute mile (5,280 ft.) rather than the more correct nautical mile (one minute of longitude or 6,080 ft.).

2. Lenski, *Acts*, p. 858.

3. Josephus, *Antiquities*, 20.9.1, §200.

4. To suggest that Luke, a Gentile, got the details all mixed up is to overlook the fact that he was present when the plan was see forth (21:13). It is safer to follow Luke here than to try to patch up a story from bits of Numbers and bits of Josephus!

5. Or chiliarch, the officer over a cohort of 1,000 men.

# Paul's Testimony to the Rioters in the Temple

In the next few episodes, Luke sets forth Paul's "defense." By letting him speak for himself, Luke gives us Paul's testimony to the rioting Jews at the Temple, to the Sanhedrin in Fortress Antonia— both of these in Jerusalem—and then in Caesarea to Felix, to Festus and to Agrippa.

*Paul Requests Permission to Speak to the Crowd.* The soldiers had managed to get Paul safely to the top of the stairs that led from the Temple court to Fortress Antonia.[1] They actually had to carry him, to keep the mob from seizing him (Acts 21:35), but now Paul was standing on his feet. Suddenly he said to the chiliarch, "May I say something to you?"

The chiliarch was surprised that Paul spoke Greek. He had already concluded that he had apprehended a dangerous Egyptian revolutionary (21:38)[2] Paul said, "I am a Jew, from Tarsus in Cilicia, a citizen of no mean city; I beg you, let me speak to the people" (21:39).

Is this scene credible? Would a Roman chiliarch, faced with a riot, permit the apparent instigator to speak to the crowd? Stranger things have happened! With Paul at the entrance to the barracks and plenty of soldiers within call, I suppose the chiliarch thought he had everything under control. Perhaps Paul's sudden request, in good Greek, caught him off guard, but we do not even need to make that assumption. The chiliarch was in need of a few facts before he could bring any charges against Paul. This might provide the facts he needed. So he gave Paul permission to speak.

Paul managed to quiet the people by motioning with his hand, and then he began to speak—in Hebrew.[3]

*Paul's Defense Before the People.* Paul's opening words in Hebrew caused the crowd to be even more quiet. Rabbis are learned men and usually excellent speakers, and the Jewish people have always admired these qualities. They did not yet know that Paul was a rabbi (they would in a moment!), but they recognized a good speaker at once.

"I am a Jew," Paul told them, "born at Tarsus in Cilicia, but brought up in this city at the feet of Gamaliel, educated according to the strict manner of the law of our fathers." What a beginning! He went on to tell them that he was "zealous for God" just as they were at that moment. He persecuted "this Way"—the Christians—to the death. He did all he could in Jerusalem to wipe out those who, in his opinion, were going contrary to the Law and the Temple. Then, armed with letters from the chief priests, he started for Damascus to continue his zealous work there. (See 22:4,5.)

What follows is the story of his conversion, which we have already covered in detail (Chapter 12, above). Let us keep in mind that on this occasion, Paul tells the story to what was, just a few minutes ago, a murderous mob. Is he trying to defend himself? Is he trying to set them straight about the charge that he brought Gentiles into the Temple? Or is he trying to convert them?

Perhaps there is an element of each purpose in the address. But we would have to admit that Paul said nothing about the charge that touched off the riot. And if he was trying to defend himself, he certainly "goofed" by bringing in that matter of being sent to the Gentiles.

It seems to me that he is trying to set forth the basic fact that Jesus is Lord of all men and has offered salvation to all, to Jew and Gentile alike.

Jesus was, as they all knew, a Jew. Paul was a Jew. Ananias, who baptized Paul, was a Jew, "a devout man according to the law, well spoken of by all the Jews who lived in Damascus." It was the will of the God of their fathers—the God of the Jews— that Paul should be a witness to all men of what he had seen and heard (22:8-16). Paul didn't add, but it was certainly true, that this was the original purpose of Israel, to be a light to the Gentiles.

Then Paul told of his vision in the Temple. He was warned that his life was in danger. "They will not accept your testimony about me," God told Paul. But Paul argued with God. Certainly they would remember that he had tried to destroy the young church. They would remember that he stood there, assenting, as they stoned Stephen to death (22:17-20).

Why did Paul put this in his speech? Was he trying to point out that the Jews had stubbornly refused to listen to God's messengers? Was he hinting that because they had failed in their mission, that mission was being given to Gentiles? Certainly the prophets had said such things centuries earlier! Certainly Jesus had made the same charge!

At that moment, when Paul was trying to convince God that he should continue to witness to his own people, God said, "Depart; for I will send you far away to the Gentiles" (22:21).

*Paul Reveals His Roman Citizenship.* When Paul mentioned the word "Gentiles," the audience once again became a mob. They "cried out and waved their garments and threw dust into the air." And they began to scream that Paul should be put to death (22:22,23).

The chiliarch, who a moment earlier thought everything was under control, suddenly had a new crisis on his hands. So he acted at once. He ordered his soldiers to take Paul into the barracks and examine him "by scourging" (22:24).

The ordeal of scourging was cruel. The prisoner's clothing was removed, except for his loincloth, and he was bound over a short pillar, so that his wrists and ankles were tied to the base of the pillar or to rings set in the pavement, and his bare back was at a convenient height for the beating. He was unable to move. The scourge was a short-handled whip of thongs, usually with bits of metal or bone imbedded in the leather thongs.⁵ After a few blows, the prisoner's back would become a mass of raw, bleeding flesh.

When they had bound Paul to the pillar, he said to the centurion, "Is it lawful for you to scourge a man who is a Roman citizen, and uncondemned?" (22:25). Now, Paul knew the answer to that question! So did the centurion. So did every Roman citizen. Scourging was reserved for slaves and non-Romans. The centurion went immediately to the chiliarch and said, "What are you about to do? This man is a Roman citizen!" (22:26). The tribune came in at once and said to Paul, "Tell me, are you a Roman citizen?"

Paul said, "Yes," he was a citizen. The chiliarch, somewhat amazed by this new factor, and possibly wondering how such a rabble-rouser could have obtained citizenship, said, "I bought this citizenship for a large sum" (22:28).

Paul replied simply, "But I was born a citizen" (22:28). That was the highest kind of citizenship.

Luke goes on to say, "So those who were about to examine him withdrew from him instantly; and the tribune also was afraid, for he realized that Paul was a Roman citizen and that he had bound him" (22:29).

*Summation.* To "suffer for righteousness' sake" is one thing. To allow yourself to become an object of ridicule when it serves no good purpose is something quite other. To be beaten for a crime committed is not the same as to be beaten by mistake when you are innocent. What could Paul possibly have gained for his Master by remaining silent?

But there is also another side to this question. To remain silent and permit the chiliarch to scourge a Roman citizen would have been to put the chiliarch's life in jeopardy, for the chiliarch would have been put to death for such an act. By revealing his citizenship, Paul was not only saving his own hide, and perhaps his life—for scourging sometimes resulted in death—he was protecting the chiliarch as well.

# Footnotes

1. Or Tower of Antonia. See Josephus, *Antiquities* 15.11.4 §§403-409, 18.4.3 §§90-95, *Jewish War* 5.5.8 §§238-247.

2. Luke's facts differ from those set forth by Josephus (*Jewish War* 2.13 §§261-263). But Josephus is notoriously bad in his figures. I refuse to accept the view that Luke has garbled Josephus here.

3. It is generally agreed that "Hebrew" means "Aramaic" in Acts. On the other hand, we now know, from the Dead Sea Scrolls, that Hebrew was in common use

4. Lenski's treatment here, I think, is excellent; cf. *Acts*, pp. 896-914

5. "Scourging," *Interpreter's Dictionary of the Bible*, 4:245 f.

# Paul's Testimony to the Sanhedrin

A chiliarch would have had no authority in a civil case; it was therefore necessary for Claudius Lysias to send the Roman citizen Paul to the procurator (or governor). Along with the prisoner he had to send a written statement giving the details of the case. At the moment, however, the chiliarch had nothing to write. So he summoned the Jewish council, the Sanhedrin, to come to Fortress Antonia, "desiring to know the real reason why the Jews accused" Paul (22:30).

The inquiry, it seems, was not held in the regular meeting place of the Sanhedrin, the Hall of Hewn

Stones on the south side of the great court.[1] It was held on the lower floor of the Fortress Antonia. Claudius Lysias brought Paul "down" to the session (22:30). When the Sanhedrin erupted into a quarrel between the Pharisees and the Sadducees, the chiliarch (who had perhaps withdrawn from the session to the upper floor) "commanded the soldiers to go down and take him [Paul] by force" (23:10).

*Paul's "Defense" before the Sanhedrin.* Since it was not a trial, this is not truly a "defense." Paul was given an opportunity to tell his story in order that the council could put together—for the chiliarch—some kind of formal charge.

Paul's first sentence was, "Brethren, I have lived before God in all good conscience up to this day" (23:1). This didn't suit Ananias the high priest, who ordered those near Paul to strike him on the mouth (23:2). Ananias was high priest from A.D. 47 to 58 or 59, and a disgrace to the office. He was greedy, he made use of violence to gain his ends; finally he was called to Rome to face charges of complicity.[2] His action with reference to Paul was completely indefensible, but it was in keeping with what we know of his character.

Paul retorted at once, "God shall strike you, you whitewashed wall! Are you sitting to judge me according to the law, and yet contrary to the law you order me to be struck?" (23:3).

Such language would be outrageous in a courtroom, and almost blasphemous in the Sanhedrin. If this had been a trial, Paul could have been punished without further ado.

Some of those present said, "Would you revile

God's high priest?" Paul replied, "I did not know, brethren, that he was the high priest; for it is written, 'You shall not speak evil of a ruler of your people'" (23:4,5).

How can we explain this scene? If it had been an official meeting, Ananias would have been sitting in the center of a semicircle, and the priests would have been formally attired. Paul, who was no stranger to the Sanhedrin in his younger days, would certainly have recognized the high priest, even if he had never seen this particular person. Or did Paul have such poor eyesight that he didn't see who had spoken? Or was he speaking with bitter irony: "You didn't talk like a high priest; how did I know you were?" All of these answers had been given. For myself, I am satisfied with the explanation that it was an informal session, and that Paul did not know that it was the high priest. His apology was genuine.

It is possible that Claudius Lysias had not told Paul that he was going to stand before the Sanhedrin, and that Paul did not know until this moment that it was the Sanhedrin. If so, that might explain his next move.

There was obviously no hope of getting any kind of favorable hearing from the Sanhedrin. But possibly he could divide the Sanhedrin, so that Claudius Lysias would have no unanimous charge to send to the governor. Paul therefore made a statement that was designed to set the Sadducees against the Pharisees: "Brethren, I am a Pharisee, a son of Pharisees; with respect to the hope and the resurrection of the dead I am on trial" (23:6).

The Sadducees did not believe in resurrection, persistence of the soul after death, or rewards and punishments in an afterlife.[3] The Pharisees did believe in these doctrines. So "a dissension arose between the Pharisees and the Sadducees; and the assembly was divided" (23:7). This dissension soon became a bitter argument, and the chiliarch feared that Paul would be "torn in pieces" by the new mob. So he ordered the soldiers to go down, take Paul by force from the council members, and bring him to the barracks (23:10).

The entire scene has caused scholars all sorts of difficulties. Even allowing for the probability that Luke has omitted much of what happened, there is no apparent sense in Paul's statement. He was charged with bringing Gentiles into the Temple, not with being a Pharisee or believing in the resurrection. Why did he bring resurrection into the argument?

Lenski, I think, has gotten to the heart of the matter.[4] Luke indicates a time lapse between verse 5 and verse 6. During this period, something had happened which led to dissension in the Sanhedrin. The discussion had become so loud that Paul had to shout to be heard (23:6). The discussion involved some points of difference between the Sadducees and the Pharisees, and Paul took the occasion to put himself on the side of the Pharisees—which won some of them to his side (23:9).

Was Paul on trial because of his hope of the resurrection?[5] Ultimately, this was true. Paul was on trial because he was obedient to the command of Jesus. Jesus could only be alive by resurrection. If

331

Paul had rejected the idea of the resurrection of the dead, he would as a matter of course have had to reject the resurrection of Jesus and with it the possibility that Jesus was able to give him authoritative and divine commands.

Further, Paul looked forward to his own resurrection because of what Jesus had done for him and in him. He did what he did because he was striving toward that goal. So his statement is essentially true. But while he had certainly thought this through for himself (when writing his letters to the Thessalonians, his great fifteenth chapter of First Corinthians, and many theological statements in Romans, Galatians, and Second Corinthians) he hardly expected his audience on this occasion to grasp the deeper implications of what he said. I think he was attempting to do what he succeeded in doing: split the Sanhedrin into dissenting groups.

After it was over, I suppose Paul might have asked himself, "What will happen next?" God met him in that hour of need. Luke reports, "The following night the Lord stood by him and said, 'Take courage, for as you have testified about me at Jerusalem, so you must bear witness also at Rome'" (23:11).

*The Plot Against Paul's Life.* The next day about forty Jews bound themselves with an oath not to eat or drink until they had killed Paul (23:12,13). They went to members of the Sanhedrin and set forth their plan. The Sanhedrin was to ask the chiliarch for another session with Paul, so they could give further consideration to his case and come to a conclusion. The session was to be held in the council chamber, apparently, for the plotters planned to ambush Paul and his guards and put Paul to death (23:14,15).

This dastardly plot seems incredible to some. However, it is exactly the kind of thing that Ananias was charged with before and it is in keeping with his character as described by Josephus.

Providentially, Paul's sister had a son who either was in close contact with the Sanhedrin or had sources of information about what was going on. He also was able to get into Fortress Antonia and tell Paul about the plot (23:16). Paul called a centurion and asked him to take the young man to the chiliarch. Claudius Lysias, in a kindly way, elicited the story from the young man (23:17-21).

The chiliarch acted at once. He called two centurions, and ordered them to get ready their centuries (200 soldiers), 200 spearmen, along with 70 horsemen and mounts for Paul, and to be ready to leave at 9 P.M.[6] for a forced march to Antipatris. He was going to get Paul into the hands of Felix the governor in Caesarea and out of his own!

Scholars object to Luke's account on the basis that the force is much too large for the task, which was to get one man safely to Caesarea. But Claudius Lysias had just had three occasions—one with the mob in the Temple, one with the mob in Fortress Antonia, and one with the Sanhedrin—that threatened to turn into a large-scale riot, and he was now faced with an assassination plot. Moreover, during the procuratorship of Felix, the situation in Judea was bad. The country was filled with robbers and impostors, and there was threat of sedition.[7] The slightest spark could set off a tremendous explosion. Claudius Lysias was taking no chances!

Scholars also tell us that it was "impossible" for a force to travel to Antipatris (about 40 miles) and back in a night and a day. That is true. Footmen move about three-and-a-half miles an hour. But Luke does not say they went down and back. He means simply that they started back to Jerusalem the next day. In other words, the trip to Antipatris took them all night. The following day, apparently without sleep, the foot-soldiers began the return march. The cavalry and perhaps the spearmen continued on to Caesarea. To any one who has traveled with infantry and cavalry this is not incredible!

Claudius Lysias sent a letter with Paul which Luke gives in full (23:26-30). It is either a verbatim copy or a close reconstruction, for it bears marks of authenticity. Its statement is not completely true. The chiliarch admits nothing that would put him in a bad light. But, as Macgregor says, "the letter is exactly what we might expect to be sent to a superior by a subordinate who wished to place his own conduct in the best possible light."[8]

We note that Lysias makes no charges against Paul: "I found that he was accused about questions of their law, but charged with nothing deserving death or imprisonment" (23:29). The reasons given for sending Paul to Felix were, first, the plot, and then the opportunity for the accusers to state to Felix their claim (23:30).

Felix read the letter and asked Paul what province he was from, in order to determine who would have jurisdiction in the case. Since Paul was from Cilicia, and since Cilicia and Judea were both technically under the proconsul of Syria, Felix could act as deputy of the proconsul in this matter. "I will hear you," he told Paul, "when your accusers arrive." So Paul was placed under guard in Herod's Praetorium (23:34,35).

*Summation.* Paul's "defense" so far leaves us wondering just what he is trying to prove. To me it seems obvious that he is not really trying to defend himself, even though he can justify every act with his own conscience. Nor is he really trying to preach the gospel to his audience. A comparison with his recorded sermons will quickly show that Paul was not preaching to the crowd in the Temple or to the Sanhedrin. He was witnessing—but for what purpose?

In a sense, he was really pronouncing a final judgment on his own nation. He had in effect pronounced the judgment of God on the Jewish nation when he testified that God had ordered him out of Jerusalem to go to the Gentiles (22:21). Setting Pharisee against Sadducee on a basic point of doctrine, he had taken his stand with the Pharisees on that point. He had declared that his hope was not in any change of heart on the part of his people, but in the Resurrection. If God's kingdom is to come on earth, it will come not through the works of Israel but by the coming of Christ and those who come with Him. This judgment on the Nation will be more clearly stated in Rome (28:26-28). It had already been spelled out in his letter to the Romans.

In Pisidian Antioch on his first mission, Paul had

begun to pronounce this judgment when he said, "We turn to the Gentiles" (13:46). Now he is in the final stage of that judgment. He is shaking off the dust of his feet as a witness against Jerusalem.

We know that he did not do so without a breaking heart (Rom. 9:3; 10:1)!

## Footnotes

1. Mishnah, *Middoth* 5.4.
2. Cf. Josephus, *Antiquities* 20.5.2 §103, 6.2 §131, 9.2,4 §§205-207,213, *Jewish War* 2.17.9 §§441 f.
3. Josephus, *Jewish War* 2.8.14 §§162-165, *Antiquities* 18.1.4 §16.
4. Lenski, *Acts*, pp. 930-936.
5. Luke's expression, "with respect to the hope and the resurrection of the dead," must be viewed as hendiadys for "the hope of the resurrection. . . ."
6. According to the Roman system, night began at sundown, hence the third hour at that time of year (May or early June), would have been about 9:30 P.M., according to *Beginnings of Christianty* 4:293. By my reckoning, if the first hour was from 6:30 to 7:30, the third hour was from 8:30 to 9:30.
7. Josephus, *Antiquities* 20:8.5-10 §§160-188.
8. *Interpreter's Bible*, 9:304.

CHAPTER 31 / (Acts 24:1-23)

# Paul's Hearing Before Felix

Antonius Felix was procurator (governor) of Judea from c.52 to c.59.[1] He was the brother of Pallas, an influential Roman who may have been instrumental in getting the appointment for Felix, and was able to keep him in office when he was accused of treachery by the Jews.[2] According to Suetonius,[3] Felix was married to three queens, one the daughter of Juba II king of Mauretania, another the daughter of Agrippa I, both of them named Drusilla; the third is not known. The procuratorship of Felix in Judea was stormy, with uprisings, assassinations, and attempted revolts. Tacitus is responsible for the famous description of Felix, "he exercised the power of a king with the mind of a slave."[4] Finally Felix was recalled to Rome by Nero.

It was Paul's lot to have his case heard by this man.

*The Accusation Before Felix.* Five days later, Ananias and some elders came down from Jerusalem to present their case to Felix. They had with them a Roman counsel named Tertullus. The fact that he spoke in the first person ("we") does not necessarily imply that he was a Jew; any good spokesman would identify himself with those he represented. Paul was called, and Tertullus made the accusation. According to Roman law, accused and accusers must meet face to face.

The first part of the speech is the *captatio benevolentiae*, which could be translated as "soft soap." It was commonly used by orators to get a favorable hearing. Actually, Tertullus didn't have much good that he could say about Felix, as the historical records show, but he made the best of it: "Since through you we enjoy much peace, and since by your provision, most excellent Felix, reforms are introduced on behalf of this nation. . . ." (We look in vain for the reforms!) "But I don't want to take up your time with such well-known kindnesses, so I'll be brief." (See 24:4.) Lenski observes, "It took a skillful rhetor to make this expert turn."[5]

Then Tertullus made the charges against Paul. He was "a pestilent fellow, an agitator among all the Jews throughout the world, and a ringleader of the sect of the Nazarenes" (24:5). So much for Paul's general character. Now, specifically, "he even tried to profane the temple, but we seized him"

(24:6). Tertullus summarized his case with these words, "By examining him yourself you will be able to learn from him about everything of which we accuse him" (24:8).⁶

It isn't much of a case, and yet it does hint at serious charges. Paul is a "pest" who causes disturbances everywhere he goes. Luke has already given us examples of the kind of "trouble" that Paul caused, and has given us the official reactions in Corinth and Ephesus. Felix undoubtedly had not heard of those decisions. On the other hand, Paul could not be tried before Felix for disturbances caused in other provinces. The charge that Paul was "a ringleader of the sect of the Nazarenes" seems vague. If the Christians had not recently caused trouble in Judea—and they seem to have been held in high respect at that time, particularly James— how would this charge impress Felix?

The most serious charge had to do with the Temple. As we know, for a Gentile to pass beyond the Court of the Gentiles was a capital offense. If Paul had caused the law to be violated, he was in serious trouble. But Tertullus does not charge him with profaning, he merely says that Paul "tried to profane" the Temple, but was prevented by the fact that "we seized him." This suggests that the Temple guards had acted.

The Jews attested that the charges were accurately presented (24:9).

*Paul's Reply to the Charge.* Paul also begins with the expected words of good will: "Realizing that for many years you have been judge over this nation, I cheerfully make my defense" (24:10). The particular ramifications of a quarrel among Jews can only be understood by one who has lived among Jews, hence the five or six years that Felix had been procurator, plus a few additional years when he served in Samaria under Cumanus,⁷ would help him understand Paul's defense.

Paul's first argument is that he was in Jerusalem no more than twelve days. The sentence structure is difficult; I suggest "It wasn't more than twelve days after I had gone up to Jerusalem to worship."

"They did not find me disputing with any one or stirring up a crowd," says Paul, "either in the Temple, or in the synagogues, or in the city." Paul adds pointedly, "Neither can they prove to you what they now bring up against me" (24:12,13). This is a blunt denial of all charges dealing with Jerusalem. What happened in other parts of the empire ("throughout the world") was not in the jurisdiction of Felix, so Paul refrained from commenting on that charge. In an actual trial it would of course be necessary to substantiate all charges in order to gain a conviction. This was only a preliminary hearing.

Turning to the matter of his relationship with the Christians, Paul says, "I admit to you, that according to the Way, which they call a sect, I worship the God of our fathers, believing everything laid down by the law or written in the prophets" (24:14). Belonging to a sect of the Jews was not a crime. Josephus calls both the Pharisees and the Sadducees "sects." The Christians worshiped the God of the Jews and held sacred the Scriptures (the Law and the Prophets) of the Jews. They were therefore considered to be a sect of the Jews.

Then Paul once again brought up the matter of hope in a resurrection (24:15), but this time he made it the basis of his "pains to have a clear conscience toward God and toward men" (24:16). In other words, it was because Paul believed in the resurrection "of both the just and the unjust," to be followed by God's judgment, that he wanted to be found blameless.

His reason for being in Jerusalem was "to bring to my nation alms and offerings" (24:17). Paul does not distinguish the Christian Jews from the rest of "my nation." The Christian Jews believed they were God's Israel, who had received the salvation which the Messiah brought. They kept the Law as good Jews. Paul never disputed that. His only quarrel was with Jews who tried to impose the Law on Gentiles.

Now as to the "disturbance." Paul says "they found me in the temple, without any crowd or tumult" (24:18). Some criticize Paul for implying that he was bringing the alms and offerings to the Temple, when as a matter of fact he had turned them over to James for the Christian community. Lenski is of the opinion that the cause of the confusion is a mistranslation. Instead of "whereupon" (*KJV*) or "amidst which" (*RV*)—or, we would now add, "as I was doing this" (*RSV*)—Lenski has "in connection with which."[8] It was in connection with his effort to conciliate the Jewish and gentile Christians (though he didn't say it this way to Felix, of course), that he was in the Temple.

Paul then points out that those who were present when this "disturbance" occurred, Jews from Asia who started it all by screaming that he had brought Gentiles into the Temple, "ought to be here before you and make an accusation, if they have anything against me." Or, since they may already have returned to Asia, "let these men themselves say what wrongdoing they found when I stood before the council" (24:18-21).

With these words, Paul turns to the subject that touched off the "disturbance" in the Sanhedrin itself. "I cried out while standing among them, 'With respect to the resurrection of the dead I am on trial before you this day'" (24:21). And by inserting this detail, Paul put the argument back into the area of theology—which, as he knew from experience, a Roman judge would refuse to handle.

*Felix's Reaction.* The Roman governor knew something about Christianity, quite likely from his Jewish wife Drusilla. He knew that differences between Christian and non-Christian Jews were not fit matters for judicial decision in a Roman court. But Felix did not want to hand down a decision that would anger the Jewish Sanhedrin. He already had been through bitter experiences with these Jews. So he "put them off," with the plausible excuse that "when Lysias the tribune comes down, I will decide your case" (24:22).

Paul was placed in custody. He was not a prisoner, and was not put in prison. He was simply being held for trial, with the proviso that he "should have some liberty, and that none of his friends should be prevented from attending to his needs" (24:23). Luke does not tell us whether Claudius Lysias ever appeared in the case (although he must have visited the procurator on occasion), and there is no indication that Felix ever again took up the Sanhedrin's charges agaist Paul. But Felix was not finished with Paul.

*Paul's Testimony to Governor Felix.* Drusilla, youngest daughter of Herod Agrippa I (cf. Acts 12), had been married at fifteen to Azizus the king of Emesa (modern Homs) in Syria. Not long afterwards, Felix saw her and fell in love with her, "for," says Josephus, "she did exceed all other women in beauty." With the help of a Cypriote Jewish magician, Felix persuaded Drusilla to leave Azizus and become his wife.[9]

It is generally assumed that Drusilla was anxious to hear Paul, about whom her people were saying so many things. At any rate, Felix sent for Paul "and heard him speak upon faith in Christ Jesus" (24:24).

Luke doesn't tell us what Paul said. We probably can reconstruct the main lines from the recorded messages of Paul in Acts. Certainly he spoke about Jesus. Perhaps he talked about the times of ignorance, and God's overlooking the sins of Gentiles—but this would not go on forever, for God had appointed a Judge for all men. He did go on to argue "about justice and self-control and future judgment." To a man notable for political corruption and marriage intrigues, the subject of justice and self-control, plus remarks about a future judgment, were quite relevant. Luke reports, "Felix was alarmed and said, 'Go away for the present; when I have an opportunity I will summon you'" (24:25).

Felix did send for Paul—often (24:26). Luke also

records that Felix "hoped that money would be given him by Paul" and indicates that this was the reason for sending for him so often (24:26). It was a serious breach of Roman law for any official to take a bribe, but it was done. Josephus tells about Albinus, who succeeded Festus (who succeeded Felix), and his common practice of accepting bribes, so that "the only persons left in jail as malefactors were those who failed to pay the price."[10] We can readily believe that Felix was given to the same practice.

*Summation.* Two years went by, and Paul continued in prison. Felix was succeeded by Porcius Festus (24:27), for the complaints of the Jews had become so great that Nero was forced to recall Felix, and only the influence of his brother Pallas kept Felix from punishment.[11] Felix could have released Paul, since his accusers had apparently failed to put forth any evidence to support their charges, but "desiring to do the Jews a favor, Felix left Paul in prison" (24:27).

These must have been trying years for Paul. Luke, we believe, spent the time collecting material for his two books. Possibly he produced the first draft of his Gospel during this period, and he may have put together the "travel document" (the "we-sections") and roughed out the first part of Acts. He had access to his sources and time to do the work.

But what of Paul? There is no indication that any of his writings came from this period. Luke tells us of no evangelistic efforts. There is not even a hint that Paul sent out any of his co-workers to continue the work. Was he ill? Was he so discouraged that he had no heart for the work? Did he accomplish a work that Luke omits because it adds nothing to the story? We do not know. He had already learned that God's grace is sufficient (2 Cor. 12:9), and God had promised that he would bear witness in Rome (Acts 23:11). He was learning, in whatsoever state God placed him, to be content.

## Footnotes

1. Some scholars put the dates at 53 and 60, cf. "Felix," *Interpreter's Dictionary of the Bible*, 2:264.

2. Josephus, *Antiquities* 20.8.9 §182.

3. Suetonius, *Claudius* 28.

4. Tacitus, *Histories* 5.9.

5. Lenski, *Acts*, p. 956.

6. Verse 7 has no support in the ancient manuscripts, and, in my opinion, it would have been in very poor taste for the accusers to make such a charge against the Roman chiliarch.

7. This takes into account Tacitus, *Annals* 12.54.

8. Lenski, *Acts*, p. 969.

9. Josephus, *Antiquities* 20.7.2 §§142f.

10. Josephus, *Jewish War* 2.14.1 §273.

11. Josephus, *Antiquities* 20.8.9 §182.

# Paul's Hearing Before Festus

Felix was recalled to Rome in disgrace, probably in the year 59.[1] He was succeeded by Porcius Festus (Acts 24:27), who seems to have been a better administrator than Felix. According to Josephus, "When Festus arrived in Judaea, it happened that Judaea was being devastated by the brigands, for the villages one and all were being set on fire and plundered." Festus moved promptly to clean up this situation.[2] In the same way, according to Luke, he handled the charges against Paul which had been left undecided by Felix.

*Paul Before Festus.* Three days after he arrived

in Caesarea to assume the office of procurator, he went up to Jerusalem. The chief priests and "the principal men of the Jews" were apparently waiting for the new governor, and they "informed him against Paul" (25:1,2).

Specifically, they asked "as a favor" to have Paul sent to Jerusalem, and Luke adds that they planned an ambush in order to kill him as he traveled to that city (25:3). We can imagine how Paul must have occupied their thoughts and plans for two years, for they were ready with a definite plot to kill him. Festus, who certainly knew nothing of the plot, but who recognized a highly irregular procedure, "replied that Paul was being kept at Caesarea, and that he himself intended to go there shortly" (25:4). He suggested that some "men of authority" should go to Caesarea with him, "and if there is anything wrong about the man, let them accuse him" (25:5).

After eight or ten days, Festus returned to Caesarea, and a delegation from the Sanhedrin also made the journey. The following day—which would be no more than two weeks after Festus had taken office—"he took his seat on the tribunal and ordered Paul to be brought" (25:6).

The Jews made "many serious charges" against Paul, but evidently they had no witnesses to support them. Paul was given opportunity to answer, and from his reply we can get a good idea of what the charges were: "Neither against the law of the Jews, not against the temple, nor against Caesar have I offended at all" (25:8). It would seem that the Jews had repeated the previous charges, that

347

Paul was a troublemaker among the Jews and that he had tried to profane the Temple. It would also seem that they had added a new charge, something that had to do with the emperor. Or possibly, as Lenski suggests,[2] Paul brought up this subject in order to underscore the fact that he had not been charged with and was not guilty of any crime against Caesar.

The case should have been dismissed then and there. Charges had been made but not proven. The defendant had categorically denied the charges. In the absence of proof he should have been declared not guilty and set free. But Festus wanted to do the Jews a favor.

Unless we have steeped ourselves in the history of the Jews from the days of the Maccabees to the First Revolt, we probably cannot understand how a Roman governor could set aside justice in order to placate the people. In the days of the Maccabees, zealous Jews had defeated a powerful gentile ruler. The Romans knew this. Rome was well aware of the fact that the Jewish people had to be handled in a special way. A Roman procurator, such as Pontius Pilate or Antonius Felix or Porcius Festus, knew when he took over his post in Judea that he was sitting on a "powder keg."

Pilate bent Roman justice, in the case of Jesus, rather than antagonize the Jews. Felix did the same, in the case of Paul. Josephus, who was a Jew but also a loyal Roman, records that other governors did the same thing in other cases. Festus had just taken office. He "had to live with these people." He certainly didn't want to get off to a bad start!

So Festus made a proposition to Paul. "Do you wish to go up to Jerusalem, and there be tried on these charges before me?" (25:9). What Festus had in mind is hard to understand.

Paul, however, refused point blank to have any change of venue. "I am standing before Caesar's tribunal, where I ought to be tried; to the Jews I have done no wrong, as you know very well. If then I am a wrongdoer, and have committed anything for which I deserve to die, I do not seek to escape death; but if there is nothing in their charges against me, no one can give me up to them" (25:10,11).

That's the governor Paul is talking to! We wouldn't talk like that even to a traffic cop! But Paul knew his rights as a Roman citizen. Moreover, he was obviously tired of waiting. So Paul took the case out of the governor's hands.

*Paul Appeals to Caesar.* A Roman citizen, since the adoption of the Valerian Law of 509 B.C., had the right of appeal. This right was somewhat altered in the five-and-a-half centuries since the law was adopted. For one thing, it now applied to Roman citizens anywhere, and not just to those in Rome. Basically, the law gave a citizen the right to take his case directly to the emperor. After an unfavorable verdict, all he had to do was to pronounce the solemn words, "*Ad Caesarem provoco*" (or, as sometimes given, "*Caesarem appello*"),' "I appeal to Caesar."

Without giving Festus a chance to reply to his bold statement of his rights, Paul proceeded to utter the words, "I appeal to Caesar!"

The effect of the appeal was to stay all action on

the case. From the moment the appeal was made, only Caesar could act on that case. The defendant and a complete report of the case had to be transmitted promptly to Rome.

Festus conferred with his council. This does not mean the Sanhedrin, for they had no authority in such a matter. Festus as procurator had a council of advisers who were familiar with the technicalities of Roman law. Possibly he simply asked them, "Is this appeal in order?," or even, "Is this man a Roman citizen?" Obviously receiving a favorable reply, Festus then pronounced the words that officially acknowledged receipt of the appeal: "You have appealed to Caesar; to Caesar you shall go" (25:12).

But before Paul could make the long journey to Rome he had one more opportunity to present his case publicly.

*Agrippa and Bernice Visit Festus.* It was proper for the Jewish "king" to pay a courtesy call on the new procurator. The office of "king" was one of the elements in the Roman accommodation to the Jewish people. The province of Cilicia-and-Syria-and-Palestine was technically under the proconsul of Syria. Palestine, however, was handled in a special way. Herod the Great had been recognized as "king" of Judea by the Roman Senate (40 B.C.). Ever since that time some member of the Herodian family was always a recognized ruler (a "king," or an "ethnarch" or "tetrarch"), even in the periods of procuratorship.

Herod Agrippa II was the present "king," having received his title from emperor Claudius and his expanded territory from Nero. He ruled over the areas once under Philip and Lysanias (cf. Luke 3:1) plus parts of Galilee, and he had located his capital at Caesarea Philippi, on the slopes of Mount Hermon. In honor of Nero he had changed the name of the capital to Neronias. In the Jewish War, Agrippa, who had tried to prevent the war, gave his loyalty to Rome.

Herod Agrippa II, following custom, went to Caesarea to pay his respects to Festus. He took with him his sister Bernice, who also fulfilled the duties of queen. Bernice, a sister of Drusilla (the wife of Felix), had a very shady record. Her life with her brother followed marriages to Marcus, the son of Alexander, and to Herod of Chalcis (who was her uncle). Because of the scandal of an incestuous relationship with Festus, Bernice persuaded Polemo, king of Cilicia, to marry her, but she was soon back with Agrippa. Later she lived with Titus, the son of emperor Vespasian. Because of her bad reputation among the Roman people, Titus was prevented from marrying her, and finally sent her from Rome, possibly when he became emperor.[5] Yet she was very "religious," and even undertook a Nazarite vow in 66 to try to stop the mad rush of the Jews into war with Rome.

Agrippa and Bernice stayed "many days" in Caesarea. One day Festus said to Agrippa, "There is a man left prisoner by Felix." He went on to tell about Paul (25:14-21). The Sanhedrin had asked a guilty verdict; Festus had told them that according to Roman law the accuser must face the accused and the accused must have opportunity to reply;

such a hearing had been held; the accusers "brought no charge in his case of such evils as I supposed," but rather the case concerned certain points of religion, and "about one Jesus, who was dead, but whom Paul asserted to be alive." It is clear that Paul had gotten through to Festus about the resurrection of Jesus!

Then the governor got down to his specific request. He was "at a loss" how to handle such a matter, and had asked Paul if he wanted to go to Jerusalem. We note that this time Festus did not say, "to be tried before me," but "to be tried there." It is possible that Festus had thought of some way of turning Paul over to the Sanhedrin. But Paul had "appealed to be kept in custody for the decision of the emperor" (25:21).

Festus didn't express his real objective, which was to get something that he could send along to the emperor that would make a case for Paul's trial.

Agrippa, however, walked right into Festus' plan. "I should like to hear the man myself," he said.

"Tomorrow you shall hear him," replied Festus.

## Footnotes

1. The dates for Festus' procuratorship are generally given as A.D. 60-62.

2. Josephus, *Antiquities* 20.8.10 §§185,188.

3. Lenski, *Acts,* p. 988.

4. Bruce points out that *provocatio,* strictly speaking, was an appeal to the emperor (earlier it had been to the Roman people), whereas the *appellatio* was an appeal to another magistrate to veto the action taken by the one hearing the case. By Paul's time the two were practically the same, an appeal to Caesar. *Commentary on Acts,* p. 478.

5. Josephus, *Jewish War* 2.11.6 §§220f., *Antiquities* 19.5.1 §?77, 20.7.3 §§145f., Tacitus, *Histories* 2.2, Suetonius, *Titus* 7.1,2, Dio Cassius *Roman History* 65.15, 66.8

# Paul's Testimony to Agrippa

We come now to the most dramatic moment in the Book of Acts. What we would give for a video-tape of the event!

Let's remember that it was not a trial. Paul had appealed his case. No one could convict him or acquit him now except Caesar. Both Festus and Agrippa recognized this fact, Festus by saying, "This man is doing nothing to deserve death or imprisonment," and Agrippa by replying, "This man could have been set free if he had not appealed to Caesar" (26:31,32).

It was a spectacle, staged by Festus for the benefit of Agrippa and Bernice, and incidentally to get something specific, if possible, to write to the emperor about the case. Festus was "showing" Paul to the Jewish king and his sister-queen. So he thought —but Paul had other ideas.

*The Stage Is Set.* "On the morrow Agrippa and Bernice came with great pomp" (25:23). In America we rarely have an opportunity to see "great pomp." Even on an occasion such as the funeral of President Kennedy or President Eisenhower, with the kings and presidents and the great of the earth assembled, we saw only a somber and subdued pomp. Agrippa and Bernice certainly were arrayed in spectacular robes, with gold and silver and precious jewels in much display. (We recall that their father, Agrippa I, had been robed in some kind of silver brocade or lamé when he addressed the Sidonians, and when the sun fell on him the sight was dazzling.)[1] They were attended, certainly, by a royal retinue. Festus, likewise, was in the full-dress of a Roman procurator, and he was attended by his aides. The five chiliarchs of the five legions which were stationed in Caesarea were there, certainly in the full-dress uniform of Roman chiliarchs. In addition, the prominent men of the city were present. Festus had only a few hours to arrange it, but he succeeded (25:23).

We can imagine the procession. Rigid protocol would be observed. Entrances were made in proper sequence. The correct interval of time would precede the next entrance. Quite possibly there were the ruffles and flourishes of drums and horns. And then at long last, when every one of the grandees was in his proper place, "Paul was brought in" (25:23).

He probably didn't have a special robe for the occasion; it was likely the same one he had worn during the two years that he was held in custody and that he had worn in Ephesus and Corinth and Philippi and Lystra—perhaps even on the way to Damascus that day. He wore no gold or silver or gems. No flourish announced his entrance. If he had an attendant, it was probably Luke or perhaps Aristarchus—but there is no indication that he was attended on this occasion. He was, if we can believe the old tradition, an unimposing figure: small in size, bald-headed, and bandy-legged. Perhaps he wore a chain—although this is not certain. But he had one possession that no one esle had in that room (unless Luke or Aristarchus was present)—he had God's Spirit.

Can't you hear some of the comments? *"That's Paul?"* "He doesn't look as if he could start a riot!" "Did Festus bring us here to hear *him*?" At the moment, Paul must have seemed like the great anticlimax.

I wonder what was going on in Paul's mind. Was he looking around at all the pomp and ceremony? Was he identifying the great persons present? Was he wishing he had been able to get a new robe, to be a little better groomed, to have put on some perfume and gargled? After reading about his reactions in Athens, we know how silly these questions are! If the grandeur that was Greece had only moved him to anger because of its idolatry, this second-rate spectacle, put on for an incestuous king and queen, must have stirred up similar feelings! Or possibly Paul was simply saying to himself, "I have appealed to Caesar; at long last I am going to Rome!"

*Paul's Witness to Agrippa.* When the whispering and the tittering had quieted down, Festus made his speech.

"King Agrippa and all who are present with us, you see this man about whom the whole Jewish people petitioned me, both at Jerusalem and here, shouting that he ought not to live any longer. But I found that he had done nothing deserving death; and as he himself appealed to the emperor, I decided to send him.

"But I have nothing definite to write to my lord about him. Therefore I have brought him before you, and especially before you, King Agrippa, that, after we have examined him, I may have somthing to write. For it seems to me unreasonable, in sending a prisoner, not to indicate the charges against him" (25:24-27).

The speech is addressed particularly to Agrippa. Festus admits that Paul is not guilty. (Why didn't he acquit him, then?) Festus "decided to send him" on to Caesar, but he had "nothing definite to write" about Paul, and it seemed "unreasonable" not to indicate the charges. (It was not only unreasonable; it was illegal!) So Festus had brought Paul before Agrippa in order to have "something to write."

It was Agrippa's turn to reply. Looking at Paul, he simply said, "You have permission to speak" (26:1).

Out of the dazzling preliminaries, Paul had

grasped at least one fact. King Agrippa was the key figure. So Paul decided to speak directly to the king.

"Concerning everything of which I have been accused by Jews, King Agrippa, I consider myself fortunate that I am about to make my defense before you today, especially since you are well informed about all the customs and questions that are particularly Jewish. Therefore I pray to you to hear me patiently." (See 26:2-3.)[2]

This is apparently a genuine statement of his feelings. Paul had to speak about things that would really be understood only by those conversant with the Jewish faith. He could do this when speaking to Agrippa. At the same time he could set forth clearly his own faith as a Christian.

The address that follows is a masterpiece. Paul talks about himself, but he does it in a way that is not offensive, while at the same time he deals with the issue.

Paul was a devout Jew. Jews knew this. They knew that he had been brought up—in Jerusalem—according to the strict tenets of the Pharisees. Part of their teaching was hope, hope in the promise which God made to the patriarchs and the prophets, hope to which the twelve tribes would attain in their earnest worship. We might think that Paul is referring to the hope of the Messiah, but he has something else in mind, as we discover when he says, "For this hope I am accused by Jews, O king! Why is it thought incredible by any of you that God raises the dead?" (26:7,8).

357

Of course, this does have to do with the Messiah. The only way that Paul could have been convinced that Jesus was the Messiah was by the resurrection of Jesus. But Paul doesn't spell that out here. He had already done so in his letter to the Romans (Rom. 1:4, etc.).

Next, Paul told about his opposition to the name of Jesus of Nazareth. This took place in Jerusalem (26:10), less than twenty-five years ago, hence there must be Jews still living who remember. Then Paul poured out his soul in what must have been to him a sore confession: he shut up many of the saints (the Christians) in prison, by authority from the chief priests; he voted for them to be put to death; he punished them in every synagogue and even compelled some to blaspheme;³ finally in raging fury he persecuted them even to foreign cities (26:9-11).

No wonder Paul considered himself less than the least of all saints! To have to live with the memory of saints that you have put to death must be terrible. But there is something worse. And that is to remember that there were some whom you caused to curse the name of Jesus—those whose faith was not strong enough and you made them deny their Saviour! Paul had to remember that he had been the Great Inquisitor.

Agrippa, of course, couldn't read Paul's conscience. He only knew that this man was saying that at one time he had been even more anti-Christian than his present accusers.

Then Paul told of his experience on the way to Damascus. Suddenly the persecution of the Church was shown to Paul in a new light. Jesus, the one who was crucified, was speaking to Paul and saying, "Why are you persecuting me?" (26:14,15). And this Jesus, speaking with the authority of God Himself, told Paul, "I have appeared to you for this purpose, to appoint you to serve and bear witness to the things in which you have seen me and to those in which I will appear to you . . ." (26:16). This Jesus went on to tell Paul that He was sending him to the Gentiles, "to open their eyes, that they may turn from darkness to light and from the power of Satan to God, that they may receive forgiveness of sins and a place among those who are sanctified by faith" in Jesus (26:18).

That certainly was clear enough to Agrippa. It may have seemed incredible, but it was not contrary to anything in the Law and the Prophets.

Paul went on, "Wherefore, O King Agrippa, I was not disobedient to the heavenly vision" (26:19). He told of his preaching, first at Damascus, then at Jerusalem, and finally to the Gentiles, "that they should repent and turn to God and perform deeds worthy of their repentance" (26:20).

It was for this reason that he was seized in the Temple by Jews (throughout the speech Paul says "Jews" and not "the Jews"—a point that translations miss), and they tried to kill him.

Then Paul testified of God's care: "To this day I have had the help that comes from God, and so I stand here testifying both to small and great, saying nothing but what the prophets and Moses said would come to pass; that the Messiah must suffer, and that, by being the first to rise from the dead, he would proclaim light both to the [Jewish] people and to the Gentiles" (26:22,23).

What a magnificent speech! Not one wasted sentence! It wasn't a sermon; it was a testimony. But it had the force of a sermon. It wasn't a defense. Paul called it an "apology"; but in his day that meant something quite different from what it means today. It was a statement designed to show that you were right. By his simple testimony, Paul was showing that he was right in taking the message of salvation to the Gentiles.

*The Reactions.* Paul was speaking to Agrippa. But Festus was listening, and apparently listening rather carefully. He was looking for something to write to Nero about this strange man. So far, he hadn't gotten much he could put in that report!

Suddenly Festus shouted in a loud voice, "Paul, you're mad; your great learning is turning you mad!" (26:24).

Paul replied simply, "I'm not mad, most excellent Festus; I'm speaking the sober truth. . . . The king knows about these things . . . I'm sure that none of these things escaped his notice, for this was not done in a corner." Then, turning to Agrippa, Paul said: "King Agrippa, do you believe the prophets? I know you believe." (See 26:25-27.)

"Then Agrippa answered Paul, 'In brief, you are trying to persuade me and make a Christian of me'" (26:25 *Williams*). A variety of translations have been made of the king's rejoinder. Whatever the exact meaning, it is clear that Agrippa did not make the leap of faith. So Paul said, "whether short or long [or better, quickly and completely], I would to God

360

that not only you but also all who hear me this day might become such as I am—except for these chains" (26:29 lit. trans.).

Was Paul in chains? Could a Roman citizen, uncondemned, be bound with chains? According to Lenski, it is unthinkable. The plural form of the word used here simply means "bondage."[4] There can be no doubt that the word is often used metaphorically, when no chains can possibly be intended.

*Summation.* The king rose, and the governor, Bernice and the others—and the spectacle was over. It was a scene that should have lived long in the memory of all who were present.

Paul did not build logical arguments. He simply told the story of his life. When a man argues, you can use counterarguments. But when he simply testifies, there is no argument. God called us to be witnesses. Paul was a good witness before kings and commoners. God promised that he would also bear witness to Him in Rome.

## Footnotes

1. See Josephus, *Antiquities* 19.8.2 §344.

2. I have tried to give an exact translation, avoiding the "woodenness" of a word-for-word translation.

3. *KJV* has "compelled to blaspheme," *RSV* "tried to make them blaspheme." However, there are two imperfects in the sentence. The second is clearly iterative, hence I make the first iterative, "I repeatedly forced, I was forcing them to blaspheme."

4. Lenski, *Acts*, p.1051f.

# The Journey to Rome

The story of Paul's voyage to Rome is thrilling.[1] Luke also made the trip (the third and last of the "we-sections" in Acts) and he describes the experience as only a true artist could. Lenski calls it a "masterpiece." Bruce says it "is a small classic in its own right, as graphic a piece of descriptive writing as anything in the Bible." Macgregor says, "If the present chapter is not in its entirety an authentic firsthand narrative, then we may well despair of finding anything in Acts that we can trust."[2]

*From Caesarea to Crete.* Festus probably assumed his post as governor about the first of July,

A.D. 60. He had acted promptly on the case and somewhere around the middle of August he was ready to send Paul to Rome. The available ship, it would seem, was a coasting vessel from Adramyttium (modern Edremit), a lovely harbor some miles south of Troas. Paul and "certain other prisoners" were delivered into the custody of Julius, a centurion of the Augustan Cohort (27:1).

According to Mommsen, confirmed generally by Ramsay, the Augustan (or Imperatorial) cohort was composed of office-couriers (*frumentarii*), who "went to and fro between Rome and the armies; and were employed for numerous purposes that demanded communication between the Emperor and his armies and provinces."[3] They drew their name *frumentarii* ("pertaining to grain") from their original purpose of controlling the supply of food, but their office came to include other duties, such as conducting prisoners to Rome and even serving as agents and spies for the emperor.

Luke and Aristarchus accompanied Paul on the journey (27:2). According to Ramsay, this could only have been possible if they had accompanied Paul as his slaves, "not merely performing the duties of slaves."[4] Lenski asks, "Would Paul have stooped to such a pretense?" Rather, he thinks that Paul's "importance and standing in the eyes of the Roman authorities," illustrated by the treatment he received from Felix, from Festus, and from Julius, suffices to explain the privilege of having two companions along with him.[5]

On their second day, after a voyage of about 70 miles, they put in at Sidon, probably to load and unload cargo. The centurion allowed Paul to visit his friends "and be cared for" (27:3). The precise meaning of this statement is unknown.

At that season of the year the Etesian winds are generally westerly or northwesterly, so they sailed "under the lee" (around the eastern tip) of Cyprus. When Luke had made the voyage to Caesarea with Paul, two years earlier, they had sailed south of Cyprus (21:3). Sailing east of Cyprus, the vessel came to the coast of Cilicia, and it hugged the shore, passing Pamphylia, until they came to Myra in Lycia (21:4,5). Yachtsmen know that favorable winds and eddy currents can frequently be found near shore when you are forced to sail into the wind.

Myra, or rather its port of Andriaca—for Myra was nearly three miles up the Andracus river—was suitable for larger ships, and the grain ships of the Empire, when winds were too strong for a more direct route from Alexandria to Rome, often put in at Myra. Julius found one of these grain ships and transferred his charges to it (27:6).

From Myra the journey was slow. They reached Cnidus, the southwestern tip of Asia Minor, "with difficulty," and headed toward Crete. They sailed around Cape Salmone at the eastern end, and hugging the south shore of Crete they finally reached "Fair Havens" near Lasea (27:7,8). A very pretty bay, called today by the same name (in Greek), *Kalous Limeōnas*, is probably the place.

*The Storm.* Luke reports that "much time had been lost, and the voyage was already dangerous." "The fast," meaning the Day of Atonement, had already gone by—in 59 it fell on October 5. The sailing season was considered "dangerous" after September 14 and closed on November 11. Therefore a council was called, or so it would seem, consisting of the navigator, the ship's captain, the centurion, and Paul (27:9-11).[6]

It seems strange that a prisoner would be invited to take part in the discussion. Here, Lenski is completely right, in my opinion. If Paul had not been of such great stature, Acts would never have been written in the first place. He was a giant. Julius recognized the fact. Paul was a veteran seafarer who had survived at least three shipwrecks. I do not find it incredible that Julius sought his advice.

Paul advised passing the winter at Fair Havens. The captain and the navigator wanted to try for a harbor that offered better protection against the winter storms. The centurion was persuaded by them. So the "majority" decided to try to make for the harbor of Phoenix. The risk was admittedly great: "on the chance that somehow they could reach Phoenix" (27:12).[7]

Some days later, "the south wind blew gently," and they weighed anchor and sailed "close inshore." They had to make only about 40 miles, but suddenly the "Northeaster," a typhonic wind, blew down from Mount Ida, and the little ship, with its sails set for a gentle south wind—doubtless with all the sail they could hoist—was caught broadside. Luke says, "We gave way to it and were driven" (27:15). They were now heading out to open sea!

Under the lee of a small island called Cauda or Clauda, they "managed with difficulty to secure" the dinghy. Luke says "we," suggesting that he gave a hand tugging on the lines to haul the swamped boat aboard. Next they set about to "undergird" the ship. And then they began to think about the next danger. Along the coast of Cyrenaica in Africa were sandbanks ("Syrtis" or "quicksands"). The wind was driving them toward these banks. So "they lowered the gear." Whatever this means specifically, we know from the results what it was they did. They set the sails for a quartering wind, lowered the steering-oars into the sea, and established a course that brought them, fourteen days later, to Malta.

Conditions were getting worse every day. The seams were opening and the ship was settling deeper in the water, so they threw overboard everything they could spare. Obviously they did not jettison the anchors, the sails, or other "gear" that was used to attempt the landing at Malta. With neither sun nor stars and no visible landfalls, navigation was practically impossible. We assume that the helmsman simply kept a course with the wind on the starboard quarter. Luke describes the storm as "no small tempest," litotes for a gale. At last, "all hope of our being saved was abandoned" (27:18-20).

At that time Paul spoke up. Reminding them that he had advised against sailing from Crete—not an "I told you so!" attitude, but a word of caution against dismissing his advice again—Paul told them that "this very night" a messenger of "the God to whom I belong" had given him a message. He was to "stand before Caesar." In other words, he would arrive safely at Rome. God had also "granted" him all

366

those who sailed with him. Everyone would be saved—but the ship would "have to run on some island" (27:23-26).

*The Shipwreck.* Paul had this vision probably on the thirteenth night of the storm. On the fourteenth night about midnight, the sailors thought they heard land approaching.[8] So they sounded and found 20 fathoms. A little farther they sounded again and found 15 fathoms.[9] Now they were afraid that the ship would run on the rocks, so they dropped four anchors "from the stern," and "prayed for day to come." By dropping the anchors from the stern, they would cause the ship to turn its bow toward the shore (27:27-29).

The sailors then lowered the dinghy and said that they were going to row out with the bow anchors.[10] Such a maneuver would have been to keep the ship from turning, so that the bow would continue to head in, regardless of wind or water currents. Luke says the sailors were seeking to escape, that they had no intention of setting the bow anchors, but were going to try to make land in the small boat. (Lenski thinks that even the captain and the ship's officers were planning to abandon ship.) Paul either heard about the plot or guessed the intentions of the sailors and he told the centurion, "Unless these men stay in the ship, you cannot be saved." Only sailors knew how to bring the ship in through the surf. The soldiers "cut away the ropes of the boat [the dinghy], and let it go" (27:30-32).

Just before daybreak, Paul urged everyone to take some food. Many had eaten nothing, whether because of seasickness or the difficulty of preparing food during the terrible storm. Paul himself set the example. He took bread, gave thanks to God publicly, broke the bread and began to eat. The others did likewise. Then, to lighten the ship, they began to throw the wheat into the sea (27:33-38).

When daylight came, the sailors could see land but they did not recognize it. They cut the ropes that held the anchors (actually, the sailors were letting the ship go). At the same time they lowered the steering-oars and hoisted the foresail. The wind would drive them onto the beach, bow-end to. Unfortunately, the ship struck a sandbar, and the bow stuck, and the stern was broken by the heavy surf (27:39-41).

The first thought of the soldiers was to kill the prisoners. If a prisoner escapes, as we learned at Philippi, the guard forfeits his life. But Julius wanted to save Paul, so he forbade the killing. Instead, he ordered those who could swim to make for land, the rest to use planks or pieces of the ship." "And so it was that all escaped to land" (27:42-44).

*On the Island of Malta.* They learned that they were shipwrecked on Malta. It was cold and raining (about the middle of November), and there were 276 persons soaked to the skin, without a thing in the world but what they were wearing. "The natives," writes Luke, "showed us unusual kindness." First they built a fire.

Meanwhile Paul was helping by gathering firewood and a viper fastened itself to his hand. The Maltese, like many another people would have done, immediately concluded that this man was a criminal who had escaped one fate but whom the gods were punishing by another. Paul shook off the viper into the fire. Then when he showed no signs of dying, the people went to the other extreme and concluded that he was a god. Lenski suggests that this was God's way of turning all eyes on Paul right from the first moment on Malta (28:1-6).

Near the scene of the shipwreck was the villa of Publius, the "first man"—that was his official title—of the island. His villa must have been commodious, for he took all 276 and gave them hospitality for three days, until, we assume, other arrangements could be made to house them for the winter (28:7).

Publius' father was sick with fever and dysentery, and Paul "visited him and prayed, and putting his hands on him healed him" (28:8). Immediately the Maltese began to bring other sick. Luke uses two different words here: Paul "healed" the father of Publius, but the people of the island who were sick "were cured." He also notes that "they presented many gifts to us." Some scholars conclude—and I am inclined to agree—that two types of healing ministry are intended here: the miraculous (by Paul) and the medical (by Luke) (28:8-10).

*Summation.* It was winter and they were on Malta. No ship would leave the island until early spring. Once again Paul was forced to wait.

We can assume that he was not idle. If he healed, we can be sure he also preached. If he preached, we can believe that some were saved. Perhaps the tradition is true that Publius became the first bishop of the church of Malta. We shall only know when the books are opened and we see whose names are written in the Lamb's Book of Life. Perhaps even the names of Julius and some of those who sailed with Paul will be inscribed there.

## Footnotes

1. For the route see *Westminster Historical Atlas*, p. 98 and plate XV or *Macmillan Bible Atlas*, map 248.

2. Lenski, *Acts*, p. 1054; Bruce, *Commentary on Acts*, p. 498; *Interpreter's Bible*, 9:331.

3. Ramsay, *St. Paul the Traveller*, p. 348. Ramsay quotes from Th. Mommsen, *Sitzungsbericht der Akademie der Wissenschaften zu Berlin*, 1895, pp. 495ff.—to which I have not had access. Several other scholars have also quoted from this work.

4. Ramsay, *St. Paul the Traveller*, p. 316.

5. Lenski, *Acts*, p. 1056.

6. Lenski says the terms should be translated "chief pilot," "sailing master" and "captain" respectively. The ship was owned by the government. *Acts*, p. 1063.

7. There is disagreement over the location of Phoenix. Some scholars think it is modern Loutro; but others do not think the situation of Loutro fits Luke's description, "facing southwest and northwest" (27:12). Admittedly such a location would give little protection from the prevailing storms. I had already concluded that *katá* here must mean "against," i.e. protection against the southwest and northwest winds, when I found that Moe came to the same conclusion. Cf. Olaf Moe, *The Apostle Paul* (trans. by L. A. Vigness, 1968), p. 444.

8. This is Luke's idiom. To a person on board a ship, land appears to be approaching.

9. To "sound" is to cast a weight on a knotted line into the sea to discover the depth of the water. A fathom is the distance between the fingers of the outstretched arms, about six feet, which is the way the leadsman measures as he hauls in the line.

10. Anchors simply dropped would be of no use. It would be necessary to row out a distance, drop them, and then, as they took hold in the bottom, to snug up the lines.

11. Macgregor points out the pronoun used is generally used of persons, and suggests that "on some of those from the ship" probably meant "on the backs of some of the crew" (*Interpreter's Bible*, 9:341).

# "And So We Came to Rome"

It was about the middle of February. A ship of Alexandria named *Dioskouroi* ("Twin Brothers," Castor and Pollux) had wintered in the harbor at Malta. It was going to Rome,[1] so Julius put his prisoners aboard. Luke does not mention the others who had been on the wrecked ship.

*The Voyage from Malta to Puteoli.*[2] Mid-February was still three weeks before the opening of the sailing season,[3] but with an early winter, they may have had also an early spring. The first leg, about 95 miles, took them to Syracuse on the island of Sicily, where they spent three days (28:12). Tradition tells us that Paul founded a church there, but this is without historical or scriptural support.

From Syracuse they sailed to Rhegium (modern Reggio di Calabria), on the "toe" of Italy. Luke's description "we made a circuit"[4] probably indicates that the journey of 75 miles was made by tacking into the wind.

They waited at Rhegium for a favorable wind, which sprang up the next day. With a south wind they could not only navigate the Straits of Messina safely, but they could also make good progress to Puteoli. The journey of about 210 miles could be made in 24 or 26 hours with a south wind. On the second day they reached Puteoli, modern Pozzuoli on the northern shore of the Bay of Naples (28:13).

At Puteoli, Luke records, "we found brethren (meaning Christians), and were invited to stay with them for seven days" (28:14). It is one more of numerous indications of his regard for Paul that Julius permitted this delay. Certainly a Roman officer had to account for his time in making a journey on government business.

*"And So We Came to Rome."* From Puteoli to Rome was about 150 miles. At Capua, Julius and his charges took the Appian Way (which went from Rome to Brundisium). Word had gone ahead from the Christians in Puteoli to the Christians in Rome that Paul was on his way, and when they reached the Forum of Appius (named for Appius Claudius, who built this part of the Appian Way in 312 B.C.) they were met by a group of Christians from Rome. At Three Taverns, about 10 miles farther along the road, another group of Christians from Rome met

372

them. These "brothers" had thought nothing of walking 30 or 45 miles to welcome their beloved Paul, and when he saw them, he "thanked God and took courage" (28:15).

Traveling by the old Appian Way, the group probably entered Rome by the Porta Capena, not by the traditional Porta San Paolo or Gate of St. Paul. Julius normally would deliver his prisoners to the Praetorian Guard.⁵ The commander of the Praetorian Guard from 51 to 62 was Sextus Afranius Burrus, "an excellent man . . . very influential in young Nero's court."⁶

*Paul in Rome.*⁷ Luke twice mentions the fact that they had reached Rome (28:14,16). Ever since his days in Corinth, perhaps earlier, this had been Paul's goal. Paul was determined to see Rome (19:21). He longed to visit the Christians there in order to impart to them some spiritual gift (Rom. 1:11). At long last he was there!

Paul was no ordinary prisoner, brought to Rome to entertain the bloodthirsty crowds by fighting beasts in an arena. He was there as an uncondemned Roman who had appealed to Caesar. Therefore he was permitted to live in his own dwelling at his own expense in the custody of just one soldier (28:16,30). Moreover, he was free to have all the visitors he wanted, and to speak whatever was on his heart (28:30,31).

The first two days in Rome were probably occupied with "getting settled." On the third day (or the fourth), "he called together the local leaders of the Jews." He gave them a brief summary of the reason why he was in Rome (28:17-20). He pointed out that he "had done nothing" against the Jewish people or their customs, that he had been delivered into the hands of the Romans, who examined him and wanted to set him free, "because there was no reason for the death penalty" in his case. However, when the Jews who were responsible for handing him over to the Romans objected, he was forced to appeal to Caesar. He was careful to add that he "had no charge to bring against" his nation.

Since it was because of "the hope of Israel" that he was "bound with this chain," he wanted to talk with the Jews in Rome. They on their part were glad to have this opportunity to talk with Paul. They had "received no letter from Judea about" him, and none of the Jews returning from Jerusalem had spoken any evil about him. They did know, however, that "this sect"—the Christian church—was everywhere spoken against (28:21,22).

So they appointed a day, and the Jews came to Paul's dwelling "in great numbers." There were eleven synagogues in Rome, and perhaps as many as ten or twenty thousand Jews. As Lenski reconstructs Paul's work in Rome, this was the beginning of a great ministry among his kinsmen, the Jews. From morning till evening he set forth one Scripture after another, from Moses and from the Prophets, "testifying to the kingdom of God," and trying to show the relationship of Jesus to this kingdom (28:23).

"Some were convinced by what he said, while others disbelieved" (28:24). In Luke's careful manner of writing this seems to say that they were about evenly divided. The disbelief caused Paul to add one more Scripture before they left. He quoted the words of Isaiah 6:9,10. To our ears the words sound harsh and judgmental. As Paul spoke them, however, I believe they were more of a warning that came from a heavy heart.

Paul loved his kinsmen, the Jews. He had great sorrow and unceasing grief in his heart because they were rejecting God's gracious offer. He could wish himself accursed, separated from Christ, for their sake (Rom. 9:3). He magnified his ministry to the Gentiles to try somehow to move his fellow-countrymen to jealousy and save some of them (Rom. 11:14). His heart's desire and his prayer to God for them was that they might be saved (Rom. 10:1).

It was only about three years ago that he had written these words to Rome. Surely what he said now in Rome must have come from the same heart!

So we read the words from Isaiah, through Paul's heart and mouth, in a different light. This was a solemn warning, designed to save some. And then, "to provoke them to jealousy" he added, "This salvation of God has been sent to the Gentiles; they will listen" (Acts 28:26-28).

When Paul wrote his letter to the Romans, there was apparently no evangelistic effort among the Jews in Rome. There were Christians in Puteoli, nearly 150 miles away, but the Jews in Rome were still in ignorance about the Church. They wanted to know more about it from Paul. There had apparently been no witness to these thousands of Jews in Rome!

Some years later, probably just before the destruction of Jerusalem (A.D. 70), the Epistle to the Hebrews was addressed to the Jewish Christians in Rome. If Lenski is right, this Jewish-Christian congregation in Rome was the result of Paul's two-year stay there. If so, it must have made his heart glad, perhaps more than all of his ministry to the Gentiles.

Paul's ministry in Rome was not limited to the room where he was "imprisoned." There was a constant coming and going of his fellow-workers, with news from and messages to the churches. The church at Colossae, which had never seen Paul's face (Col. 2:1), had problems, some of them involving the doctrine of the person of Jesus Christ. Paul wrote them a letter and sent it by Tychicus (Col. 4:7). Tychicus, we assume, had come to Rome and brought Paul word about Colossae. In his letter, Paul mentions that Aristarchus and Luke were with him, as well as Mark (!), Jesus Justus, Epaphras, and Demas (Col. 4:10-14).

Onesimus, who journeyed back to Colossae with Tychicus (Col. 4:9), was a runaway slave from the household of Philemon in Colossae. Somehow he had made his way to Rome and met Paul. Paul sent him back, now converted to Christ, along with a letter to his owner (Philem. 1). Paul wrote that letter about the same time as the one to Colossae, and he mentions Timothy, Epaphras, Mark, Aristarchus, Demas, and Luke (Philem. 1,23,24).

Paul wrote another letter at that time, which we know as "Ephesians." Some scholars believe that it was a circular letter intended not only for Ephesus but for all the churches in Asia. If so, it may be the same as the letter to Laodicea that Paul mentions (Col. 4:16). The letter to Colossae set forth Jesus Christ as the head of the Church, Ephesians presents the Church as the body of Christ. Tychicus also carried this letter (Eph. 6:21). We can date all three letters about A.D. 60, or around the middle of Paul's two-year stay in Rome.

Toward the end of that time he wrote another letter. It was written to the church at Philippi, to thank them for the gifts which they had sent to him, and to clear up a few matters that were disturbing the church. Epaphroditus, a member of the church in Philippi, had brought a gift to Paul from that church, and then had been taken deathly sick in Rome (Phil. 2:25,27). News that he was seriously ill had gotten back to Philippi, and word of their concern had come back to Rome (2:26), so we have to allow several months for this exchange of messages. Timothy was with Paul when he wrote the letter (Phil. 1:1), and so were other unnamed "brethren" (Phil. 4:21). We can be certain that Luke was not there or he would have been mentioned by name. It is possible that Luke was the "true yoke-fellow" that Paul addresses (Phil. 4:3), and that he was back in Philippi. If Luke and Aristarchus had been considered as Paul's slaves, we should note that Epaphras is designated as "fellow-prisoner" in Philemon (v. 23). It is possible that Epaphras "relieved" Luke in this capacity, so Luke could return to Philippi. Of course, the expression "fellow-prisoner" could have other interpretations.

Paul, in his letter to the Philippians, speaks in a very optimistic way of his bondage in Rome. While he does not yet know definitely what the outcome will be (Phil. 1:19-24), he is convinced that he will "remain" in this life and come to see them again (1:25,26). He had already sent Epaphroditus to them (2:25), and hopes to send Timothy to them "shortly" with news of the final outcome of his appeal. In fact, he expresses the hope that he himself also will be coming shortly (2:24).

In an incidental way, Paul lets us know another part of his ministry in Rome. He was chained to one of the Praetorian Guard, but the guards were changed at regular intervals. Paul tells the Philippians, "I want you to know, brethren, that what has happened to me has really served to advance the gospel, so that it has become known throughout the whole praetorian guard and to all the rest that my imprisonment is for Christ . . ." (Phil. 1:12-14).[8] When Paul had visitors, we can be sure he was telling them about Christ. When he had no visitors, he was telling his guard about Jesus. And meanwhile, his care for all the churches continued.

*Summation.* So we come to the end of the Book of Acts. We have followed the course of the Christian witness from the very first Pentecost in Jerusalem to Paul's arrival in Rome. We have seen the growth of the Church from 120 souls in Jerusalem, to unknown thousands spread across the Roman Empire. We have seen the marvels of its ministry, both in the salvation of souls and in the healing of bodies. We have seen the ministry of the Holy Spirit in the Church.

We have also seen some of the Church's struggles. Beginning with what now seems a minor problem between Hebrews and Hellenists, we have seen the growth of the spirit of schism. We have seen how God's grace overruled, so that there was one Church and not two. Gentiles were brought into the Church as Gentiles, and were neither compelled to become Jews nor relegated to second-class citizenship.

We have seen something of the hostility of the world against the Church. At first it was simply a command not to preach or teach in the name of Jesus. But it soon became a madness that screamed, "Kill! Kill!" Men who killed thought they were serving God. Nor was this hatred limited to Jews who opposed the gospel. In gentile cities, Gentiles stoned the preachers, Gentiles brought charges against them, Gentiles complained because humanitarian deeds in the name of Christ were destroying pagan profits.

We have seen how one of those who thought he was serving God by persecuting the Church was brought by the grace of God into the very Church he had hated, to serve the very same Jesus he had persecuted. And we have traveled with this apostle as he went out, in obedience to the Lord Jesus, to tell of his salvation, to witness to men in many cities —to Jews and Gentiles, to common people who are nameless and to priests and governors and kings— to establish churches and to commission fellow-workers in those churches, until the name of Jesus was named in every part of the empire.

This is the story of how the Church began. To God be the glory!

# Footnotes

1. Ships for Rome landed their passengers at Puteoli; their cargo was transferred to small boats at Ostia at the mouth of the Tiber.

2. See *Westminster Historical Atlas* plate XV for a good map.

3. Unless we follow Pliny's statement (*Natural History* 2:47) that sailing was resumed on February 8. The authority for the commonly-accepted dates of November 11 and March 10 is Vegetius, *On Military Affairs* 4:39.

4. *KJV* "fetched a compass" is misleading to modern-day readers. The magnetic compass, of course, was not yet known in that part of the world, and the word "compass" in Elizabethan language could mean a line drawn by a compass, hence, a circuitous course.

5. *KJV* includes the statement, "the centurion delivered the prisoners to the captain of the guard," but this statement is found in no manuscript earlier than the ninth century; nevertheless, even though the evidence is very late, the truth of the statement is generally accepted.

6. Lenski, *Acts*, p. 1105.

7. For map and photos, see *Atlas of the Classical World,* map 56 and photos 349-362.

8. Moe believes that at the end of the two years Paul was transferred from his private dwelling to the barracks of the Praetorian Guard *(The Apostle Paul,* p. 480). I reject any theory that Philippians was written from Ephesus or Caesarea. The contents of Philippians just do not fit any other period of Paul's life or any other location, than the two years in Rome.

# Epilogue

We have finished our study of Acts, but someone will ask, "What happened to Paul?" Luke does not tell us. Are there other sources of information? Is it possible to reconstruct the rest of the story of Paul's life?

For one thing, we know that there was no case against Paul. Felix practically admitted as much (Acts 24:22-27), and Festus certainly did (26:31). Festus could hardly have sent a letter with Paul that would have contained a serious charge. Julius, the centurion who took Paul to Rome and who must have had to report on the prisoner's conduct, could not say anything that would have been detrimental to Paul! If the Jews in Rome had received no letters concerning Paul, we may assume that the Sanhedrin had sent no letter or a representative to present their case against Paul. (A representative by traveling overland, could have gotten there before Paul did.) Without any support of the original charges against Paul, the case would have gone by default. Roman law is clear on this point.[1]

Then there are the letters to Timothy and Titus, the "Pastoral Epistles." It is true that a very large majority of scholars reject the tradition that Paul wrote them. They claim that the language and style are not Paul's and that the ecclesiology (or doctrine of the church) in the Pastorals is much too advanced for the seventh decade of the first century. In my opinion, the arguments against Pauline authorship are not sustained. A number of modern scholars, while rejecting Pauline authorship, admit that the Pastorals contain historical material.

If we accept this material, whether written by Paul or not, we find that Paul was continuing his ministry. He visited Ephesus and Macedonia (1 Tim. 1:3), Crete (Tit. 1:5), and by inference Nicopolis (Tit. 3:12). He had left Titus in Crete, hence Titus must have been traveling with him (Tit. 1:5), and he had left Timothy in Ephesus (1 Tim. 1:3). No place in the life of Paul prior to his first Roman imprisonment has room for these events.[2]

Possibly Paul went to Spain, as he once had planned to do (Rom. 15:24). Clement, who wrote to the Corinthians from Rome in 95 or 96, records that Paul "was released from the world and went to the holy place"—i.e., he died and went to his reward—"after he had come to the boundary of the West."[3] Some take this to refer to Spain, others think it could mean Rome. The Muratonian Canon (c.120) and the apocryphal Acts of Peter (Vercellenses) (c.200) also include the tradition that Paul visited Spain.[4] According to Moe, this journey was made soon after Paul's release from Roman imprisonment, and afterwards Paul visited the regions of the eastern Mediterranean. To attempt to reconstruct his route and destination in Spain is to build a theory on a theory, and is of little worth.[5]

Second Timothy is, by its own statement, Paul's last word. From beginning to end it breathes the last breaths of one expecting to die. Paul says: "For I am already on the point of being sacrificed; the time of my departure has come. I have fought the good fight, I have finished the race, I have kept the faith. Henceforth there is laid up for me the crown of righteousness . . ." (2 Tim. 4:6-8).

He had already had his "first defense," and "no one took my part" (4:16). He was alone, except for Luke (4:11). Some, like Demas, had deserted him. Others had probably been sent on missions, for example Crescens to Galatia and Titus to Dalmatia (4:10).

Paul was practically alone, but there was still a Christian community in Rome, and they managed somehow to keep in touch with him. Eubulus, Pudens, Linus, and Claudia sent their greetings to Timothy, as did "all the brethren" (4:21). Priscilla and Aquila, however, had moved back to Ephesus, which is where Timothy obviously was at this time, since he was to give Paul's greetings to them (4:19).

These details, incidentally, make me skeptical of the theory that Paul's last imprisonment and death occurred as part of the aftermath of the Fire of Rome. True, some had forsaken him, but there was too much coming and going, too much open activity of Christians, for a time of extensive persecution. I find it hard to believe, for example, that Paul would urge Timothy to come to him at a time when Christians were being hunted down.

Paul urged Timothy to come to him soon, "before winter" (4:21), and to bring with him the cloak that Paul left in Troas, as well as the books, "and above all the parchments" (4:13). Whether Timothy arrived before Paul's execution we do not know.

The tradition that Peter and Paul had been imprisoned together in the Mammertine Prison for nine months has been rejected even by Roman Catholic scholars. Paul makes no mention of Peter in Second Timothy. Second Peter, on the other hand, written when Peter was expecting death (2 Pet. 1:14,15), does mention Paul (3:15). It is possible that Peter was executed before Paul was.

According to tradition, Paul was beheaded outside Rome, on the Ostian Way at the third milestone at a place now called Tre Fontane (Three Springs). The traditional date is A.D. 67. A number of modern scholars, who accept the two-imprisonment theory, link Paul's arrest and execution with the persecution that broke out after the fire of the summer of 64. If we assume that Paul's first imprisonment was 59-61, this would allow about three years for Paul's later ministry, which would seem to be quite long enough, even to include a journey to Spain. If, on the other hand, we accept the traditional date of 67, we must be prepared to answer the question: Why didn't Paul write any letters in this long period of time?

The fact that Luke was with Paul when Paul wrote Second Timothy (2 Tim. 4:11), raises another question, Why didn't Luke tell us at the end of Acts what happened to Paul? Obviously if he was with Paul at some time during the second imprisonment, he knew the outcome of the first. We might, of course, go even further and point out that since Luke wrote both the Gospel and Acts he must have lived on beyond 64 or even 67. Why, then, didn't he finish the story of Paul's life?

The obvious answer—obvious, but disregarded by many scholars—is that Luke was not writing a Life of Paul. He was writing the story of the beginning of the Church, and the limits he set on the work—as his own literary devices make clear—are from the beginning in Jerusalem until the gospel reaches Rome. Once Paul arrived in Rome, Luke's story was concluded.

## Footnotes

1. Cf. Lake in *Beginnings of Christianity* 5:330f.
2. See Moe, *The Apostle Paul*, pp. 490f.
3. 1 Clement 5:5-7.
4. Acts of Peter 1:3.
5. Cf. Moe, *The Apostle Paul*, p. 494.

# Acts 15 and Galatians 2

In our discussion of the Jerusalem Conference, we made no reference to Paul's account in Galatians 2:1-10. This was not an oversight. Nor was it an effort to evade the problem.

It is a fact, however, that excellent scholars who are equally committed to the inspiration and authority of Scripture, can arrive at quite different conclusions concerning the interrelationship of Acts and Galatians.

Rather than complicate, and perhaps invalidate, our study of Acts 15 with an attempted correlation of Luke's account and Paul's—and, after all, they may not be talking about the same event!—I have chosen to handle Luke's account by itself. Now I propose to set forth the facts, along with various possible solutions, concerning Acts 15 and Galatians 2. Perhaps we shall not reach satisfactory conclusions. We shall at least have the data available for reference.

*Paul's Visits to Jerusalem: Galatians.* In Galatians
1:11–2:10, Paul describes his post-conversion visits to
Jerusalem. He had, of course, been in Jerusalem when
he first persecuted the Church (Gal. 1:13). Then had
taken place the miracle of miracles for him: God's Son
had been revealed to him (1:16). He does not tell us
here that this was on the way to Damascus to persecute
the Church there, but we can infer it from 1:17. Following the conversion, he went to Arabia, and returned
again to Damascus (1:17).

Paul's first visit to Jerusalem following his conversion
was "after three years." At that time he went "to visit
Cephas" (Peter), "and remained with him fifteen days"
(1:18). He saw no other apostles "except James the
Lord's brother" (1:19). Then he went to Syria and Cilicia (1:21).

Paul's second visit took place "after fourteen years"
(2:1), but it is not clear whether Paul is counting from
his conversion or from the first visit. The language
seems to mean that it was fourteen years after the first
visit. To complicate the problem a bit more, it is not
clear whether Paul uses the inclusive or exclusive system of counting years. We shall return to this complex
problem later.

On this visit, Paul went "with Barnabas, taking Titus
along" with him (2:1). Paul says, "I went up by revelation; and I laid before them (but privately before those
who were of repute) the gospel which I preach among
the Gentiles" (2:2).

The circumcision question must have been raised, for
Paul says, "But even Titus, who was with me, was not
compelled to be circumcised, though he was a Greek"
(2:3). There was some kind of opposition, for "false
brethren" had been "secretly brought in, who slipped
in to spy out our freedom which we have in Christ
Jesus" (2:4). It is certain from Paul's further discussion
that the "bondage" into which these false brethren
would have brought him and his companions was some
form of Judaizing. Bondage of the law is the subject

390

discussed in Galatians 3, and circumcision is discussed in 5:2-12.

*Paul's Visits to Jerusalem: Acts.* In Acts, Luke records five visits of Paul to Jerusalem after his conversion. The first is recorded in Acts 9:26-29. Paul "attempted to join the disciples" but "they were all afraid of him" (9:26). Barnabas interceded "and brought him to the apostles" and told of his conversion and his preaching at Damascus (9:27). Luke adds, "So he went in and out among them at Jerusalem, preaching boldly in the name of the Lord." He "disputed with the Hellenists" until they laid a plot against his life, and then the "brethren" took him to Caesarea and "sent him off to Tarsus" (9:28-30).

Paul's second visit to Jerusalem, as recorded in Acts, was at the time of the prophecy by Agabus (11:28), that there was to be a famine. This occurred in Antioch-on-the-Orontes, and Paul (or Saul) was there. The church in Antioch decided "to send relief to the brethren who lived in Judea" and they sent this "to the elders by the hand of Barnabas and Saul" (11:29,30). The famine took place "in the days of Claudius,"( A.D. 41-54), although it is possible that the offering, like the prophecy, preceded the actual time of the famine. "Barnabas and Saul returned from Jerusalem when they had fulfilled their mission, bringing with them John whose other name was Mark" (12:25). Since Luke inserts the accounts of the martyrdom of James, the imprisonment and miraculous release of Peter, and the death of Herod between the accounts of the journey of Barnabas and Saul to Jerusalem and the return journey, it is possible to date the famine-relief mission in late 43 or early 44. Some scholars, however, do not understand Luke's arrangement to have any necessary chronological significance.[1]

Paul's third visit to Jerusalem, in Acts, was at the time of the Jerusalem Conference (15:1-29). We have just discussed this (Chapter 21).

Paul's fourth visit to Jerusalem, according to Acts,

followed the Second Missionary Journey. Luke gives a very brief account in these words, "When he had landed at Caesarea, he went up and greeted the church, and then went down to Antioch" (18:22). (In my opinion it is beyond argument that Luke meant that Paul "went up to Jerusalem.") This visit to Jerusalem was later than the beginning of the proconsulship of Gallio (18:12), which can be dated with high probability between July of 51 and July of 52.

The final visit of Paul to Jerusalem was at the end of the Third Missionary Journey (21:17), when Paul and his company took the offering from the gentile churches to the church in Jerusalem. Luke scarcely mentions this offering (cf. Acts 24:17), but it is written large in Paul's letters. On this occasion, Paul was the cause of a riot in the Temple which subsequently led to his arrest, his imprisonment at Caesarea, his appeal to Caesar, and his journey to Rome.

*Correlation of the Visits in Acts and in Galatians.* Is it possible for us to correlate these two sets of data? Some scholars have completely despaired of any solution. Of these, some assume that Luke's account is the more reasonable. Most modern scholars, however, would say that we must accept Paul's own account and reject Luke's.

Other scholars believe a correlation is possible, but they are not in agreement in their results. However, let us look at possible correlations.

The first post-conversion visit in Acts (9:26-29) is undoubtedly the same as that described by Paul in Galatians 1:18-23.[2] There are discrepancies in the accounts, we must frankly admit, but these can be attributed to the differing purposes of the two authors. Paul says he went to visit Peter and stayed fifteen days. He saw no other apostle except James the Lord's brother. He was not known by sight to the churches of Christ in Judea. Luke says that Saul (Paul) attempted to join the disciples (probably meaning the members of the church in Jerusalem), that Barnabas acted on his behalf and brought him to the apostles, that he preached boldly and went in and out among "them at Jerusalem," again probably meaning the church, and that he disputed with Hellenists until he aroused their fury. I shall not try to harmonize these two accounts here, as it lies beyond the purpose of this study.[3] Many scholars have attempted harmonizations, and succeeded to their own satisfaction, and published their efforts in their commentaries.

Our major concern is with the second visit in Galatians. Was it the famine-relief visit of Acts, or was it the Jerusalem-Conference visit?

Paul seems to say that the visit "after fourteen years" was his second visit. Some scholars put great weight on his words. "In what I am writing to you, before God, I do not lie!" (Gal. 1:20). Paul, they tell us, is terribly serious and therefore exceedingly careful. If he says this was the second visit, it must have been the second visit. But *does* he say it was his second visit?

Luke and Paul agree that Barnabas accompanied Paul on the second visit in each account. Luke, however, seems to imply that only Barnabas and Saul were delegated to take the offering. Paul says he took Titus with him. Paul's statement that he went up "by revelation" is taken by Bruce to refer to the revelation given by Agabus, and Bruce also finds reference to the famine-relief purpose of the visit in Galatians 2:10.[4] Both of these interpretations, I think, are somewhat forced.

A number of other facts are used to support the view that the second visit in Galatians was the famine-relief visit. Perhaps most significant, when Paul undertook to answer the charges brought against him by the Judaizers in Galatia, he made no reference at all to the "Apostolic Decrees" or the Jerusalem Conference. This, we are told, would have been his most important defense. Since he did not use it, we must assume that the Jerusalem Conference had not yet taken place. Bruce holds that "Galatians was written shortly before the Council of Jerusalem."[5]

A second corroborating bit of evidence is Paul's rebuke to Peter (Gal. 2:11-14). Certainly, we are told, Peter would never have taken such action after the Jerusalem Conference had delivered its decision! However, in my opinion, for Peter to act this way (separating himself from eating with Gentiles) at any time after God gave him the vision on the housetop followed by his experience in the house of Cornelius, is unthinkable. Yet, on Paul's word, he did withdraw from table-fellowship with Gentiles. This is Peter! If he could do this after the housetop vision, he could do it after the Jerusalem Conference. And he could just as quickly repent of the deed. Peter in Acts has not lost all of the characteristics of Peter in the Gospels.[6]

Scholars who identify the second visit (according to Galatians) with the Jerusalem Conference have frequently held to the "North Galatian" theory. Scholars who reject the North Galatian theory in favor of the South Galatian theory have sometimes intermixed their arguments. If we are to hold to the South Galatian theory, they would suggest, we must reject the identification of Acts 15 with Galatians 2. But this is a logical *non sequitur*. According to the North Galatian hypothesis, the cities addressed in the letter to the Galatians were Pessinus, Ancyra, and Tavium. These are not mentioned in Acts, in Paul's letters, or elsewhere in the New Testament. The only possible time Paul could have visited these cities is included in Acts 16:6. Here the context allows no time for establishing churches, for the Spirit was obviously driving the apostles on to Troas and to Macedonia. Scholars contending for the North Galatian theory often use the argument that the characteristics of the Galatians are those of the Celts, and the Celts were located in North Galatia.[7] This argument is worthless. The South Galatian theory rests on the geographical evidence given in Acts.[8] I fail to see any reason why a person who holds to the South Galatian theory must therefore identify Galatians 2 with the famine-relief visit.

When we attempt to identify the second visit of Galatians with the Jerusalem Conference, we likewise run into difficulties. In Galatians, Paul says he went up by revelation. This, however, is not inconsistent with Luke's statement that Barnabas and Paul and some of the others were appointed to go to Jerusalem.

In Galatians, Paul said he presented his arguments privately to "those who were in repute." His account seems to imply (although his sentence structure is badly broken) that this private session was with "James and Cephas and John" (Gal. 2:9), and that it ended with their cordial acceptance of Paul and Barnabas as apostles to the Gentiles. The Acts account, however, refers to a meeting with the church (Acts 15:4). If there was a smaller session (beginning with 15:6), it included "the apostles and the elders," and even if we consider James to be an elder, this expression would not be suitable to describe a group consisting of James, Peter, and John.

It would be possible to assume that Paul, Barnabas, and Titus had a private meeting prior to the Jerusalem Conference, as a number of scholars have suggested. Bruce objects that this would involve Paul in a suppression of the truth.[9]

I frankly admit that I cannot, with the data available, completely harmonize Acts 15 with Galatians 2. However, we must bear in mind one very important fact: we do not have the full story. We have only that part which Luke included for his purpose and that part which Paul included for his purpose. And the sum of these two parts does not equal the whole. Paul's purpose was to show that his apostleship did not depend on other apostles, that he did not get his gospel from men. Luke's purpose was to show how the Church approached this great crisis. Paul was strongly motivated to show the independence of his office over against the other apostles. Luke was motivated to show the unity of the Church in the decision it reached. Neither one falsified. Each one was true to the facts in the light of his purpose. If we had the complementary data I am sure we could harmonize the accounts. Lacking those data we cannot.

*Setting the Accounts in Perspective.* There is a way, however, to approach the problem that may get us nearer to a solution, and this is to attempt to put the accounts in their proper perspective.

To hold the view, for example, that Galatians 2 is the famine-relief visit poses a number of serious problems that lie beyond simple textual statements. First, there is the matter of date. When Bruce arrives at a date of A.D. 46 for the famine-relief visit, for example, he is adjusting Luke's arrangement to fit the needs of his theory. Luke seems to be telling a rather straight-line story. The relief journey to Jerusalem is placed before the death of Herod (A.D. 44), and the return journey is placed after. But A.D. 44 is too early for the Judaizer problem to have reached such significance. Evangelization of the Gentiles first became an issue in the Jerusalem Church when the church in Antioch entered into the effort (11:10-22). Barnabas was sent to Antioch to investigate; he was happy with the effort and went to Tarsus to look for Saul. The two of them spent a year in this effort in Antioch. I maintain that this did not provide the opportunity for the problem to become acute. It was the deliberate evangelization of totally pagan areas that brought the issue to a head. If Saul and Barnabas had started out on their First Mission with Galatians 2 behind them, would the Jerusalem Conference have been necessary? And if so, would it not have developed in a different way?

The background of Galatians 2 requires a Judaizer controversy. It is not merely a debate over Paul's qualifications as an apostle, although the Judaizers at Galatia had strongly attacked his apostleship. There is no evidence of a Judaizer controversy at the time of the famine-relief visit in Acts.

The suggestion that Galatians was written prior to the Jerusalem Conference, likewise, does not fit the proper background. Galatians was written, it would seem, after Paul had visited Galatia a second time[10]—at least, this is the most obvious meaning of the words, "You know that it was because of a bodily ailment that I preached the gospel to you the first time"[11] (Gal. 4:13). This same verse, incidentally, makes the North Galatian theory impossible, for there is no room in the Acts account for two North Galatian journeys.

It may be asked, Then why did Paul not refer to the Conference? The obvious answer: It did not suit his purpose. He was attempting to defend the divine origin of his apostleship; he would not do so by calling on an apostolic or church decision for support. It may also be asked, Why did not Luke include the incident about Titus? There may be two reasons, but the most obvious is that the example of Cornelius proved everything that could be proved by offering Titus in evidence, and certainly carried more weight in the Jerusalem context.[12] In fact, it could be argued that the reason why Titus was not required to submit to circumcision was that God had accepted uncircumcised Cornelius. Just the reverse, namely the acceptance of Titus (who might loosely be called "Paul's Cornelius") by the Jerusalem pillars, would be Paul's best argument to the Galatians.

One very important question must be answered, namely: If Galatians 2 is identified with the Jerusalem Conference, why did Paul omit reference to the famine-relief visit? Does this not involve him in a deliberate falsification of history? Again, I think an author's purpose justifies his inclusion and exclusion of material. Paul was concerned with refuting attacks by Judaizers on his apostolic authority. His apostleship came, he argues, not from men but from God. Then he proceeds to list the only contacts which he had with apostles in Jerusalem, to show that he could not have gotten either his apostleship nor his gospel from them, and to show that both his apostleship and his gospel were accepted by them.

If the famine-relief visit was, as Luke seems to indicate, at the time of the Herodian persecution (late 43 or early 44), there were few apostles in Jerusalem. James the brother of John was there; he was seized and martyred. Peter was there; he was seized and thrown into prison, and became the second Christian martyr. No other apostles are mentioned, either at the prayer meetings in Peter's behalf, or in Peter's message after his miraculous release; only James (who presided at the Jerusalem Conference) is mentioned, and James was not one of the Twelve.

*The Chronological Approach.* Perhaps we can work toward a solution from chronological details. In Galatians 1:18 Paul puts his first visit to Jerusalem "after three years." In 2:1 he refers to a visit "after fourteen years." It is not clear whether he is using the inclusive (in.) or exclusive (ex.) method of counting years.[13] Nor is it entirely clear whether he means "fourteen years after the first visit" or "fourteen years after the conversion." The language seems to support the interpretation, "fourteen years after my first visit. For the first I shall use the symbol "3+14" and for the second "3,14". The most probable combination of the variables is the inclusive system and the 3+14, but I have put down all possible combinations. For our base line, I use the purely arbitrary figure of 30 for Paul's age at the time of his conversion. since to use an arbitrary date would complicate our table. We can therefore tabularize the possibilities as follows:

| Paul's Age[14] | 30 | 31 | 32 | 33 | 34 | 35 | 36 | 37 | 38 | 39 | 40 | 41 | 42 | 43 | 44 | 45 | 46 | 47 |
|---|---|---|---|---|---|---|---|---|---|---|---|---|---|---|---|---|---|---|
| (A) 3+14 ex. | 0 | 1 | 2 | 3 | 1 | 2 | 3 | 4 | 5 | 6 | 7 | 8 | 9 | 10 | 11 | 12 | 13 | 14 |
| (B) 3+14 in. | 1 | 2 | 3 | 2 | 3 | 4 | 5 | 6 | 7 | 8 | 9 | 10 | 11 | 12 | 13 | 14 | | |
| (C) 3,14 ex. | 0 | 1 | 2 | 3 | 4 | 5 | 6 | 7 | 8 | 9 | 10 | 11 | 12 | 13 | 14 | | | |
| (D) 3,14 in. | 1 | 2 | 3 | 4 | 5 | 6 | 7 | 8 | 9 | 10 | 11 | 12 | 13 | 14 | | | | |

The Jerusalem Conference can be dated around A.D. 49. This is based on two data. When Paul reached Corinth on his Second Mission, Priscilla and Aquila had recently come there from Rome as the result of the Claudian edict against the Jews (Acts 18:1,2). That edict is dated 49-50. Further. the proconsulship of Gallio in Corinth, which is dated 51-52, has to be synchronized with Paul's eighteen-month mission in Corinth (18:11,12). From the wording, we assume that the charges against Paul were made soon after the beginning of Gallio's term as proconsul, or in mid 51. Paul therefore probably arrived in Corinth in 50, and started on the Second Mission either in late 49 or early 50. Since he traveled overland, we need not be concerned with the sailing season.

Working backwards from A.D. 44 (the known date of death of Herod Agrippa, for the famine-visit), from A.D. 46 (following Bruce's date for the famine-visit), and from A.D. 49 (the approximate date of the Jerusalem Conference), we get the table on the following page.

Any theory that requires the conversion of Saul prior to A.D. 33 is, in my opinion, questionable, and before 32 is highly improbable.

All things considered, the chronological approach would seem to support the view that Galatians 2 is to be identified with the Jerusalem Conference.

*Attempts at Solution.* The suggestion has been made that the famine-relief visit and the Jerusalem Conference visit were one and the same; Paul rightly refers to only one visit; Luke is responsible for the "goof." But any attempt to get rid of a problem that resorts to such drastic treatment of the text is not acceptable, for if a scholar does not take the text seriously, how can we consider his work as a study of the text? It would be easy to rewrite the Book of Acts without any textual problems. But that would be of no value for textual study.

Other scholars have suggested that Galatians 2 is to be identified with the fourth visit recorded in Acts (i.e. 18:22). If it is difficult to harmonize Galatians 2 with Acts 15, this is even more difficult, for then we would have to explain why Paul makes no reference to his visit at the time of the Conference. Moreover, Paul and Barnabas had separated prior to the Second Mission, and there is no indication that they ever joined forces again. I find nothing to commend this theory.

399

# CHRONOLOGICAL TABLE

| A.D. | 27 | 28 | 29 | 30[1] | 31 | 32 | 33[2] | 34 | 35 | 36 | 37 | 38 | 39 | 40 | 41 | 42 | 43 | 44[3] | 45 | 46[4] | 47 | 48 | 49[5] |
|---|---|---|---|---|---|---|---|---|---|---|---|---|---|---|---|---|---|---|---|---|---|---|---|
| (A) | 0[6] | 1 | 2 | 3[7] | 1 | 2 | 3 | 4 | 5 | 6 | 7 | 8 | 9 | 10 | 11 | 12 | 13 | 14 | | | | | |
| (B) | | | 1[6] | 2 | 3[7] | 2 | 3 | 4 | 5 | 6 | 7 | 8 | 9 | 10 | 11 | 12 | 13 | 14 | | | | | |
| (C) | | | | 0[6] | 1 | 2 | 3 | 4 | 5 | 6 | 7 | 8 | 9 | 10 | 11 | 12 | 13 | 14 | | | | | |
| (D) | | | | | 1[6] | 2 | 3[7] | 4 | 5 | 6 | 7 | 8 | 9 | 10 | 11 | 12 | 13 | 14 | | | | | |
| (A) | | | 0[6] | 1 | 2 | 3[7] | 1 | 2 | 3 | 4 | 5 | 6 | 7 | 8 | 9 | 10 | 11 | 12 | 13 | 14 | | | |
| (B) | | | | | 1[6] | 2 | 3[7] | 2 | 3 | 4 | 5 | 6 | 7 | 8 | 9 | 10 | 11 | 12 | 13 | 14 | | | |
| (C) | | | | | | 0[6] | 1 | 2 | 3[7] | 4 | 5 | 6 | 7 | 8 | 9 | 10 | 11 | 12 | 13 | 14 | | | |
| (D) | | | | | | | 0[6] | 1[6] | 3[7] | 4 | 5 | 6 | 7 | 8 | 9 | 10 | 11 | 12 | 13 | 14 | | | |
| (A) | | | | | | | | | | 1 | 2 | 3[7] | 4 | 5 | 6 | 7 | 8 | 9 | 10 | 11 | 12 | 13 | 14 |
| (B) | | | | | | | | | | | 2 | 3[7] | 4 | 5 | 6 | 7 | 8 | 9 | 10 | 11 | 12 | 13 | 14 |
| (C) | | | | | | | | | 0[6] | 1 | 2 | 3[7] | 4 | 5 | 6 | 7 | 8 | 9 | 10 | 11 | 12 | 13 | 14 |
| (D) | | | | | | | | | | 1[6] | 2 | 3[7] | 4 | 5 | 6 | 7 | 8 | 9 | 10 | 11 | 12 | 13 | 14 |

[1] Probable date of Crucifixion
[2] Traditional Date of Crucifixion
[3] Date of Herod Agrippa's death; famine-visit late 43 or early 44
[4] Bruce's date for famine-visit
[5] Date of Jerusalem Conference
[6] Year of Saul's conversion
[7] Year of Saul's first post-conversion visit to Jerusalem

*Summation.* In spite of the difficulties, and they must be frankly admitted, the identification of Paul's "second" visit in Galatians 2:1-10 with the Jerusalem Conference of Acts 15 seems preferable. I have followed this correlation, but not without great respect for those who identify Galatians 2:1-10 with the famine-relief visit.

# Footnotes

1. W. L. Knox, *The Acts of the Apostles* (1948), pp. 36-37; cf. Bruce, *Commentary on Acts*, p. 257.

2. Most scholars readily accept this identification.

3. It is not acceptable to me to harmonize the accounts by saying that Paul was known "by sight" to churches in Jerusalem but not in the rest of Judea. Paul's statement in Gal. 1:22 and Luke's statement in Acts 9:28,29 constitute a major problem.

4. Bruce, *Commentary on Acts*, p. 244.

5. Bruce, *Commentary on Acts*, p. 298.

6. It will be objected that Barnabas also dissimulated, and Barnabas does not exhibit such a mercurial personality. But Barnabas was always trying to find the good in every person. See my *Great Personalities of the New Testament* (1961), p. 126-127.

7. Cf. J. B. Lightfoot, *Saint Paul's Epistle to the Galatians* (7th ed., 1881), pp. 1-17, and W. J. Conybeare and J. S. Howson, *The Life and Epistles of Saint Paul* (1877), p. 187.

8. A very clear study of the geographical data is found in *Hastings Dictionary of the Bible* (rev. by F. C. Grant & H. H. Rowley, 1963), p. 312.

9. Bruce, *Commentary on Acts*, p. 299.

10. One way this problem has been met is to take the outward and homeward visits of the First Journey as two visits. Cf. *Hastings Dictionary of the Bible* (Revised), p. 313. To me, this seems forced.

11. Literally, "on the former [visit]."

12. The second possible reason, and the reason why Titus is not mentioned at all in Acts could be that Titus was Luke's brother. See chapter 2, "The Author and His Work."

# A Suggested Chronology for the Study of Acts

(This should only be used along with the discussions of the problem of dates which are scattered through the entire study.)

The Crucifixion, Resurrection, Pentecost    spring A.D. 30

Martyrdom of Stephen    possibly A.D. 33

Conversion of Saul of Tarsus    A.D. 34

Saul's first post-conversion visit to Jerusalem    A.D. 36

Famine-visit of Barnabas and Saul to Jerusalem    A.D. 43-44

Martyrdom of James ben Zebedee    early A.D. 44

Death of Herod Agrippa I    A.D. 44

Famine in the days of Claudius    A.D. 44-48

The "First Missionary Journey"    A.D. 47-48

The Jerusalem Conference    A.D. 49

Edict of Claudius, expelling Jews from Rome    A.D. 49/50

The "Second Missionary Journey"   A.D. 49-51
Gallio Proconsul of Achaia   A.D. 51-52
Writing of First and Second Thessalonians from
    Corinth   A.D. 50/51
The "Third Missionary Journey"   A.D. 52-57
Paul in Ephesus   autumn 53—summer A.D. 56
Writing of Galatians,
    First Corinthians from Ephesus   A.D. 53-55
Writing of "Severe" letter,
    brief visit to Corinth   perhaps A.D. 55
Writing of
    Second Corinthians from Macedonia   autumn A.D. 56
Writing of Romans from Corinth   winter A.D. 56
Farewell visit with
    Ephesian elders at Miletus   spring A.D. 57
Antonius Felix Procurator of Judea   c. A.D. 52-59
Paul's arrest in Jerusalem   late spring A.D. 57
Paul's imprisonment in Caesarea   A.D. 57-59
Porcius Festus Procurator of Judea   possibly A.D. 59-61
Paul's journey to Rome
    on appeal to Caesar   fall 59—spring A.D. 60
Paul's (first) Roman imprisonment   A.D. 60-61
Writing of Colossians,
    Ephesians, Philemon from Rome   A.D. 60
Writing of Philippians from Rome   A.D. 61
Paul's later journeys   possibly A.D. 61/62—63/64
Writing of First Timothy and
    Titus possibly from Macedonia   A.D. 62/63
Paul's second Roman imprisonment   A.D. 63/64
Writing of Second Timothy from Rome   fall A.D. 63/64
Death of Paul   possibly A.D. 64/65

# For Further Reading

*(The Author's Selected Bibliography)*

Note: *Needless to say, I do not agree with everything that appears in the following works. A man would be shallow indeed if he limited his reading to that with which he is in full agreement. Differing viewpoints stimulate our thinking, and the man of faith is never afraid of truth.*

## Works on Acts

F. F. BRUCE, *A Commentary on the Book of Acts.* (*The New International Commentary on the New Testament.*) Grand Rapids: Wm. G. Eerdmans Publishing Co., 1956. 555 pp. [In many ways the most satisfactory single volume on Acts, with great scholarship and deep devotion.]

F. J. FOAKES JACKSON and KIRSOPP LAKE, editors, *The Beginnings of Christianity.* London: Macmillan and Co., 1922. 5 vols. [Excellent scholarship and thorough, but frequently based on presuppositions which I cannot accept and which, in my opinion, are unwarranted.]

G. CAMPBELL MORGAN, *Acts of the Apostles.* New York: Revell, 1924. 547 pp. [One of the best works of one of the great Bible expositors of all time.]

R. C. H. LENSKI, *The Interpretation of the Acts of the*

*Apostles.* Columbus: Lutheran Book Concern, 1934. 1126 pp. [Careful exegesis of the Greek text, colored by a strongly Lutheran theology, but an excellent (but difficult) help for studying Acts.]

CHARLES R. ERDMAN, *The Acts.* Philadelphia: Westminster Press, 1930. 176 pp. [Based on careful scholarship, yet simply written and very helpful to the layman.]

RICHARD B. RACKHAM, *The Acts of the Apostles.* (*Westminster Commentaries.*) 13th ed. London: Methuen, 1947, 524 pp. [A scholarly work, reverent and devotional, from an Anglican point of view. If we would get a full-orbed view of the Church, we must become familiar with all of the viewpoints within the Church.]

C. S. C. WILLIAMS, *A Commentary on the Acts of the Apostles.* (*Black's New Testament Commentaries.*) London: Adam & Charles Black, 1957. 301 pp. [An up-to-date treatment of recent critical views, with a healthy viewpoint; useful to gain a sympathetic view of, and valid replies to, some critical positions.]

*The Interpreter's Bible.* Volume 9: Acts—Romans. 668 pp. Introduction and text by G. H. C. Macgregor; Exposition by T. P. Ferris. Nashville: Abingdon-Cokesbury Press, 1954. [Many practical applications, but sometimes based on the Lake-Jackson work mentioned above, and therefore open to a similar criticism.]

J. M. STIFLER, *An Introduction to the Study of the Acts of the Apostles.* New York: Revell, 1892. 287 pp. [An older work, with much good material. Older works frequently must be updated by more recent studies.]

*The Expositor's Greek Testament,* Volume 2: Acts—I Corinthians. Reprinted, Grand Rapids: Wm. B. Eerdmans Publishing Co., n.d. 953 pp. [The commentary on Acts is by R. J. Knowling and is highly scholarly. It is very difficult for the average layman.]

GEORGE T. PURVES, *Christianity in the Apostolic Age.* New York: Scribner's, 1926. 343 pp. [A fine historical treatment of Acts, well balanced, out of date in places.]

W. L. KNOX, *The Acts of the Apostles*. Cambridge: University Press, 1948. 121 pp. [Discussions of some of the problem-areas of Acts.]

E. M. BLAIKLOCK, *The Acts of the Apostles*. (*The Tyndale New Testament Commentaries.*) Grand Rapids: Wm. B. Eerdmans Publishing Co., 1959. 197 pp. [Good, but at times too brief.]

F. F. BRUCE, *The Acts of the Apostles*. 2d edition. Grand Rapids: Wm. B. Eerdmans Publishing Co., 1952. 491 pp. [A scholarly study based on the Greek text.]

F. F. BRUCE, *The Dawn of Christianity*. London: Paternoster Press, 1950. 183 pp. [Very helpful background material.]

## Bible Dictionaries

*The New Bible Dictionary*, edited by J. D. Douglas, Grand Rapids, Mich.: Wm. B. Eerdmans Publishing Co., 1962. 1375 pp., 16 plates, 17 maps. [The best one-volume Bible dictionary in English, in my opinion; conservative in theology, excellent in scholarship.]

*The International Standard Bible Encyclopaedia*, edited by James Orr et al. Reprint, Grand Rapids: Wm. B. Eerdmans Publishing Co., 1960 (original edition revised 1930). 5 vols. [An excellent work, now being revised.]

*A Dictionary of the Apostolic Church*, edited by James Hastings. New York: Charles Scribner's Sons, 1915. 2 vols. [Many articles of superlative value; the factual details may need updating.]

## Atlases

G. E. WRIGHT and F. V. FILSON, eds., *The Westminster Historical Atlas to the Bible*. Revised edition. Philadelphia: Westminster Press, 1956. 130 pp., XVIII plates. [Pages 95-107 are pertinent. An excellent work.]

L. H. GROLLENBERG, *Atlas of the Bible*. Translated and edited by Joyce M. H. Reid and H. H. Rowley. New York: Thomas Nelson and Sons, 1956. 165 pp., 35 maps, 408 photographs. [An outstanding atlas, but disappointing in its coverage of Acts and the Early Church.]

A. A. M. VAN DER HEYDEN and H. H. SCULLARD, eds., *Atlas of the Classical World*. New York: Nelson, 1959. 221 pp., 73 maps, 475 photos. [Very useful for the Greek and Roman background.]

F. VAN DER MEER and CHRISTINE MOHRMANN, *Atlas of the Early Christian World*. Translated and edited by Mary F. Hedlund and H. H. Rowley. New York: Nelson, 1958. 215 pp., 42 maps, 614 photos. [In the same series as the previous two titles; however it has little to offer on the First Century A.D.—which leaves a serious gap in this series of Nelson atlases.]

JOHANAN AHARONI and MICHAEL AVI-YONAH, editors, *The Macmillan Bible Atlas*. New York: The Macmillan Company, 1968. 184 pp., 264 maps. [A map with brief notes for almost every significant event in the Bible. Maps 239-248 deal with material in Acts.]

CHARLES F. PFEIFFER, ed., *Baker's Bible Atlas*. Grand Rapids, Mich.: Baker Book House, 1961. 333 pp., 26 maps in color, 18 maps in black-and-white, many illustrations. [A useful work, but not exactly an "atlas" in the usual sense. Pages 207-230 pertain to Acts.]

## Geographies

CHARLES F. PFEIFFER and HOWARD F. VOS, *The Wycliffe Historical Geography of Bible Lands*. Chicago: Moody Press, 1967. 588 pp., 9 maps, 459 illustrations. [A very useful tool with a good index, as well as bibliographies on each area. Since the arrangement is geographical rather than biblical, you will have to look around for what you want—but it's not hard to find.]

GEORGE ADAM SMITH, *The Historical Geography of the*

*Holy Land.* 25th edition. New York: Harper and Brothers, 1931. 744 pp., 8 maps. (Paperback, London: Fontana Library, 1966; 512 pp., no maps.) [The classical work, but restricted to Palestine, hence of limited value for the student of Acts.]

*The Geography of Strabo.* (*Loeb Classical Library.*) Greek text and English translation by Horace Leonard Jones. Cambridge, Mass.: Harvard University Press, 1930. 8 volumes. ["An encyclopaedia of information concerning the various countries of the Inhabited World as known at the beginning of the Christian Era." Strabo lived from c.64 B.C. to after A.D. 21.]

## Background Material

A. C. Bouquet, *Everyday Life in New Testament Times.* New York: Charles Scribner's Sons, 1954. 236 pp., 102 illustrations. [The emphasis is more on the life of the Greco-Roman world. The illustrations are helpful.]

*Josephus.* Complete Works, translated by William Whiston. Grand Rapids: Kregel Publications, 1960 (reprint). [I have generally quoted from the *Loeb Classical Library* edition, which is unnecessarily expensive for the person not working in the Greek text. Whiston's translation is often archaic, but not inaccurate. The careful scholar will check with the Loeb edition. I have included references to both editions.]

H. V. Morton, *In the Steps of St. Paul.* New York: Dodd, Mead & Company, 1955. 499 pp. [Originally published in 1936. A charming work, with lots of background material which, unfortunately, is not documented. I have sometimes spent hours searching for the sources of some statement in Morton—and not always successfully!]

Jack Finegan, *Light from the Ancient Past; the Archeological Background of Judaism and Christianity.* 2d edition. Princeton: Princeton University Press, 1959. 638 pp., 204 illustrations, 6 maps, 4 plans. [A valuable work, fully documented in extensive footnotes. Pages 247-384 are pertinent to our study.]

JAMES SMITH, *The Voyage and Shipwreck of St. Paul.* 4th ed. London: Longmans, Green, and Co., 1880. 293 pp. [Now a classic, and a delightful account as well as a careful study of the text. It was, of course, written before the critical work of Westcott and Hort on the New Testament text was available.]

W. M. RAMSAY, *St. Paul the Traveller and the Roman Citizen.* 3d ed. (1897), reprinted, Grand Rapids: Baker Book House, 1960. 402 pp. [Ramsay wrote many works, all quite disorganized, all helpful. I have selected this title because it more consistently follows the account in Acts than his other works. But many important details of his research and recorded observations have to be filled in from other volumes, as my footnotes will indicate.]

J. GRESHAM MACHEN, *The Origin of Paul's Religion.* London: Hodder & Stoughton, 1921. 329 pp. [Not as widely known as it deserves to be, and ignored by too many critical scholars, this work is built on magnificent scholarship.]

## Tools for the Scholar

W. F. ARNDT and F. W. GINGRICH, *A Greek-English Lexicon of the New Testament and Other Early Christian Literature.* Translated and adapted from the 4th ed. of Walter Bauer's *Griechish-Deutsches Wörterbuch usw.).* Chicago: University of Chicago Press, 1957. 909 pp. [The best, and only up-to-date, lexicon in English for studying the Greek New Testament.]

*Theological Dictionary of the New Testament,* edited by G. Kittel, translated by G. W. Bromiley. Grand Rapids: Wm. B. Eerdmans Publishing Co., 1964 ff. 7 vols. to date. [An incredible amount of material on the vocabulary of the New Testament. The scholar who fails to use it is certainly denying himself of great riches.]

# Index

A

417

# F

failure 316
"Fair Havens" 364, 365
faith 52, 53, 136, 179,
    201, 221, 228, 229,
    230, 237, 357
falsification 394
Famagusta 198
family 260
farewell to the elders 307
fasting 190, 364
fathom 370
fear God 209
fear of the Lord 145
Feast of Booths 9
Feast of Harvest 43
Feast of Weeks 9, 43
Felix 333, 334, 338,
    339, 342, 343, 344,
    346, 348, 351, 381
fellowship 32, 34, 53,
    68, 76, 122, 135, 178,
    187, 228, 291, 314
    in the sufferings of Christ
    69
    nature of 54
    of goods 69
    with each other 37
    with the Risen Lord 33
Festus 237, 347, 348,
    349, 350, 351, 352,
    353, 356, 360, 362,
    381
filled with the Spirit 66
First Book of Maccabees 89
first Christian convert in
    Europe 256
First Church 31, 40, 57
First Corinthians 277,
    299, 303
first day 305
First Missionary Journey
    197, 213, 222
First Peter 242
first preaching 42, 54
First Thessalonians 282
forbidden degrees of mar-
    riage 234

food 155, 233
"foreign divinities" 274
forgiveness 53, 61, 207
fornication 233
Fortress Antonia 319, 322,
    328, 329, 333
forty days 33
Forum of Appius 372
freedmen 98
freedom 247
*frumentarii* 362
fulfillment 102, 103, 104

# G

Gaius 12, 175, 220, 296,
    302
Gaius Julius Caesar
    Octavianus 12
Galatia
    203, 214, 219, 220,
    240, 246, 248, 383
Galatian churches 288
Galatians 299, 386, 387,
    390, 391
Galatic and Phrygian region
    289
Galatic Phrygia 248
Galen 86, 253
Gallio 280, 283, 284
Gamaliel 8, 134
Gate of St. Paul 373
gear 366
gentile churches 304
gentile converts 227
gentile evangelization
    202, 235
gentile ministry 317
gentile world 12, 233
Gentiles 49, 89, 93, 100,
    113, 151, 152, 153,
    154, 157, 158, 160,
    209, 222, 224, 225,
    231, 235, 317, 319, 325,
    359, 375, 379
gift of prophecy 171
gift of the Holy Spirit
    121, 158
gifts 93

418

# I

Iconium 214, 215
idolatry 270, 272
idols 270, 274
Ignatius 308
ignorance 278
illness 204, 253
Illyricum 302, 308
imperial provinces 12
imprisonment 177
Incarnation 49
inclusive method 396
inclusive or exclusive
    system of counting
    years 387
independent missionaries
    222
individual salvation 260
infallibility 320
"infant baptism" 119
inspiration 25, 26
"interpreter" 11
Ionia 251
Isaiah 210, 231, 375
Israel 88, 210
Israelites 88
"Italian" 14
Italian cohort 152

# J

jailer 259, 260, 261
James 316, 317, 391
James and John 147
James, the apostle 149,
    176, 177
James, the brother of John
    176, 181
James, the Lord's brother
    39, 179, 180, 231, 232,
    237, 386, 388
Jason 263, 264
Jeremiah 43, 231
Jeremias, J. 17
Jerome 107
Jerusalem 100, 114, 115,
    168, 190, 226, 312, 316,
    333, 346

Jerusalem Christianity
    172
Jerusalem church 227, 228
Jerusalem Conference 224,
    247, 316, 385, 389, 390
Jerusalem Council 235
*Jerusalem Megillah* 17
Jesus 103
Jesus and "Resurrection"
    274
"Jesus and the resurrection"
    271
Jesus Christ 23
Jesus Justus 375
Jewish dispersion 5
Jewish faith 356
Jewish "king" 349
Jewish world 4
Jew(s) 88, 100, 113, 154,
    158, 209, 245, 263, 358
Jews in Rome 373, 374
Jews of the Diaspora 99
John 387, 391, 177
John Mark 73, 178, 180,
    197, 239
Joppa 146, 147, 148, 154,
    155, 157
Joseph Barsabbas 39
Josephus 116, 152, 162,
    171, 173, 180, 181, 183,
    237, 320, 326, 335, 339,
    342, 343, 344, 345, 347,
    351, 360
Joshua 103
Journey to Rome 194
Judaea 345
Judaizer problem 227,
    235, 236, 392
Judaizers 159, 225, 231,
    245, 255, 389, 393
Judaizing 225, 386
Judas 136
Judas Barsabbas 234, 235,
    242
Judas the Galilean 84
Judean 88
judge 158, 274
judgment 201, 210, 334,
    340, 342

420

424

426

427

428